Gerry Stahl's assembled texts volume #8

Essays in Personalizable Software

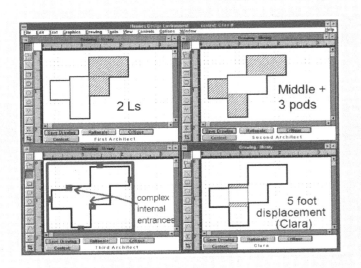

Gerry Stahl

Gerry Stahl's Assembled Texts

1. *Marx and Heidegger*

2. *Tacit and Explicit Understanding in Computer Support*

3. *Group Cognition: Computer Support for Building Collaborative Knowledge*

4. *Studying Virtual Math Teams*

5. *Translating Euclid: Designing a Human-Centered Mathematics.*

6. *Constructing Dynamic Triangles Together: The Development of Mathematical Group Cognition*

7. *Essays in Social Philosophy*

8. *Essays in Personalizable Software*

9. *Essays in Computer-Supported Collaborative Learning*

10. *Essays in Group-Cognitive Science*

11. *Essays in Philosophy of Group Cognition*

12. *Essays in Online Mathematics Interaction*

13. *Essays in Collaborative Dynamic Geometry*

14. *Adventures in Dynamic Geometry*

15. *Global Introduction to CSCL*

16. *Editorial Introductions to ijCSCL*

17. *Proposals for Research*

18. *Overview and Autobiographical Essays*

19. *Theoretical Investigations*

20. *Works of 3-D Form*

21. *Dynamic Geometry Game for Pods*

Gerry Stahl's assembled texts volume #8

Essays in Personalizable Software

Gerry Stahl

Gerry Stahl

Gerry@GerryStahl.net

www.GerryStahl.net

Introduction

Much of my work in computer science at the University of Colorado in Boulder can be characterized as explorations of *personalizable software*. For me, that term increasingly meant designing hypermedia systems that would allow people to explore information from different *personal perspectives*. This theme persisted in my research from the time that I joined Gerhard Fischer's lab as a beginning graduate student in 1989 and became a research assistant for Ray McCall in 1990 until I transitioned into educational software upon graduation in 1993. The switch to educational software stretched across many years and several roles, including software developer, post-doc and research professor. The development of WebGuide played a central role in the transition, since WebGuide applied the mechanisms of personalizable software and computational perspectives to an educational application.

While the highlights of this work are presented in *Group Cognition* (Stahl, 2006), a number of writings that did not make it into that volume fill in important aspects of my explorations of personalizable software. The present volume has been assembled to make those essays available in an organized way.

This book is structured in four sections, corresponding roughly to phases in the development of my research on personalizable software:

1. As a research assistant for Ray McCall, I rewrote his Phidias software system for design rationale capture. This became my dissertation Hermes system with perspectives. The concept behind these systems was to provide a multimedia hypertext system, including an English-like query language for browsing design rationale and associated artifacts or information. I added the idea of allowing different people to personalize their access to this structured hypermedia from their own perspectives, as defined by the query language. This became the basis for my doctoral dissertation (Stahl, 2010b).

2. Following the completion of my dissertation work on Hermes, I developed several other personalizable software systems, such as WebGuide. In a series of technical reports, I considered the nature of personalizable software, using these prototypes as "objects to think with."

3. WebGuide was designed in collaboration with Thomas Herrmann and his assistants. The goal was to combine my perspectives mechanisms with his negotiation-support mechanisms. This goal was never realized until considerably later after I left Colorado and worked on the BSCL system

(see Chapters 7 and 8 of *Group Cognition*). However, during this period I developed the perspectives mechanism further.

4.   In later years, I often returned to the concept of personalizable software, exploring its potential in a variety of application areas. I worked with other people to investigate potentials and issues involved in applying personalization mechanisms to their domains.

Part I. Structured Hypermedia

The first essay presents the structured hypermedia system of Phidias, with its end-user query language (Stahl, 1991; Stahl, McCall & Peper, 1992). It situates this system within the field of artificial intelligence by comparing it with rule-based expert systems, which were all the rage at the time. This research was under a Colorado Advanced Software Institute (CASI) state grant to Ray McCall in the College of Environmental Design in collaboration with Geri Peper at IBM's Boulder research lab. I published it as Technical Report in the Computer Science Department in November 1991 and revised it in August 1992. Peper presented it at an IBM conference in October 1992.

The next essay grew out of work under a second CASI grant, this time in collaboration with Johnson Engineering, a local NASA subcontractor (Stahl, 1992a). In this grant, we adapted our structured hypermedia system to support design of lunar habitats. As preliminary work on my dissertation, I reviewed theories of design and approaches of artificial intelligence as related to our system. I also began to develop a conceptualization of alternative personal perspectives as views on the design knowledge captured in the hypermedia.

This research culminated in my doctoral dissertation proposal (Stahl, 1992b). I proposed the Hermes system, which built on ideas from McCall's Phidias system and from the work on Janus by a number of dissertation projects in Fischer's lab on domain-oriented design environments (DODEs). This, of course, led to my computer science dissertation (Stahl, 1993; 2010b). The Hermes system defined an underlying structured hypermedia system that could support all the components of a DODE as different views of the hypermedia information. A hierarchy of perspectives could also be defined, further structuring and personalizing these views. The personalization was controlled through an end-user definable query language.

Part II. Personalizable Software

After graduation, I became the Director of Software Development at Owen Research, a small research firm conducting SBIR grants. There, I developed a prototype Teacher's Curriculum Assistant (TCA) (Stahl, Sumner &

Owen, 1995). I also prototyped an application of perspectives to a system for corporate usage, the `Collaborative Information Environment` (CIE), working with another software start-up. These experiences led me to expound a theory of personalizable software (Stahl, 1995). The major statement of this theory discussed the examples of TCA, the `Agentsheets Remote Exploratorium` (ARE) and a proposed `Personalizable Learning Medium` (PLM). This paper has never been published before. It is the conceptual centerpiece of this volume.

When I returned to the University of Colorado as a post-doc, I presented the idea of personalizable software, now applied to the World Wide Web, which was becoming popular with the availability of browsers (Stahl, 1996). Here, I discussed `Hermes`, TCA, PLM, and CIE. In addition, I included `WebNet`, a system that I was developing with colleagues in Fischer's lab. `Hermes`, TCA and `WebNet` are discussed separately in *Group Cognition*, chapters 4, 1 and 5, respectively.

This section closes with a summary of the approach to personalizing software (Stahl, 1999c). It presents `WebNet`, TCA and CIE as three models incorporating mechanisms from `Hermes`.

Part IIII. Software Perspectives

The first paper in this section situates my perspectives mechanism from `Hermes` in the context of critiquing systems within the DODEs of Fischer's lab (Fischer et al., 1993a). Co-authored with the people who wrote dissertations with me in that lab, this paper was the first that I presented at an international conference. The perspectives mechanism was here introduced in terms of a third form of critic, an interpretive critic, in addition to generic and specific critics.

The next paper expanded the conference paper into a journal-length presentation, published in the *Knowledge Engineering Review* (Fischer et al., 1993b) and later reprinted in *Readings in Intelligent User Interfaces* (Fischer et al., 1998). This provides an overview of the theory of DODEs including the latest examples, approaches and mechanisms.

In 1999, I gave a number of conference presentations (Stahl, 1999a). They particularly emphasized the potential of personalization techniques for Web applications. Earlier DODEs had been heavyweight desktop applications, most of them requiring special Symbolics LISP machines to run the prototypes. The Web provided a venue for lightweight applications that could be deployed to users relatively easily. It seemed ideal for supporting collaboration. The `WebNet` system for network administrators (see *Group Cognition* chapter 5) was a first exploration of this while I was a post-doc working with Jonathan Ostwald and Gerhard Fischer. As a Research Professor, I began work on `WebGuide` for students (see *Group Cognition* chapter 6), and that was the prime example in this paper.

The next paper presented more detail on the implications of the WebGuide system in my CSCL 1999 presentation (Stahl, 1999b). It illustrated a number of issues for personalizable, Web-based systems, using the perspectives mechanisms of WebGuide as a model. It developed the notion of collaborative knowledge-building environments, which then became a central theme in research funding proposals that I submitted in subsequent years (Stahl, 2010a).

The work on WebGuide was initiated with Thomas Herrmann and a couple of his assistants, who visited Boulder at different times and met with me during my visits to Dortmund, Germany. In a paper for GROUP 1999, Herrmann and I discussed the planned synthesis of perspectives and negotiation mechanisms in WebGuide (Stahl & Herrmann, 1999).

Part IV. Applications to Health Care, Education and Publishing

My ideas about computer support for collaboration and personalization appealed to Dr. Paul Ullig, a cardiology surgeon who was experimenting on family-centered and patient-centered post-cardiac care by a team of health care providers. He contacted me about helping to design computer support systems for this approach. This led to observations and discourse analyses by Alan Zemel and Wes Shumar of my lab at Drexel. I produced a series of observations and proposals based on this (Stahl, 2005).

As part of my work at Owen Research, I developed TCA in collaboration with Tamara Sumner. In a paper I delivered as the closing paper of the first CSCL conference, we discussed this educational application along with Agentsheets (Stahl, Sumner & Repenning, 1995). Agentsheets is an end-user programming environment for creating simulations, using an end-user programming language. It was developed by Alexander Repenning, who graduated with me and later shared an office when we were both research professors. The paper shows how the two systems incorporate parallel mechanisms.

The final example looks at a structured hypermedia approach to academic journal reviewing and publication. Co-authored by Elizabeth Lenell, a PhD student working with Sumner and me, the paper provides a critical assessment of *JIME*, an online journal founded by Sumner and colleagues (Lenell & Stahl, 2001). My paper on WebGuide (reproduced in Group Cognition chapter 6) first appeared in *JIME*.

This Volume

It may seem ironic that I am now organizing my writings into fixed volumes of a series of my collected works. When printed in books, the flexibility of hypermedia is lost. As files on my website, one could reassemble and reorder sets of papers, based on personal and/or thematic preferences. Live links on index pages or in the online versions of the papers could interconnect texts, inviting readers to pursue flexible paths of reading. Of course, the electronic versions are still available and this volume is available electronically for e-readers.

There is a trade-off between personalized flexibility and organized guidance. The DODEs were cumbersome to build and to master; the perspectives mechanism could create considerable confusion; the mass of papers available on the Web can be overwhelming, rather than personally inviting. So, different presentations are appropriate for different audiences. While an author may not ultimately be the best judge of his or her own writings, the author is often the only one with the understanding, overview and motivation to undertake a systematic gathering like this. The goal is to scaffold the reader's access to the ideas contained herein with the hope that you will then forge your own way.

References

The essays in this volume were originally published as: (Stahl 1991; Stahl, McCall & Peper 1992; Stahl 1992a; 1992b; 1995; 1996; 1999a; Fischer et al. 1993a; Fischer et al. 1993b; Fischer et al. 1998; Stahl 1999b; 1999c; Stahl & Herrmann 1998; 1999; Stahl, Sumner & Repenning 1995; Stahl 2005; Lenell & Stahl 2001; Kintsch et al. 2000; Collazos et al. 2007; Stahl, Rohde & Wulf 2006; Stahl 2000)

Stahl, G. (1991). *A hypermedia inference language as an alternative to rule-based systems* (No. CU-CS-557-91). Boulder, CO: Department of Computer Science, University of Colorado. Web: http://GerryStahl.net/publications/conferences/1990-1997/ibm92/InfLang.html.

Stahl, G., McCall, R., & Peper, G. (1992). *Extending hypermedia with an inference language: An alternative to rule-based expert systems.* In the proceedings of the IBM ITL Conference: Expert Systems. Yorktown Heights, NY. Proceedings pp. 160-167. Web: http://GerryStahl.net/publications/conferences/1990-1997/ibm92/ExtHyper.html.

Stahl, G. (1992a). *A computational medium for supporting interpretation in design* (No. CU-CS-598-92). Boulder, CO: Department of Computer Science, University of Colorado. Web: http://GerryStahl.net/publications/techreports/design/Design.tr.html.

Stahl, G. (1992b). *Toward a theory of hermeneutic software design: Dissertation proposal* (No. CU-CS-589-92). Boulder, CO: Department of Computer Science, University of Colorado. Web: http://GerryStahl.net/publications/dissertations/Proposal.html.

Stahl, G. (1995). *Supporting personalizable learning* (No. CU-CS-788-95). Boulder, CO: Department of Computer Science, University of Colorado. Web: http://GerryStahl.net/publications/techreports/personalize/.

Stahl, G. (1996). *Personalizing the Web* (No. CU-CS-836-96). Boulder, CO: Department of Computer Science, University of Colorado. Web: http://GerryStahl.net/publications/techreports/www6/PAPER82.html.

Stahl, G. (1999a). *Supporting personalization and reseeding-on-demand.* Unpublished manuscript. Web: http://gerrystahl.net/publications/ideas/gerry_pp.html.

Fischer, G., Nakakoji, K., Ostwald, J., Stahl, G., & Sumner, T. (1993a). *Embedding computer-based critics in the contexts of design.* In the proceedings of the Conference on Human Factors in Computing Systems (INTERChi '93). Amsterdam, NL. Proceedings pp. 157-164. Addison Wesley. Web: http://GerryStahl.net/publications/conferences/1990-1997/chi93/CHI93.html.

Fischer, G., Nakakoji, K., Ostwald, J., Stahl, G., & Sumner, T. (1993b). Embedding critics in design environments. *Knowledge Engineering Review. 4*(8), 285-307. Web: http://GerryStahl.net/publications/journals/ker/index.html.

Fischer, G., Nakakoji, K., Ostwald, J., Stahl, G., & Sumner, T. (1998). Embedding critics in design environments. In M. T. Maybury & W. Wahlster (Eds.), *Readings in intelligent user interfaces.* (pp. 537-561). New York: Morgan Kaufman. Web: http://GerryStahl.net/publications/journals/ker/index.html.

Stahl, G. (1999b). *Pow! Perspectives on the Web.* In the proceedings of the WebNet World Conference on the WWW and Internet (WebNet '99). Honolulu, HA. Proceedings pp. 91-99. Web: http://GerryStahl.net/cscl/papers/ch08.pdf.

Stahl, G. (1999c). *Reflections on WebGuide: Seven issues for the next generation of collaborative knowledge-building environments.* In the proceedings of the International Conference on Computer Supported Collaborative Learning (CSCL '99). Palo Alto, CA. Proceedings pp. 600-610. Web: http://GerryStahl.net/cscl/papers/ch09.pdf.

Stahl, G., & Herrmann, T. (1998). *Verschrankung von perspectiven durch Aushandlung (in German; translated by G. Stahl as: The sharing of perspectives by means of negotiation).* In the proceedings of the Interaktion in Web: Innovative Kommunikationsformen. Marburg, Germany. Proceedings pp. 95-112. Web: http://GerryStahl.net/publications/conferences/1998/verschrankung/index.html and http://GerryStahl.net/publications/conferences/1998/sharing/sharing.html.

Stahl, G., & Herrmann, T. (1999). *Intertwining perspectives and negotiation.* In the proceedings of the ACM SIGGROUP Conference on Supporting Group

Work (Group '99). Phoenix, AZ. Proceedings pp. 316-324. Web: http://GerryStahl.net/cscl/papers/ch07.pdf.

Stahl, G., Sumner, T., & Repenning, A. (1995). *Internet repositories for collaborative learning: Supporting both students and teachers*. In the proceedings of the International Conference on Computer Support for Collaborative Learning (CSCL '95). Bloomington, Indiana. Proceedings pp. 321-328. ACM Press. Web: http://GerryStahl.net/cscl/papers/ch06.pdf.

Stahl, G. (2005). *Reflections on supporting and studying collaborative team formation in post-cardiac surgery care*. Philadelphia, PA: College of Information Science & Technology, Drexel University. Web: http://GerryStahl.net/pub/collabcare.pdf.

Lenell, E., & Stahl, G. (2001). *Evaluating affordance short-circuits by reviewers and authors participating in on-line journal reviews*. In the proceedings of the European Computer Supported Collaborative Learning Conference (E-CSCL '01). Maastricht, NL. Proceedings pp. 406-413. Web: http://GerryStahl.net/publications/conferences/2001/ecscl2001/ecscl.html.

Kintsch, E., Steinhart, D., Stahl, G., Matthews, C., Lamb, R., & the LSA Research Group. (2000). Developing summarization skills through the use of LSA-backed feedback. *Interactive Learning Environments.* 8(2), 87-109. Web: http://GerryStahl.net/publications/journals/ile2000/ile.html.

Collazos, C. A., Guerrero, L. A., Pino, J. A., Ochoa, S., & Stahl, G. (2007). Designing collaborative learning environments using digital games. *Journal of Universal Computer Science. 13*(7), 781-791. Web: http://GerryStahl.net/pub/jucs2007.pdf.

Stahl, G., Rohde, M., & Wulf, V. (2006). Introduction: Computer support for learning communities. *Behavior and Information Technology (BIT). 26*(1), 1-3. Web: http://GerryStahl.net/pub/bit_intro.pdf. Doi: http://dx.doi.org/10.1080/01449290600811495.

Stahl, G. (2000). Review of "professional development for cooperative learning: Issues and approaches" [book review]. *Teaching and Learning in Medicine: An International Journal. 12*(4) Web: http://GerryStahl.net/cscl/papers/ch18.pdf.

Contents

Part I: Structured Hypermedia

1.   A Hypermedia Inference Language as an Alternative to Rule-based Expert Systems

Abstract

This paper reports on the development of a hypermedia inference language designed to strengthen the ability of hypermedia systems to be used effectively in applications that might otherwise require cumbersome rule-based expert systems. The inference language grew out of a primitive query language, which provided the mechanism for navigation in a hypertext system. As the language gained logical and computational capabilities it became increasingly embedded in the nodes and links. A new paradigm of intelligent hypermedia emerged, incorporating "smart" nodes and links that were dynamically computed by means of the inference language. The language itself provided an end-user programming facility that was English-like enough in appearance to be readily comprehensible to non-programmers. An application in the domain of academic advising was developed to compare the inferencing language approach to expert system alternatives.

Overview of Report

This report will start by reviewing the actual progression of the research. It will begin with the original assumptions and goals and show how they were explored. A series of discoveries during the year's work led to further ideas and techniques. In the end, certain technical difficulties that had not been envisioned were overcome and a conception of intelligent hypermedia was fashioned. The creation of test applications embodying the new system revealed how its power might best be exploited.

The history of the research will provide an introduction to the system of intelligent hypermedia that emerged and a context for understanding its significance. This will be followed by illustrations of the use of the language in sample applications.

They should give a good feel for the system's usability as well as its utility. The inference language will be described next. The content and structure of this language embodies the real power of the system. Much of the research time was spent in the design and development of the language. An important emphasis of the research was trying to keep the appearance of the inferencing language as English-like as possible and to keep its use intuitive. Finally, implications of the research will be discussed and conclusions drawn.

Comparing Rule-Based Expert Systems with Hypermedia

Expert systems are most useful in well-defined domains in which the rules can be made explicit. However, a study by researchers at IBM (Peper, et al, 1990) identified a number of problems with traditional rule-based expert systems. The design of systems of rules is difficult and problem-laden. Even more of a concern is the issue of maintaining rule-bases. Maintenance is always a primary concern in the software lifecycle, as both the rules of the domain and the needs of the users evolve. Expert-system shells, designed to obviate the need for specialists with computer-programming expertise, have not eliminated these difficulties.

There are a number of reasons for the problems with rule-based systems. The first step, encoding and ordering the rules, is a major challenge. This is because the syntax of the rules is non-intuitive and hence hard for users to understand and modify as well as awkward to encode. Furthermore, because of the nature of the inferencing process in the expert system engines, the ordering of the firing of rules is critical. The firing of rules can also have unwanted side effects. In particular, conflicts between which rules to fire can arise, creating what is perhaps the most significant problem for maintenance of expert systems: conflict resolution. In addition, even once the rules have been adequately debugged, special procedures often still need to be programmed in source code (e.g., Lisp). Finally, expert systems tend to be inflexible. They pursue a fixed line of inquiry entirely under the computer's control. Thus, it is not possible for the user to introduce new information unless explicitly prompted for it, or to explore the information in the system in an unrestricted manner.

The IBM study showed that hypermedia navigation could often provide an effective alternative to rule-based inference systems. Such an approach gives users greater control and allows them to explore the knowledge base. The study concluded that a hypermedia system could be just as effective and easier to create and maintain. Also, the hypermedia system can run faster and require less computer resources than rule-based expert systems.

The original idea led to **HyperWin**, an IBM product. Applications are, indeed, easy to construct, understand and maintain with it. They can be used in an exploratory way with no training. Several applications have been developed in **HyperWin**, including an academic advising system for Auburn University.

Hypermedia represents an appealing alternative for situations in which all the knowledge can be laid out as a network of textual nodes and links for traversal by the user. However, there are many applications in which inference by the system would also be desirable or necessary. Hypermedia represents an appealing alternative for situations in which all the knowledge can be laid out for the user as a network of textual nodes and links. However, there are many applications in which inference by the system would also be needed.

Extending Hypermedia with Inferencing

It was decided to add the power of inference to the elegance of hypermedia navigation. Some expert system applications can be defined as a network of nodes for navigating without inference. Others are wholly reliant upon inference computations. But many applications fall between these two extremes and might best be served by combining the two approaches.

The project began by building on an existing hypermedia system called **Mikroplis** (McCall, 1989), with an English-like query language that has been successfully used for several years. The **Mikroplis** query language is a comparatively simple language for navigating across links in a hypermedia document. It has a total of 12 syntactic options and a limited potential complexity, compared to over a hundred options in the inference language developed in this research. It allows the system to select links from a node and to check the content of nodes for the inclusion of a substring of characters.

To support a wide range of inferencing, the language had to be extensively expanded to include true/false conditionals, numerical calculations, comparison operations and nesting of phrases. (See the appendix for a listing of the abstract syntax of the new language, with the options from **Mikroplis** underlined.) A typical request in the new language -- taken from the test domain of academic advising -- might look like the following:

> Display all courses of Sandra which have studio_types and which also have less than 3 prerequisites, with their prerequisites.

To evaluate this statement, the system would navigate from the student node, Sandra, across all its courses links; check which nodes arrived at had at least one studio_types link and also had less than three prerequisites links;

and output a list of the course nodes that satisfied these conditions, along with a sublisting of their prerequisites. The output might look like this:

```
***COURSES:
1. ENVD 2110 Architectural Studio
   *** PREREQUISITES:
   1. ENVD 1000 Environmental Design Studio
   2. ENVD 1014 Intro to Environmental Design
2. ENVD 2120 Planning Studio
   *** PREREQUISITES:
   1. ENVD 2110 Architectural Studio
```

The structure of statements in the inference language and their method of evaluation are based on the structure of hypermedia. The queries investigate the node and link structure, rather than the content of a database and their evaluation proceeds by navigation across the links from initial nodes. In this sense, the research represents an effort within the hypermedia paradigm. The thrust of the effort is to exploit hypermedia mechanisms to achieve certain functionality of artificial intelligence and information retrieval technologies. Thus, the goal was to expand hypermedia to include:

- Some of the inferencing capability of **Prolog**, but without the comprehension difficulties of predicate calculus and explicit variables;

- Some of the querying ability of SQL, but without the inefficiency of relational joins;

- Some of the advantages of semantic databases, but allowing semantic relationships to be defined between instances as well as types; and

- Some of the utility of semantic networks, but without restriction to a pre-defined set of types.

A Navigation Language for Nodes

The original approach relied heavily on the idea of *smart nodes*, in which the inferencing power is embedded in the nodes of the hypermedia. This was conceived primarily in terms of *virtual structures*, an extension of the fixed structures of textual or graphical nodes in traditional hypermedia systems, suggested by Frank Halasz (1988). The navigational (or structural) approach to query evaluation was used, as found in the **Mikroplis** language and embedded the language in the hypermedia nodes. This was done to avoid simply gluing together two different paradigms (e.g., hypermedia and **Prolog**, or hypermedia and **SQL**, or **HyperCard** and

HyperTalk) and to develop the querying or inferencing capability out of the hypermedia paradigm itself.

The content of a smart node is not limited to the text or graphic originally entered into it. Instead the content is determined by the results of a query or conditional phrase associated with the node. The query traverses the hypermedia network, so its result depends upon the current state of the network: the existence of other nodes, their links and their current content. When smart nodes are displayed, the appearance of the hyperdocument itself changes dynamically.

Two forms of smart nodes were explored: *conditional nodes* and *virtual structures*. A conditional node contains a conditional phrase in the inference language and normal text or graphics. If the condition evaluates to true, the text is displayed. If the condition is false, nothing is displayed. For instance, in the academic advising application a node with the text, `"Are you interested in a studio course?"` might have the condition, `If there are courses which have studio_types`. Then the text would be displayed only if there actually were studio courses for the student to choose from.

A virtual structure differs from a conditional node in that it contains only a query. Instead of fixed text, the system displays the result of the query. So, in the previous example, if there were studio courses and the user responded to the question with a "yes," then the yes response might be implemented as a link to a virtual structure node with the query, `Display all courses which have studio_types`. The user would not see the statement of the query, just the results.

Conditional nodes and virtual structures add significant flexibility to hypermedia. They allow specific nodes to be responsive to changing conditions in other nodes of the hyperdocument. For instance, decision trees can be implemented using smart nodes by basing new decisions on nodes that contain the results of previous decisions.

The major surprise of this research was an important limitation of smart nodes. Suppose you had defined an inference computation for a specific node, embedded it in that node and found that it worked fine. But now you wanted to apply the same computation to other nodes without explicitly entering the condition or query in each of the other nodes. More generally, suppose you wanted to apply the computation as an operation on an arbitrary list of nodes. This turned out to be a critical concern because it was important to be able to do this within the inferencing language itself.

Adding Smart Links

Smart *links* or *predicates* solved the limitation of smart *nodes*. Smart links are different from primitive links or defined link types. When a hypermedia system is designed, a set of link types is defined. For instance, in the academic advising application there might be links of type `proposed_courses` from a student's node to his or her chosen course nodes and other links of type `prerequisites` from course nodes to other course nodes. A smart link would then be a virtual link that was computed based on the definition of a predicate. For instance, a predicate might be defined as:

required_prerequisites = proposed_courses which have prerequisites, with their prerequisites.

`Required_prerequisites` would not be a primitive defined link type, but a computation or an inference.

This is an example of a query using normal primitive links:

Display the proposed_courses for Sandra.

It would be evaluated by following the `proposed_courses` links from the student node `Sandra` and displaying the nodes reached:

```
*** PROPOSED_COURSES:
1. ENVD 2110 Architectural Studio

. . . .
```

This is an example of a query using smart links:

Display the required_prerequisites for Sandra.

It would be evaluated by substituting the definition for the computed link type into the query and displaying the result:

```
***PROPOSED_COURSES:
1. ENVD 2110 Architectural Studio
   *** PREREQUISITES:
   1. ENVD 1000 Environmental Design Studio
   2. ENVD 1014 Intro to Environmental Design

   . . . .
```

The idea of substituting a definition for a term in a query is known as *macro expansion*. The definition of smart links as macros turns out to be an extremely powerful mechanism for the inferencing language. Because of the way the substitution is implemented, recursive definitions of smart links are possible. This allows simply stated queries to evaluate tree structures and easily display transitive closures, in both breadth-first and depth-first order -- an accomplishment not matched by relational query languages like SQL.

During the research, the process was refined to distinguish between macros and predicates. A predicate is like a macro; however, when its results are displayed, they are labeled to appear as though the predicate were a primitive link type. This is critical for the user. Now when the user says,

Display the required_prerequisites for Sandra.

the user does not need to know that `required prerequisites` is anything but an ordinary link type. The result is displayed like this:

*** REQUIRED_PREREQUISITES:
1. ENVD 2110 Architecture Studio
2. ENVD 1000 Environmental Design Studio
3. ENVD 1014 Intro to Environmental Design
. . . .

So now there are three kinds of links:

- Primitive links, which are the traditional link types of hypermedia.

- Macros, which add significant inferencing power.

- Predicates, which use the power of macros but hide the complexity from the user.

Predicates like `required prerequisites` had to be defined and the differences between types, macros and predicates had to be considered during system development, but the eventual user can use the computational power without knowing that no links exist between student nodes and their required prerequisites. The predicates look like simple links to the user. Therefore, they are called smart, computed or inferred links.

Smart links overcome the limitation of smart nodes. Because macros and predicates are syntactically equivalent to primitive link types, they can be bound to arbitrary nodes or lists of nodes as if they were actual links coming out of those nodes. Smart links turned out to be so powerful and flexible that the academic advising application was primarily developed with them. Smart nodes were incorporated for only a few special situations. (The application will be described later in this report.)

The Future: Intelligent Hypermedia

The implementation of smart nodes and smart links in effect defines a new paradigm of intelligent hypermedia, in which the elements of the system -- the nodes and the links -- are not necessarily fixed text (or graphics), but can in general include any query results. The inferencing language is thereby conceptualized as integral to the system elements. The new paradigm of intelligent hypermedia represents a leap of abstraction with major practical implications. These implications will need to be explored in the future.

The major consequence of the new paradigm is that all nodes can be conceptualized as query results. This means that the inferencing language and the hypermedia built on it must incorporate all media on an equal footing, so that query results can display text, numbers, truth values, drawings, bit maps, animation, sound, etc. Inferencing and computation mechanisms must be fully polymorphic, so they can be applied to content from any medium. Furthermore, if nodes can contain query results, then they are typically lists of elements rather than single elements of text, graphics, etc. This means all node processing must be list-oriented.

An example of a query in the future system might be,

> Display the kitchen with appliances which are less than 6 feet high but more than 3 feet high and are seen from the doorway.

This might result in the display of several graphical objects representing appliances meeting the stated conditions and viewed from the specified perspective. That is, this query -- which might be the content of a node which the user can navigate to -- evaluates to a computed list of graphical objects (each of which might itself be computed).

The new paradigm has particularly broad consequences for graphics. Composite drawings, rather than being conceived as fixed arrangements of polylines, could be thoroughly reconceptualized to integrate inference language queries. Correspondingly, the syntax of the inference language could be extended to encapsulate computations of scale, spatial transformations in 3-D, hidden plane removal, etc. Detail-on-demand could similarly be incorporated, so that only details above a specified or calculated extent would be displayed.

A follow-up grant to the research reported here is supporting research-exploring mechanisms for virtual copying of parts of the hypermedia network, implementing a kind of local versioning. This work introduces the notion of inheritance. Inheritance has proven to be a fundamental concept for other AI work. It could conceivably have broad use in intelligent hypermedia. In addition to inheritance of specific networks of nodes and links, the node and link types could participate in inheritance hierarchies. Thus, for example, the `studio_courses` type could be a kind of the `courses` type. Then inference about `studio_courses` could take advantage of this relationship as well as those defined by primitive and smart links in the network.

The envisioned form of intelligent hypermedia has sufficient power that all displays in an application could be defined as queries in the inference language. Then there would be no system-defined screens, like general browsers in which the user can become "lost in hyperspace." All application screens would be under the complete control of the user through the formulation of appropriate queries. (This report will discuss features of the current version of the language that make it plausible that a non-expert user could reasonably be expected to handle such a powerful inferencing language.)

An Example of Inference

Having reviewed the goals, progress and implications of the research project, let us take a closer look at the new paradigm of hypermedia and its inference language.

A textbook example from logic programming like Prolog provides a good illustration of how predicates can be used in the inference language to break down and solve a typical inference problem. Take the problem: given a network of `people` nodes linked by `son` and `daughter` links, infer `cousin` relationships. Inference is defined as the combining of facts to deduce new facts. Here, facts about sons and daughters are combined to produce facts about who is a cousin of whom. This is a non-trivial task for humans, generally requiring people to consciously articulate part of the computation (e.g., "Let's see, her mother is my father's sister. . . .")

In the new inference language, the problem could be solved by the definition of the following predicates:

```
children = sons and daughters.
parents = converse sons and converse daughters
siblings = children of parents which are not self which
     contain no duplicates.
cousins = children of siblings of parents.
```

Of course, these definitions require some explanations about the language -- although far less explanation than corresponding definitions in a traditional programming language like Lisp or Prolog. The `children` predicate includes nodes linked by both `sons` and `daughters` primitive links. Converse links are primitive links traced backwards, like from the son back to the person whose son he is. The definition of `siblings` is inherently tricky. Most likely, the definer of this predicate would discover an adequate definition through a series of successive refinements. If one defines `siblings` as just `children of parents`, one discovers upon first use of the predicate that the original people are always included among their own siblings, because they are sons or daughters of their parents. Therefore, a condition must be added to exclude the original person from the result list. Similarly, there will usually be duplicate names on the list of siblings because they are children of both the mother and the father of the original child. The simplest way of solving this problem while maintaining the ability to handle children of multiple marriages is to simply eliminate duplicates from the final list of results.

The complexity of the definition of siblings is telling. Although the task of determining cousins is difficult for people, the problem does not lie in the definition of `siblings` but rather in the sequence of steps that must be put together. People naturally exclude the extra results that pop up surprisingly when the `siblings` predicate is incompletely defined. This is symptomatic of the fact that programming in any language in any domain is going to require some steps of logical analysis and some efforts at debugging. No language, however English-like can entirely avoid that. The primary advantage of the inference language described here is that once predicates are successfully defined, it is clear what they mean, even for someone with little training in the language. The definition of siblings is about as obscure as any statement in the language need be.

Given the above definitions, the following computations can now be evaluated:

Display the cousins of Sandra.
Display all people which have cousins and which also have less than 3 cousins, with their cousins.

Furthermore, these definitions have begun the creation of a domain language for family relationships. It is an easy matter to add predicates for brothers, aunts, grandparents, etc.

A particularly interesting definition is that of descendants:

descendants = children with their descendants.

A programmer would recognize this to be a *recursive* definition. That is, it not only lists the descendants of the starting node, but the descendants of those descendants, the descendants of descendants of descendants, etc. until there are no more generations. A non-programmer might be able to see that this definition would produce such a result, without having studied recursive function theory in the abstract. Again, the non-programmer might not be able to generate recursive definitions easily from scratch, yet might understand them when seen.

Styles of Computation Using the Inference Language

Recursive programming is a potentially powerful technique. The language Lisp (the traditional language for artificial intelligence programming) relies almost exclusively on recursive processing. This technique is particularly useful for processing trees of data, like family trees. In the academic advising application, tree structures appear in the list of course prerequisites. The full set of tree elements is called the *transitive closure*.

The two primary approaches to enumerating a transitive closure by navigation through a tree structure are *depth-first* and *breadth-first*. Both of these approaches can be programmed in the inference language. The following definition and query produce a nested, depth-first listing of the transitive closure of course prerequisites:

```
prerequisite_trees = prerequisites with their prerequisite_trees.
Display ENVD_4550 and ENVD_4560 with their prerequisite_trees.
```

The following definition and query produce a flat, breadth-first listing of course prerequisites:

```
prerequisite_lists = prerequisites and prerequisites of prerequisite_lists.
Display the prerequisite_lists for ENVD_4550 which contain no duplicates.
```

The computation through trees has important applications in practical problems. For instance, in a hypermedia system of issues, subissues of the issues, subissues of the subissues, etc., it is useful to define the issue_trees, a depth-first listing of the whole tree of issues. If the issues can each have answers and arguments for the answers (as in the popular hypertext IBIS systems), then one wants to list deliberations -- the tree of arguments on the issue tree. This is straightforward to do in the language. It is trickier to produce a list of the *terminal* issues, that is subissues at the leaves of the issue tree, which have no subissues themselves. This can be done with a predicate for terminal_issues:

```
terminal_issues = terminal_issues of issues if there are issues of issues, else
issues.
```

The inference language is also designed to take advantage of *defeasible reasoning* in an intuitive way. Defeasible reasoning allows a system to be designed with certain default behavior, which results unless explicit action is taken to change it. Suppose in a hypertext network of issues and answers one wants to allow a user to accept, reject or ignore answers by attaching status links to nodes containing words like "accept", "reject", "ignore", "don't care" or no links. One might also want to allow multiple status links from any given answer node. So there may be contradictory information attached to an answer or no information at all. Suppose further that one wants to display an_important_issue unless all its answers have been explicitly rejected with status links to "reject". This would require defeasible reasoning, a very robust approach. The following query could be used:

Display an_important_issue if there are not answers of an_important_issue which have no statuses which equal reject.

Another important programming technique -- particularly for expert system applications -- is *decision trees*. A typical example of using a decision tree is categorization of fauna and flora. One proceeds through a sequence of questions posing alternatives. Based on one's answers, the choices lead down a path through the tree of decisions to the answer, e.g., the name of the animal or plant corresponding to the choices. Here is an example from the domain of academic advising, implemented with virtual structure smart nodes. For purposes of the example, most of the nodes have been given names like node_4 to make it clear that they are (smart) nodes; in a realistic setting, they would have more meaningful names. Suppose we have the query,

Display the suggestion.

And suppose the node named "suggestion" contains the following query:

Display node_2 if envd_semester of student is less than 3, else node_3.

Assuming that the proposition (if envd_semester of student is less than 3) turns out true, node_2 is evaluated. It contains the query,

Display node_4 if completed_courses of student do not contain ENVD_1000, else node_5.

Suppose we take the branch of the tree to the simple node_5, which contains the text, "Take ENVD 1000." Then this text is displayed in response to the original query. The virtual structure nodes have implemented a decision tree in a way that is relatively easy to understand and to modify if necessary. The links through the hypermedia defined by the embedded queries reflect in a very straightforward way the structure of the abstract tree of decisions. Here again, the system requires some analysis to set up, but once defined in the inference language it is rather self-documenting.

While the above implementation of a decision tree is appealing, it demonstrates the limitation of smart nodes as well as their power. Note that in the last two queries the node student was referred to by name. If one next wants to evaluate the decision tree for another student, the new student information must be substituted in the hypermedia network that contains the smart nodes. The decision tree cannot be simply applied somehow to other existing nodes, let alone to arbitrary lists of nodes (the way predicates can). This is a form of the general binding problem, a consequence of avoiding the use of variables in order to keep the language easy to understand. In the inference language one cannot say "If envd_semester of X is less than 3," except by defining a predicate to encapsulate that computation and applying the predicate to an arbitrary subject. That is why predicates are used so extensively in applications using the inference language.

But predicates have their own *binding problem*. When it is used in the evaluation of a query, a predicate is implicitly (automatically) bound to whatever subject it is applied to. Therefore, any unbound relationship in the predicate definition is implicitly bound to that subject as well. However, predicates can have whole queries embedded in them and so a question arises concerning the subjects of these embedded queries. If there is an explicit subject node named in the embedded query, then there is no problem. However, predicates draw much of their power from binding to implicit subjects, as explained in the previous paragraph. Therefore, the inference language permits leaving the subject unnamed in an embedded query. In such a case, the implicit subject of the embedded query is bound to the last explicit subject of a query (i.e., to the subject of the query in which the embedded query is embedded, or if that query has no explicit subject then the subject to which its subject is bound). This procedure is based on the usual assumptions of the English language, so that inference statements behave the way English-speaking users would expect them to, without the user having to think in programming terms.

For an example of the two binding mechanisms presented in the previous paragraph, consider the problem of determining what problems a student has with missing prerequisite courses. The query for this can be based on a predicate named "prerequisite_problems" which contains a predicate named "prerequisites_not_taken":

> prerequisites_not_taken = prerequisites which are not contained in Display the courses_taken.
> prerequisite_problems = proposed_courses which have prerequisites_not_taken, with their prerequisites_not_taken.
> Display the prerequisite_problems for Sandra.

In this query, "prerequisite_problems" is bound to the explicit subject of the query, Sandra. The other predicate used in its definition, prerequisites_not_taken, is applied to proposed_courses through composition. So prerequisites in its definition is bound to proposed_courses (i.e., we are concerned with the prerequisites of the proposed courses). The issue arises with courses_taken. These are not courses taken by the proposed courses, but by Sandra. According to the syntax of the query, `courses_taken` is part of an embedded query: `Display the courses_taken by` X. The subject is left implicit, which to English speakers means it refers to the previous main subject, Sandra. This is in fact the rule used for binding implicit subjects of embedded queries in the inference language as well.

The inference language solves the binding problem through the two mechanisms illustrated above. This allows predicates to exercise their power of leaving their subjects implicit, to be bound at runtime. The solution maintains the language's English-like quality by corresponding to the intuitions of non-programmers. While it cannot handle arcane examples requiring binding to multiple or obscure subjects, it handles reasonable, humanly comprehensible examples -- including arbitrarily deep embedding of queries. The example of `prerequisite_problems` is a realistic one, occurring in the main test application described below.

The Academic Advising Application

The IBM HyperWin system provided not only the starting point for this research, but also the sample application for testing the results of this research: an academic advising system. The HyperWin version allowed a user to navigate through a hypermedia database of information about courses at Auburn University. This system asked the user about interests, courses already taken, etc. and responded to answers chosen by the user with appropriate further information.

To demonstrate the inference language, an application was created using information about the curriculum of the College of Environmental Design at the University of Colorado. This information included not only lists of offered courses, but other facts and rules used by the College's official student advisor. Courses were linked to their prerequisites and to their categories, such as which curriculum they belonged to and which elective breadth requirements they satisfied. Other, less formal factors were also included, like which courses were particularly labor intensive.

The centerpiece of this application was the definition of a predicate named `advice`. This predicate was built on a combination of several specific kinds of advice, which in turn used predicates to compute inferences across the hypermedia. The idea was that a student, Sandra, could enter her name, curriculum option, semester number, completed courses, current courses and proposed courses into the hypermedia system. By clicking on the Advice button, Sandra would initiate the query,

Display the advice to Sandra.

The query critiques Sandra's proposed list of courses. This is a typical result:

Here is some advice on your choice of courses:
The following courses each require a lot of work. It would be wise not to take them in the same semester:

> ENVD 3220 Planning Studio 2
> MATH 1300 Calculus

The following courses are not designed for your curriculum option:

> ENVD 3220 Planning Studio 2

You have not taken the listed prerequisites for the proposed courses:

> ENVD 3220 Planning Studio 2

With your proposed courses you will not satisfy the following elective breadth requirements:

> science

It would be wise to take a course in one of these areas rather than the following proposed courses in elective areas for which you have already satisfied the breadth requirements.

> FINE 1012 Art History

The above is the actual system output for a sample student. Relatively intricate computations have been performed to check, count and list courses meeting or not meeting certain conditions. In particular, for instance, the advice about breadth requirements is only displayed if the proposed courses include an elective in an area that has already been satisfied and do not include one in an unsatisfied area. This kind of inferencing facilitates the offering of important information tailored to a particular user in a way that is impossible in a purely navigational hypermedia system. It begins to look like a rule-based expert system, but without many of the problems of such systems.

Developing an application of this level of complexity requires some system designing expertise. One needs to know how to represent the knowledge in hypermedia and how to build up a sequence of modular definitions. This is probably inevitable in any system. Once designed, however, the system is significantly easier to understand, modify and extend than alternative implementations would be. While the result of the advice predicate looks like the output from a traditional expert system, the flexibility is still there to explore the underlying knowledge base by navigation. Alternatively, one can reformulate the major query or execute a series of simpler queries using components of the advice predicate.

The Inferencing Language

An abstract syntax defining the structure of the inference language is included in the Appendix. The language consists of a number of options for various clauses of a query: Subjects, Relationships, Filter conditions, Boolean propositions and Queries. The interface for constructing queries allows the user to choose from appropriate options at each step. Although the language is in fact tightly constrained, statements of queries always look very English-like. The options are displayed in ways that make programming of the language as intuitive as possible.

The general form for a query is defined as:

Q::= display R of S which F if B with their R', else Q.

Each of the capitalized symbols in this definition stands for a clause, which can be chosen from a number of options. An example of this form is the following, in which slashes have been inserted to distinguish the major clauses:

Display those proposed_courses / for Sandra / which have prerequisites_not_taken / if there are more than 3 proposed_courses / with their prerequisites_not_taken, / else display proposed_courses of Sandra with their prerequisites.

The ordering and phrasing of clauses is designed to give an English-like expression to the query. The actual evaluation of the query is implemented in a very different order:

if B then R' (F (R (S))), else Q

That is, first the Boolean propositional clause is evaluated to see whether it is even necessary to evaluate the following clauses. Then, the system starts with the Subject clause to determine where to begin in the hypermedia. From there the Relationship clause is applied to the list of subject nodes to follow specified primitive or smart links. The Filter clause is subsequently applied to the nodes reached to see which of them contain the specified contents. Finally, with their R' is applied to the current results, typically to produce recursive sublistings of nodes traversed to by relationship R'. Thus, although it is not necessarily apparent to the user, the language is implemented through mechanisms based on navigation of the hypermedia structure.

The language itself is applicative and declarative, rather than procedural. This allows query clauses to be successively applied without restriction -- imposing finer and finer information filters. Applicative programming also simplifies things by requiring no variables or state changes. This eases the cognitive load on the user, who need not be concerned about variables -- or even understand what a variable is. The absence of state change substantially reduces the possibility of side effects of rule firing, which are so problematic in rule-based systems. In effect, the language lets the user specify *what* should be done by successively applying conditions, without worrying *how* the task should be accomplished by the computer -- the way a programmer does who writes a sequence of procedural commands in a programming language. This, again, makes the inference language more like an English language communication than like a traditional computer programming language. The user can concentrate on what is desired in domain terms, rather than worrying about details of computer hardware and software. It is true that the user needs some familiarity with how the hypermedia is structured, but that structure should correspond closely to a representation of the domain, so being aware of the hypermedia structure should not distract too much from the user's focus on domain concerns.

The development of the software architecture to support this very flexible and powerful language required a complete re-write of the Mikroplis hypermedia and query language system, which had explored some of these approaches. The new implementation is object-oriented, fully modularized and consistently applicative. Each clause has its own methods for being evaluated and displayed. Polymorphic techniques allow the methods for the selected clause option to be executed. This allowed the rapid expansion of the language through the successive implementation of new features and options. It also allows arbitrarily deep nesting of clauses within clauses, making the language infinitely generative and as complex as one wishes. The expressive power of the language is further enhanced by the recursive potential of macro and predicate smart links.

Most of this complexity can be hidden from the user. Queries, macros, predicates and other syntactic clauses can be defined once and stored with a descriptive name (like `"cousin"` or `"advice"`). From then on, the user can treat the name as a primitive term -- or reuse and modify its definition. Typically, names will be taken from the user's application domain. In this way, statements of queries will read like English sentences in the domain:

> Display the cousins of David.
> Display advice for Sandra.

Viewed the other way, the relationships of a domain can be programmed into a vocabulary of user-defined node types, link types, macros, predicates and queries. This may be assisted by a system designer programming a *seed* vocabulary for the domain as a basis for the user to start with. At any rate, the vocabulary is always open-ended so that users can add their own concepts as needed. These terms embody the semantics of the domain in a form that can be used naturally by anyone familiar with the domain whether or not they have any programming experience.

Using the Language

While the inferencing language is meant to give the appearance of natural English, it is in fact tightly constrained in its syntax. The vocabulary is less constrained than the syntax, in that it is primarily based on node and link types, which are named by the user when they are defined. The syntax of statements in the language is constrained operationally through the user interface. While a point-and-click interface is now available in Windows, the original interface consists of textual menus. The older menu interface will be used here to illustrate the process of defining a predicate and a query statement.

Suppose we first want to define the following predicate:

cousins = children of siblings of parents.

Assume that children, parents and siblings have already been defined as predicates. Then from the main menu we first select the option, Define a predicate. The following menu is displayed. (Because predicates are just a form of Relationships, this menu is used for Relationships and predicates.) The options in this menu correspond to the options for Relationships in the language syntax (cf. Appendix):

```
0 = EXIT (nil)
1 = everything
2 = a relationship type
3 = converse T
4 = R which are not self
5 = the Nth R
6 = R which F if B with their R, else R
7 = R of R
8 = R and R
9 = a named predicate
10 = a named macro
number: __
```

We are trying to define children of siblings of parents, so we select option 7 = R of R, a composition of two Relationships. This choice results in the same menu being displayed to select the first of the two composed Relationships. Again we choose 7 = R of R, thereby defining the syntax of our predicate as: (R of R) of R. Next we will be given the menu for Relationships three more times, to define each of these three Relationships. In these cases, we will select 9 = a named predicate and type in "children," "siblings" and "parents" respectively. (In the Windows interface they are selected from a mousable pick list.) The system now displays the defined predicate and asks for the user to name it.

Having defined cousins, we are ready to define a query using this predicate. Suppose we want to define the following query:

Display all cousins of Sandra which have children.

From the main menu we select `Define a query`. The menu for queries is:

```
0 = EXIT (nil)
1 = display Art R Prp S which F if B, with their R', else Q
2 = the Nth result of Q
3 = Q and Q
4 = a named query
number: __
```

We choose option 1, the general form for a query. We are then successively prompted with menus for the components of this syntactic form: Article (a, all, an, that, the, those), Relationship (menu options as above), Prepositions (about, by, for, from, in, of, on, over, to, under), Subject, Filter, Boolean, Relationship, Query. We select the following: `all`, `cousins`, `of`, `Sandra`, `have Qop R which F`, nil, nil, nil. Note that the article and preposition chosen by the user, as well as the word "`Display`" which is prepended to the query statement are purely cosmetic and have no significance for the query evaluation. The same is true for the connective English terms in the syntax, like "`which`" or "`with their`".

The Filter clause (`have Qop R which F`) shows how clauses can be nested to arbitrary depths. The Relationship or the Filter could be defined through various sequences of menus for choosing their constituents. For our example query, we keep things simple and choose for Qop (the quantity operator): "`at least one`"; for R (Relationship): "`children`"; for F (Filter clause): nil. Thus, our defined query is: "`all cousins of Sandra which (have at least one children which nil) if nil, with their nil, else nil`". The nil clauses are not displayed or evaluated. By convention, the "`at least one`" is kept implicitly, but is not displayed. So the defined query is displayed back to the user as: "`Display all cousins of Sandra which have children.`"

An end-user programming language statement thereby appears in an English-like form. The menu system has stepped the user through the process of formulating a query without either pretending that the user can say anything he or she wants to in English or allowing the user to enter anything which is ungrammatical in the inferencing language. The point is not to pretend that English is being used by the computer, but to make the statements in the language easy for an English-speaking user to comprehend.

Because the language has an object-oriented implementation, the query can be constructed while it is being defined by the user. Therefore, no parsing routine is necessary and the syntax is not required to be unambiguous. The binding and nesting of clauses is done based on the order of the defining steps, so an intuitive approach by the user generally results in the intended meaning of the query.

The query is an object, whose data consists of Article, Relationship, Preposition, Subject, Filter, Boolean and Query objects. They are each defined as the user makes the corresponding selections for them or for their components. Each type object has methods to display and to evaluate themselves. For instance, a Query object displays itself by first displaying the word "Display", then having its Article object display itself, then having its first Relationship object display itself and so on. Similarly, a Query object evaluates itself by first having its Boolean object evaluate itself and then (assuming that evaluates to True) having its Subject evaluate itself, etc. This approach allows a flexible, infinitely generative language to be built up from a limited number of carefully crafted elements.

Research Directions

This research is situated in three distinct traditions: expert systems, hypermedia and design environments. The focus of the work reported here was on developing intelligent hypermedia as an alternative to rule-based expert systems, following the lead of HyperWin and extending that with an inferencing capability. That approach seems to have considerable promise for the future. One possibility for developing that alternative is in the direction of *design environments*. Another possible direction is defined by the hypermedia community itself. First, this section will consider issues for the future of design environments and then for the future of hypermedia.

The paradigm of intelligent hypermedia built around an inferencing language seems like a useful approach for implementing design environments. A design environment like Janus (Fischer, et al, 1989) is an alternative to an expert system for designers. It is a software system that supports the work of designers by providing a construction kit of parts for building a design in a specific domain. It also supplies design rationale information when it is appropriate in the design process and critiques the design as it evolves. Hypermedia can provide the text and graphics for design rationale and for design drawings. The language can supply a domain-oriented and fully extensible vocabulary for describing, evaluating and critiquing the design. A design environment represents a more fundamental alternative to expert systems than merely extending a HyperWin system with an inferencing language.

However, design environments suffer from a lack of integration. The most advanced design environment architecture described to date, Hydra (Fischer, et al, 1991), consists of half a dozen different components, all representing domain and design information. Special additional components are required to coordinate the primary components: for instance, a Catalog Explorer links the Specification and the Construction components with the Catalog. Intelligent hypermedia built around the inference language provides a form of knowledge representation that can be used by all of the primary components of a design environment. Then the role of linking is done by the formulation of statements in the inference language. Thus, a statement can request a display of catalog elements that meet conditions defined by textual nodes in the Specification sub-network and by graphical nodes in the Construction sub-network.

Design environments have also suffered from the lack of a user-defined domain language. **Janus**, for instance, has been used in the domain of kitchen design. However, it has no language for the user to discuss features of kitchens. Both critics in the system and specification forms use terms like `"is_safe"` or `"is_flammable"`. But these terms (as well as the critic rules) must be coded in **Lisp**. Similarly, attempts in **Hydra** to integrate the content of hypermedia design rationale with filters for selecting from the catalog are problematic because of the lack of a user-definable domain language that could be used in the design rationale and also in query statements.

Generally, design environments have suffered from the lack of an end-user programming language. In an attempt to make these programs usable by non-programmers, developers of design environments have adopted the model of direct manipulation applications. However, such systems are ultimately limited, as argued by Eisenberg (1991). The developers of **Janus** have recognized this and added an end-user-modification capability (Fischer, et al, 1990). Unfortunately, this capability is limited to certain components of the system and requires knowledge of Lisp. By contrast, the inference language described here pervades the intelligent hypermedia system, because it is embedded in its nodes and links, as well as formulating queries which control displays and navigation throughout the system. It also has the advantage of being English-like in appearance and intuitive in how it works.

The research presented here builds directly on the **Phidias** system, which has always been intended as a design environment. (McCall, 1990) However, the discoveries in this research have wide-reaching implications for re-designing a system like **Phidias** as a well-integrated system based on intelligent hypermedia. This involves above all a re-thinking of the graphics system. Currently, graphics in **Phidias** are conventional vector graphics. They should be re-programmed as composite objects, which can include query results. This would be part of a thoroughgoing conversion to hypermedia, in which text, vector graphics, bitmaps, numerical data and truth values (also sound, animation, etc.) would all be handled uniformly. It would complete the re-write of the system as object-oriented and the integration of all information in a single hypermedia network, stored to disk in an object-oriented database.

The fully integrated system suggested by the new paradigm of intelligent hypermedia would integrate all components (critics, palette of parts, catalog of design examples, textual rationale, graphic design, specification). This would permit the display of any one component to be filtered by information from any of the other components. In the kitchen domain, for instance, a palette of appliances would not display dishwashers if there was already a dishwasher in the graphic design, if the specification didn't call for one or if the design rationale had clearly opted against one. Perhaps more importantly, the user would have full (programmable!) power over all the displays by means of the language. Thus, the user could, at any time, add new concepts to the language and use these in critic rules, specification forms, design rationale or display definitions. This kind of programming power goes beyond the use of HyperTalk scripts in HyperCard because the HyperTalk sequential, procedural programming language is primarily oriented to controlling the appearance of the user interface, rather than providing an intuitive language for talking about a domain and doing computations in the domain.

The issues for the future of design environments correspond closely to the seven issues proposed by Frank Halasz for the next generation of hypermedia systems. (Halasz, 1988) It is worthwhile comparing the results of the research reported in this report with the vision outlined by this leading spokesman for the hypermedia community. He lists the following issues:

1. Search and query in a hypermedia network.

2. Composites -- augmenting the basic node and link model.

3. Virtual structures for dealing with changing information.

4. Computation in (over) hypermedia networks.

5. Versioning.

6. Support for collaborative work.

7. Extensibility and tailorability.

The status of these issues for the paradigm of intelligent hypermedia explored in this research is:

1. The inference language provides a primary access mechanism for search and query.

2. Composites seem particularly important as a way of implementing complex graphics.

3. Virtual structures have been implemented and explored in this research. The discovery of the limitations of smart nodes and the solution with smart links goes beyond Halasz' view.

4. The inference language performs computation over hypermedia networks.

5. Versioning will be explored in follow-up research on hypermedia network inheritance.

6. Support for collaborative work can be approached through design environments.

7. The inferencing language provides the kind of programmable extensibility that Halasz has in mind; the predicates and queries can be modified and tailored by the user; and the types, etc. are user-defined and always open-ended.

Thus, of the seven issues for hypermedia, four have been directly and successfully addressed in this research and the remaining three are high on the list of priorities for the future.

A final concern for future work relates to user testing. A central priority of this research has been the attempt to keep the system as easy as possible for non-programmers to use, so it can indeed provide an attractive alternative to rule-based expert systems. As additional power and generality is added to the system, it is important to monitor its usability empirically. This means realistic user testing. The inference language is currently in a primitive prototype version. The menu-based interface is adequate for internal debugging, testing and demos, but is not adequate for users. In particular, a construction kit approach to building, testing and modifying queries would be valuable for facilitating use of the language. A much larger, realistic application would also need to be developed in a domain of interest to users, containing information or computations not already available to them.

The software discussed here was developed in an object-oriented extension to **Pascal** in the MS-DOS operating system. It was subsequently ported to the Microsoft Windows 3.1 environment and enhanced with a graphical user interface for defining predicates and queries in the language and for navigating through the hypermedia using smart nodes and links.

The language is currently being embedded in a high-functionality design environment. (McCall, 1990) The specific application domain for this is lunar habitat design, a form of space-based architecture. (Stahl, 1993) This work entails three main aspects:

- Building a software environment to support designers, based on the kind of intelligent hypermedia discussed here.

- Extending the inferencing language to be multi-media, incorporating CAD-style vector graphics, bit mapped graphics, boolean conditionals and numeric expressions, as well as text.

- Developing a hypermedia-based inheritance mechanism for type inheritance, virtual copying, perspectives and versioning.

Conclusions

The goal of this work has been to show that hypermedia has more computational potential than is generally thought. Hypermedia is often regarded merely as a user-friendly way of browsing "canned" information. The implementation of predicates shows that the link traversal mechanisms inherent in hypermedia also have the potential for knowledge-based computation. The key to exploiting this potential is twofold: 1) the creation of a powerful query language and 2) the embedding of queries at nodes to create virtual structures. Given a custom implementation of fine-granularity hypermedia, which is object-oriented and designed with the language in mind, only minor changes were needed to make the hypermedia perform full-blown inference once a powerful retrieval language was implemented.

Inference is defined as the combining of facts to derive new facts. In the approach to hypermedia reported here, primitive nodes and links are combined by means of embedded predicates and queries written in the inference language to deduce new (virtual) nodes and links. The end effect for a user is the same as that created in expert systems by means of sophisticated inference engines, namely to infer logical or computational results. The *intelligent hypermedia* approach avoids the need for a separate inference module and spares the user the difficulties of formulating rule bases. The computational mechanisms are handled by extending the normal navigational mechanisms of hypermedia.

The power of intelligent hypermedia was demonstrated in a suggestive way through the implementation of a realistic application, academic advising. Experience with this application and other test cases showed that the development of systems runs up against complications inherent in the domain. No matter how natural the language, an application may require the initial assistance of an experienced programmer or system analyst. However, for simpler tasks and, what is more important, for understanding, modifying and extending existing applications, the inferencing language appears to be quite easy for users.

The inference language allows users to build a vocabulary of terms for their domain (or for their personal way of looking at things). This vocabulary is open-ended and can be modified or extended at any time. The naming of macros, predicates and queries allows the system designer or user to conceal technical complexities. Definitions can be built up step by step in a modular way to divide complex concepts. In the end, statements can be formulated in a simple, natural way. The underlying details are always available to the interested user for exploring aspects of an overall problem or for tweaking a definition.

The research uncovered an unanticipated limitation of the original idea of smart nodes. It overcame this limitation with the notion of predicates. Instead of using approaches from procedural programming, the problem was solved in a way that is transparent to the user and results in intuitive results without the user having to be concerned with the use of variables. Using smart links implemented as predicates turned out to be a very powerful and useful notion. The power of this mechanism and of the inference language generally is discussed at length in (Stahl, 1993).

Academic advising is an example of a domain that could be modeled in a rule-based expert system or in navigational hypermedia. The use of intelligent hypermedia combines the computational power of the former with the flexibility of the latter. The inference language will continue to evolve in scope, power and elegance as it is applied in new computational contexts and new application domains. The goal is to develop a language that can be written and read easily by people who are not experienced computer programmers. This will require considerable experience in observing the language in use in a variety of situations.

References

Eisenberg, M. (1991). Programmable Applications: Interpreter Meets Interface.

Fischer, G., McCall, R., Morch, A. (1989). JANUS: Integrating Hypertext with a Knowledge-Based Design Environment. *Proceedings of Hypertext '89*. New York: ACM.

Fischer, G., Girgensohn, A. (1990). End-User Modifiability in Design Environments. *Human Factors in Computing Systems, CHI '90 Conference Proceedings (Seattle, WA)*. New York: ACM.

Fischer, G., Grudin, J., Lemke, A., McCall, R., Ostwald, J., Reeves, B., Shipman, F. (1991). Supporting Indirect, Collaborative Design with Integrated Knowledge-Based Design Environments. Submitted to *Human- Computer Interaction*.

Halasz, F.G. (1988). Reflections on Notecards: Seven Issues for the Next Generation of Hypermedia Systems. *Communications of the ACM*, Vol. 31, No. 7.

McCall, R. (1989). Mikroplis: A Hypertext System for Design. *Design Studies*, 10 (4), 228-238.

McCall, R., Bennett, P., d'Oronzio, P., Ostwald, J., Shipman, F., Wallace, N. (1990). Phidias: A PHI-based Design Environment Integrating CAD Graphics into Dynamic Hypertext. *Proceedings of the European Conference on Hypertext (ECHT '90)*.

Peper, G., MacIntyre, C., Keenan, J. (1990). Hypertext: A New Approach for Implementing an Expert System. *IBM Internal Technical Liaison Conference on Expert Systems, 1989.*

Stahl, G. (1993). Supporting Interpretation in Design. *Journal of Architecture and Planning Research*, Special issue on Computational Representations of Knowledge. Forthcoming.

Acknowledgments

The ideas in this report grow out of several years of research by Ray McCall of the School of Environmental Design. He was the principal investigator for the grant that supported this work and most of the theoretical insights of the research originated with him. He also contributed many ideas to this report and reviewed an earlier draft of it.

The report benefited from comments at a presentation to the Human-Computer Communication group and at a CASI Research Symposium.

The research reported here was supported in part by a grant from the Colorado Advanced Software Institute (CASI) for 1990-91. CASI is sponsored in part by the Colorado Advanced Technology Institute (CATI), an agency of the State of Colorado. CATI promotes advanced technology education and research at universities in Colorado for the purpose of economic development.

Appendix: Abstract Syntax of the Inference Language

Following is the abstract syntax in BNF notation of the version of the inference language discussed in the paper. The options that existed in the original Mikroplis query language are underlined.

QUERY OPTIONS

Q : Query   Q::= display Art R Prp S which F, if B, with their R, else Q. | the Nth result of Q | Q and Q

S : Subject   S::= all items | all K | Z | Q | S and S

R : Relationship   R::= everything | T | converse T | R which are not self | the Nth R | R which F if B with their R, else R | Z | R Prp R | R and R | R as a macro | R as a predicate

F : Filter   F::= Eop C | Eop Q | have Qop R which F [, with them] | are Cop N | e Cop N R which F [, with them] | F Lop F | F and which also F | contain data type Top | contain no duplicates

MEDIA OPTIONS

C : Character   C::= String | {text of} Z | substring of C from N for N | C append C

N : Number   N::= Real | the count of results of the query: (Q) | N Nop N | Z

B : Boolean   B::= true | false | N is Cop N | C Eop C | Q Eop Q | not B | B Lop B | Pop Q | R of S which F

HYPERMEDIA OPTIONS

K : Kind   K::= node kind

T : Type   T::= link type | macro | predicate

Z : Node   Z::= C | C if B | Z if B | Q

L : Link   L::= Z linked to Z

OPERATOR OPTIONS

Nop : Numerical   Nop::= plus | minus | times | divided by

Cop : Comparison   Cop::= more than | less than | the same as | at least | no more than | not the same as

Lop : Logical   Lop::= and | or | exclusive or | nand

Qop : Quantity   Qop::= no | all | (at least one) | most | several | a few

Pop : Proposition   Pop::= there are | there are not | there are several

Top : Type   Top::= numeric | non-numeric

Eop : Equality   Eop::= equal | are not equal to | do not contain | contain | are contained in | are not contained in

Prp : Preposition   Prp::= of | about | by | for | from | in | on | over | to | under

Art : Article   Art::= | a | all | an | that | the | those

2.   A Computational Medium for Supporting Interpretation in Design

Introduction

Theorists of design methodology have described facets of design and problem solving that call for computer support. However, their assessments conflict in fundamental ways with the techniques of artificial intelligence, the discipline within computer science concerned with these issues. For instance, pivotal writings about design have argued as follows:

1.   While computers should be used to help manage the complexity of today's problems, they should not replace or restrict the role of human intuition. (Alexander)

2.   The conceptualization of design problems should be allowed to evolve through public deliberation; computers can support communication and critique as long as they do not impose closed frameworks. (Rittel)

3.   Designers construct the design situation, including its patterns and materials; computers can aid in this if they do not restrict things to pre-established ways of viewing. (Schoen)

These statements express a troubled tension between (human) *interpretation* and (computer) *representation*.

Artificial intelligence traditionally plays upon the computational power of formal representations. A recent shifting from autonomous expert systems to critiquing systems may help to re-establish the role of people in problem solving, but still retains too heavy a reliance on rigid, objective representations. Many of the fields most in need of computer support are exploratory domains that cannot be reduced to systems of formal rules and manipulations of primitive symbols. Lunar habitat design is one example of this.

Hermes is a computer system to support interpretation in the design of lunar habitats. This research prototype features a special language for defining terms, conditions, critics and queries to display design information from the human user's interpretive perspective. Hierarchies of interpretive contexts facilitate the sharing of these perspectives. All textual, graphical and other information is integrated and inter-related by a form of hypermedia incorporating these language and context mechanisms. This provides a computationally active medium for expressing, storing, communicating and critiquing design interpretations..

The message of **Hermes** is that computers can support human creativity in design rather than automating or rigidifying the design process. To do this, a new approach to software is needed that heeds the deeper principles of design methodology and the nature of human interpretation.

Design Methodology from the Perspective of Computer Support

Alexander: Balancing human intuition with computation

Deliberation on the question of whether and how computers should be used to support the work of designers has raged for several decades now. The issues go to the heart of what design is and should be. In his now classic *Notes on the Synthesis of Form*, Christopher Alexander reviewed the history and even the prehistory of design in order to argue that the field has reached a second watershed in the mid-twentieth century. The profession of design had originally emerged when society started to produce new needs and innovative perspectives too rapidly to allow forms to be developed through "unselfconscious" activities of slowly evolving traditions. Now, the momentum of change has reached a second qualitatively new stage:

> Today more and more design problems are reaching insoluble levels of complexity. This is true not only of moon bases, factories and radio receivers, whose complexity is internal, but even of villages and teakettles. In spite of their superficial simplicity, even these problems have a background of needs and activities which is becoming too complex to grasp intuitively. (Alexander, 1964, p.3)

The management of complexity must become a primary concern of the field of design. The level of complexity that Alexander had in mind is characterized by the fact that it exceeds the ability of the unaided individual human mind (intuition) to handle it effectively. Various methodologies can help and this is where the abstract logical structures, diagrams or patterns that Alexander proposed come in. He saw a major advantage of the systematic use of such logical structures in what he referred to as a "loss of innocence."

When design first became a profession with rules that could be stated in language and taught, there was, according to Alexander's account, a first such loss of innocence. More recently, when the Bauhaus designers recognized that one could design for mechanized production, another accommodation was made with changing times. The use of systematic methodologies to help manage complexity would, Alexander claimed, entail an analogous acceptance of the limitations of the individual designer's intuitive powers. This would bring with it a significant opportunity for progress of the profession. When the design process is formulated in terms of logical structures it becomes much more readily subject to public criticism than when it is concealed in the mysteries of the lonesome genius' artistry, just as the earlier formulation of previously unselfconscious design into explicit plans, articulated processes and stated justifications laid the basis for a science of design which could be refined through on-going debate. Loss of innocence entails the removal of an outmoded barrier to the kind of critical reflection required for a profession.

But Alexander did not see the issue one-sidedly. He did not propose that design methods substitute for the practice of design or for the designer's practical intuitions. Rather, he recognized that intuition was necessary and argued for a proper balance: "Enormous resistance to the idea of systematic processes of design is coming from people who recognize correctly the importance of intuition, but then make a fetish of it which excludes the possibility of asking reasonable questions." (*Ibid*, p.9) Alexander felt that the fetishism of intuition as some kind of inalienable artistic freedom of the designer functioned as a flimsy screen to hide the individual designer's incapacity to deal with the complexity of contemporary design problems. As a consequence of the designer ignoring these limitations, the unresolved issues of complexity get passed down to engineers who have been trained to work out details rather than to grasp complex organization synthetically; the product that results tends to be a monument to the personal idiom of the creator rather than an artifact with a good fit to its function.

The questions posed by Alexander three decades ago for design methodology generally still confront the particular task of figuring out how best to use computers for supporting the work of designers. Consider his first example above, that of designing a moon base. Clearly, this is an overwhelmingly complex task. One needs to take into account technical information about supporting humans in outer space, including issues that may not have previously been thought of and investigated (such as the practicality of using lunar rocks as building materials). One must also consider the mission goals of the base, both stated and implicit. Then there are social and psychological issues concerning the interactions among groups of people who are confined in an alien environment for a prolonged period. All of these factors interact with the more common issues of designing a habitat for working, eating, socializing and sleeping -- resulting in a design problem of considerable complexity.

This paper will focus for its example on the specific project of developing a computer system for lunar habitat design. A primary concern will be to fashion the system so that it supports the intuitive powers of human designers. That is, the system will not be intended to replace the human designer, as has been the goal in traditional artificial intelligence and expert systems. At the same time, it should not simply provide computational power that is tangential to the process of design. Rather, the computer system should simultaneously aid the designer to manage the complexity of the project and to articulate his or her intuitions about the emerging design. In keeping with the balance called for by Alexander, the computer should give free reign to the human designer's intuitive powers even while it helps to document the central issues and decisions of the design process so they are rendered publicly available.

Rittel: Tackling wicked problems through argumentation

When Horst Rittel declared in his *Dilemmas in a General Theory of Planning* that "planning problems are inherently wicked," (Rittel, 1972, p.10) he thereby spelled out that characteristic of planning and design tasks that has subsequently become the central source of perplexity in trying to imagine a computer system that can effectively support the challenging aspects of design. For, computer programs have traditionally been devised in accordance with the classical paradigm of "tame" science and engineering problems -- precisely the paradigm that Rittel argued is not applicable to the problems of open societal systems with which planners and designers are generally concerned. This paradigm assumes that a problem can first be formulated in a clear, unambiguous and exhaustive manner. Then, based on such a problem statement, all possible solutions can be evaluated to see which are optimal solutions to the problem. Computer programs based on this paradigm try to represent in advance the space of problems and solutions for a well-defined type of design problem in an explicit and exhaustive manner. Their contribution to solving a problem is to take a complete statement of the problem as input and to compute the optimal solution to it by means of a search through the set of all possible solutions.

Rittel claimed that the wicked problems of planning could not be thoroughly understood in the first place unless one already had ideas for solving them. Suppose, for instance, that you are asked to plan a mission to the moon for four astronauts for a period of 45 days. According to NASA, the purpose of the mission is to explore long-term stays for crews of international backgrounds and mixed gender; there is to be some scientific research and some site work to prepare for future moon bases. In thinking about the design of the lunar habitat for this mission, you might begin to discuss the importance of privacy issues with other people on your design team. You might feel that not only was some physical privacy needed for cultural reasons, but psychologically there would be a need to structure a careful mix of public and private spaces and opportunities. These privacy issues might become paramount to your design even though they had not been included in the original problem statement. In this way, the set of issues to be investigated and concerns to be balanced would emerge and evolve as the planning process took place.

In opposition to the then dominant methods of operations research which tried to compute optimal solutions from static and well-defined problem statements, Rittel called for a model of planning as "an argumentative process in the course of which an image of the problem and of the solution emerges gradually among the participants, as a product of incessant judgment, subjected to critical argument." (*Ibid*, p.13) This is a very different model of the profession. In the operations research approach, it was assumed that problems could be formulated up front and that the dimensions of possible solutions could, at least in principle, also be enumerated once and for all. Solving a planning or design problem then consisted in making that combination of choices among the given options that maximized some objective quantitative measures of the criteria specified in the problem statement. In no sense should the value of a solution be determined by the process of its discovery or by the individuals involved in formulating it. This was a model made for computerization. In fact, one might suspect that this model was influenced by the computer model in the first place: only those elements were accepted as scientific and objective which could be easily reduced to algorithmic processes.

By contrast, Rittel rejected the notion that even the underlying concepts in terms of which a problem or its solution could be formulated were objective in this sense. The language used in real, significant planning processes is itself the result of discussion and debate among various parties, each of whom uses subjective judgments to criticize hidden assumptions and to reconstrue implicit meanings of terms. No one view has a necessary priority; every view must be capable of standing up to critique by opposing views. Solutions arise through this process of critique, in which new issues and possibilities can arise at any moment and new criteria can be introduced or old concerns reinterpreted. Rather than worshipping some theoretical notion of objectivity, Rittel's approach recognizes that people's perspectives on problems are based in subjective conditions such as their individual value systems and political commitments or their personal roles *vis a vis* the proposed solutions:

> For wicked planning problems, there are no true or false answers. Normally, many parties are equally equipped, interested and/or entitled to judge the solutions, although none has the power to set formal decision rules to determine correctness. Their judgments are likely to differ widely to accord with their group or personal interests, their special value-sets and their ideological predilections. (*Ibid*, p.15)

Consider again the concept of privacy in the lunar habitat. A design team might start from the idea of visual privacy. Through discussion of the implications of life in this confined space, they might want to include protection from the noise of flushing toilets and snoring neighbors. But then the team member concerned with medical contingencies might introduce a notion of privacy for an injured astronaut who needs to recuperate. A psychologist on the team might insist that crew members have an opportunity to communicate in private via radio with family members back on Earth, or that there be ways for pairs of astronauts to confide in each other without being monitored by ground control. Because the crew will be international, a sociologist would bring up culturally diverse definitions of privacy that must be taken into account as well. Different members of a design team come to the common task with different perspectives; their constructive criticisms of each other are part of what makes a team more insightful than the sum of its parts. Given a methodology that builds on the strengths of design as an argumentative process, these differences can contribute to a robust solution that takes into account a variety of competing and interacting insights, not all of which could have been anticipated in advance.

Computer support for planning and design processes as Rittel conceived of them must allow team members to articulate their individual views and judgments, to communicate these to each other and to forge shared perspectives. It must support deliberation or argumentation. Rittel himself made some initial attempts to define computerized issue base information systems, leading to recent systems like gIBIS (Conklin, et al, 1988) and Phidias (McCall, et al, 1991). Somehow, the dimensions of the design problem must be allowed to emerge and change as different perspectives are brought to bear, as initial approaches are subjected to critique and as solutions gradually emerge. Computer systems may be useful for storing, organizing and communicating complex networks of argumentation -- as long as they do not stifle innovation by imposing fixed representations of the ideas they capture.

Schoen: Dialogs of discovery

Alexander and Rittel have suggested the importance of the individual designer's intuitions and of public processes of deliberation for the development of good design. This is at least implicitly a rejection of the model of technical rationality based on the methodology of the natural sciences. Donald Schoen made this rejection even more explicit in his influential study of the design profession, *The Reflective Practitioner* (1983). Here he argued that much design knowledge is tacit, rather than being rule-based. He viewed the design process as a dialog-like interaction between the designer and the design situation, in which the designer makes moves and then perceives the consequences of these design decisions in the design situation (e.g., in a sketch). The designer manages the complexity that would be overwhelming if all the constraints and possibilities were formulated as explicit symbolic rules by using professionally trained skills of visual perception, graphical sketching and vicarious simulation.

Schoen recently took up the question of computer support for design in a paper with the descriptive title, *Designing as reflective conversation with the materials of a design situation*. In this article, he argued for a necessarily limited role for computers in design because one of the most important things that designers do is to create the design situation itself. Not only is this something that computers cannot do by themselves, but it also precludes computer programmers from pre-defining the design situation for the computer.

Before trying to discuss potential computer roles, Schoen takes time to review several experiments supporting his thesis that designers construct the design situation. In one experiment, several experienced architects are shown a 14-sided, dimensioned polygon with door locations indicated and asked to design a library with that shape as its footprint. One architect saw the figure in terms of simple end entrances and complex middle entrances; another saw it as three pods surrounding a middle; a third saw two Ls back to back. Clara, another subject, discovered a five-foot displacement in the layout that complicated the spatial relationships considerably for her. Schoen concludes from these and other studies that designers construct the problem by seeing the situation *as* defined in a certain way:

> In one sense, the 5 ft displacement that Clara noticed is there to be discovered. However, not everyone who tried the library exercise discovered it. Clara did. She noticed it, named it and made a *thing* that became critically important for her further designing. In this sense, her treatment of the library exercise shows her not only discovering but *constructing* the reality of a design situation. For designers share with all human beings an ability to construct, via perception, appreciation, language and active manipulation, the worlds in which they function. . . . Every procedure and every problem formulation, depends on such an ontology: a construction of the totality of things and relationships that the designer takes as the reality of the world in which he or she designs. (Schoen, 1992, p.9)

Other experiments showed that designers also construct the materials, site and relationships (or prototypes) in a similar way to how Clara constructed the crucial patterns of the project. In this sense, then, there is no given design problem which is explicitly and exhaustively defined before the designer comes to it. Correspondingly, there can be no well-defined problem space for the designer (or for some automated version of the designer) to search through methodically. Rather, the designer's subjective, personal or intuitive appreciations shape the problem by constructing its patterns, materials and relationships. The design project is solved by the designer experimenting with tentative moves within the constructed design situation and discovering the consequences of those moves.

Clearly, a computer program cannot on its own construct a design situation the way an architect does, picking out, naming and focusing upon critical patterns, materials and relationships. To the extent that the role of a designer includes applying intuitive, perceptual and linguistic skills to see the situation creatively and to converse with it reflectively, a computer cannot do what a human designer does. Assuming that Schoen is correct that these skills are necessary for real design, a computer can also not accomplish the design task using alternative methods to those used by humans, because programs as we know them are based on predefined representations of fixed and strictly delimited ontologies. Computer programs for design are therefore limited to solving problems in well-defined microworlds or else working with human designers to support their human skills.

The Hermeneutics of Design

Adrian Snodgrass and Richard Coyne of the Faculty of Architecture in Sydney have begun to articulate a philosophical basis for artificial intelligence in design by arguing that design is hermeneutical. "Hermeneutics" is the study of interpretation and today refers primarily to the philosophy of Martin Heidegger and its explication by Hans-Georg Gadamer. Snodgras and Coyne argue that design is a human science in contrast to a natural science and therefore must be founded on human understanding rather than on objective method. This has profound implications for the attempt to provide computer support for design, as well as for the more general attempt to comprehend the design process. The ideas of hermeneutic philosophy provide a conceptual framework for further explicating Alexander's ideas about intuition and public critique, Rittel's views on wicked problems and the need for argumentative processes involving personal interests and Schoen's analysis of tacit knowledge and the designer's dialogue with the constructed design situation.

As a human science, design is based in human understanding gained through processes of interpretation, rather than being based in knowledge, that is, in propositions and explicit rules. In fields like design, claims are not proven by appeal to objective facts and rigorous methods, but by reference to further interpretations (Rittel's argumentative process). A given claim reflects a certain interpretation of the design situation, a certain way of seeing it or constructing it, as Schoen would say. It is always legitimate to question a design move and to demand some justification. But the justification will always be from the perspective of an interpretation, which can be questioned further. There are no axiomatic starting or stopping positions, such as those sought by the rationalist tradition. No claims form absolute starting positions for arguments that cannot themselves be questioned; the chain of justifications based on interpretations ends only when one concedes that the argument is plausible or convincing from the perspective that one has been persuaded to adopt.

The model is indeed one of persuasion, not of hypothesis testing. One is always already in an interpretive context. From within this context, one then understands new arguments, claims and interpretations. Being in an interpretive context is not like tentatively accepting a propositional hypothesis that one may later flatly reject as false based on some discovered objective facts. It is more like having a framework through which one can first understand arguments and facts and thereby modify one's own framework. In Heidegger's terminology, we are always already thrown (*Geworfen*) into a certain way of being in the world and from this position we project (*Entwerfen*) new interpretations of the world. We project a future based on our past history. Interestingly, the German term for projecting is also used in its noun form for a project, design or sketch: a design is a projection of a possible future artifact.

According to Heidegger (1927), the projecting of interpretation takes place based on three dimensions of preliminary understanding:

- Pre-judice: we already have a wealth of tacit, culturally acquired skills and practices that we bring with us as historical (thrown) beings.

- Fore-sight: we see our situation in terms of a conceptual framework and language in terms of which things can be disclosed to us.

- Pre-conception: we have a tentative expectation of what it is that we are about to interpret.

Most of the time, we form interpretations without being aware of this three-fold background of assumptions. That is why the interpretive process of design seems so mysterious and intuitive. As we are forced to justify or reflect critically upon the assumptions of our interpretive stance, we gradually make more and more of the underlying background explicit. We can be prompted to do this by what Schoen calls "breakdowns" in the design process. For instance, we make a move in our design sketch and then we see that a problem occurs as a result. Perhaps seeing the problem brings to our attention a certain need or constraint of the project that has been violated and that we were not formerly aware of. Breakdowns of relationships in our situation are a common way in which our circumstances are explicitly disclosed to us. Dialog with other team members is another way in which tacit assumptions are brought to light, in explaining and arguing for one's own views in order to bridge the gap to someone else's perspective. Critical self-reflection while engaged in a design task is yet another way:

The process of design is thus a disclosure, in two senses. Firstly, it is a disclosing of the artifact that is being designed; and secondly and simultaneously, it is an unfolding of self-understanding, since it reveals one's preunderstandings. It uncovers the preconceptions that are constitutive of the design outcome and at the same time brings to light the prejudices that are constitutive of what we are. (Snodgrass & Coyne, 1990, p.15)

This conception of design as a dialog that discloses involves a very different notion of language than that of the natural sciences. "On the one hand there is the model of formalized language, the language of primary units that are combined according to the rules of logic to form meaningful structures; and on the other hand there is the metaphor of the language of conversation, which is the language of interpretation." (*Ibid*, p.16) This presents a serious problem for any attempt to provide computer support for design. Computers speak the formalized language, while designing requires the language of conversation. Computer programs consist quite precisely of algorithms encoded in a formal language, data structured as primary units and operations performed in accordance with the rules of logic. Even software environments like **Janus** (Fischer, et al, 1990) which try to end-run this problem by communicating with designers via graphical images which represent objects in the design domain provide only a fixed palette of primary units whose semantics are not open to debate.

The Approach of Artificial Intelligence

Simon: Searching through the solution space

Most work in the history of artificial intelligence (AI) can be characterized as an attempt to create computer programs to solve problems by using formalized language, primary units and the rules of logic. Herbert Simon, a major proponent of this tradition, tried in a well-known article on *The Structure of Ill-structured Problems* to finesse his way around Rittel's argument. Rittel had claimed that most interesting problems are wicked problems that are not susceptible to solution by methodical search through some purported solution space, partly because the definition of the problem shifts as the solution develops. Simon's strategy revolves around the example of a chess-playing program. He argues that the problem for this program shifts from move to move as the features of the board (attacks, opportunities, strengths) change. So even chess is a wicked problem. Yet, a computer can play chess using traditional AI techniques. Therefore, wicked problems can be solved by these techniques. QED.

Of course, this is mere sleight-of-hand. The point is that chess is a well-defined domain with explicit, unambiguous rules. In no sense does a chess program reinterpret the rules as the game proceeds. The representation of game states and therefore the universe of possible chess moves is fixed for all games. When Simon finally does consider domains in which the situation must be interpreted, he goes off on spurious tangents to discuss problems of information retrieval, natural language processing and perceptual pattern recognition. With typical AI bravado, he was as reassuring that these still open computerization problems would be solved as he was that ill-structured problems in general could be solved with mechanisms that are not qualitatively different from the ones already being used in AI schemes.

For a brief moment at the end of the article, Simon allows a glimpse of the real issue. If a program needs to acquire external information about the problem situation, then it must force that information into its fixed representational framework. Simon admits that this is a weakness, but concludes that it is really for the best:

> [The process of acquiring external information] is an aid [to the process of understanding that information] because it fits the new information to formats and structures that are already available and adapts it to processes for manipulating those structures. It is a limitation, because it tends to mold all new information to the paradigms that are already available. The problem-solver never perceives the *Ding an sich*, but only the external stimulus filtered through its own preconceptions. . . . The world perceived is better structured than the raw world outside. (Simon, 1973, p.163)

The whole point of Rittel's analysis of wicked problems was that there is no adequate set of formats and structures already available before one acquires the information about a situation. Rather, an argumentative process is needed to respond to the flow of information in ways that transform the paradigms that were already available. Schoen's reflective conversation with the materials of a design situation makes no sense if the materials have been fit to a mute format. Although Heidegger would agree that the world is perceived through existing preconceptions, he would not agree that this is a "better" structure if the tentative original expectations are not allowed to respond and be transformed by the raw world.

Perhaps Simon realized that planners and designers need to take approaches that are qualitatively different from the methods of traditional AI, but he could not imagine how to extend computer technology to support those activities. More recently, in a lecture on *Social Planning*, he recited a series of anecdotes that illustrated how complex planning processes hinge in large part on not assuming a fixed representation of the problem, but letting it evolve with the solution. For instance, in establishing the Marshall Plan after World War II the people involved in setting it up proposed six different and largely contradictory conceptions for its role. Simon underscores the observation that different conceptualizations of the problem would imply various ways of organizing the agency and consequently quite different programs emphasizing different results. He concludes, "what was needed was not so much a 'correct' conceptualization as one that could be understood by all the participants and that would facilitate action rather than paralyze it." (Simon, 1981, p. 166) What was needed, in other words, was an argumentative process among the participants to reach a common understanding, not some formally rigorous representation framework. Although Simon manages to propose a series of methodological approaches to issues of social planning, these are strikingly less formal than the tools he had proposed for well-structured domains. Significantly, he did not discuss the possible implementation of AI programs that might be able to support these methods of social planning.

From expert systems to critiquing

It seems clear that planning and design problems cannot be solved by means of automated methods without the active involvement of humans. Whether one thinks of Alexander's references to intuition, Rittel's insistence on the role of personal interests, Schoen's emphasis on tacit knowledge, or Snodgrass and Coyne's focus on interpretation, one finds the essence of designing in skills that are distinctively human. These skills are to be strictly contrasted with the *modus operandi* of computer programs. During the past decade, AI research has begun to explore ways of supporting human expertise with computer systems that preserve a central role for people. This can be seen in the shift from autonomous expert systems programs to "expert critiquing systems."

In his survey of expert critiquing systems, Barry Silverman defines the term "critic" as a computer program that critiques human-generated solutions. Thus, rather than the program coming up on its own with a solution by following a set of rules that have been gleaned from domain experts, a critic program responds to a solution proposed by a human user of the program. Consider, for instance, an expert system such as Simon discussed for playing chess. It would operate by accepting as input a board position and responding with an optimal move. A chess critic, by comparison, would allow a human user to make a move in response to the board position and would then critique that move. The critic might say that the proposed move violated the rules of chess, or that it put the player in some danger, or that it missed the opportunity for some better move. Most often, the critic would probably be silent and let the human continue to play uninterrupted. The idea of using critics is to allow human intuition to guide the solution process -- recognizing the appropriate role of the human -- while at the same time bringing to bare the computer's ability to recall facts, rules and constraints which the person might easily have forgotten.

As Silverman's presentation makes clear, critics are a straightforward modification of expert systems. They require the same ability of the computer to solve the problem, but merely delay the announcement of the computer's solution until the user has had a chance to try:

> The conversion from an expert system to a critiquing process primarily involved adding a differential analyzer that would: suppress the expert system's diagnosis until after the user had also input his or her own diagnosis (the machine would request that input), compare its diagnosis to that of the human user and determine if the human deviated significantly enough from the machine's ("optimal") diagnosis and plan, to warrant interrupting the human to explain the problem it had uncovered. (Silverman, 1992, p.111)

This approach can be effective in simple, well-defined domains that can be captured in a number of explicit rules or look-up tables. Spelling checkers can be viewed as a particularly successful example, with grammar checkers being more interesting examples, but less useful tools. Perhaps the best application is intelligent tutoring programs, where the user is not likely to be aware of even the rules of a domain that can be formulated in expert system rule bases. AI systems are really only "intelligent" compared to novices who are learning the basic rules, not to domain experts whose skills far exceed the realm of rules.

As the name suggests, critics can represent a first step in a paradigm shift toward the model of critiquing as a dialog process. In fact, Silverman claims critiquing should be a two-way, interactive, communicating, view-sharing process. Unfortunately, when one looks at the implementation details he proposes, this dialog reduces at best to a limited user model in terms of which the program's explanatory output is adjusted to the represented skill level of the user. In other words, the program somehow classifies the user (perhaps by asking the user to select a skill level) and then prints out the text that had been programmed as an explanation for the current "user deviation" for that level user. This is scarcely an argumentative process in Rittel's sense or a dialog in the hermeneutic sense.

In fact, the work Silverman reviews is still very much in the rationalist tradition. Most critic systems require that the domain be well-defined in terms of the following criteria: explicit rules can be specified for each type of wrong answer; the rules for assessing user solutions are objective; only one or two possible correct solutions exist for each task; and subtasks can be critiqued independently of each other. Silverman's own contribution to the theory of the critic approach is to emphasize the importance of clarity (a watchword of rationalism since Descartes). The first thing that critics should do in his opinion is to eliminate ambiguity. "Ambiguous statements which have more than one meaning cannot be clearly confirmed logically," he warns, "nor can they be completely disproven empirically. They may be true according to some interpretations." (*Ibid*, p.107) Although Silverman's critics have introduced people back into the problem-solving loop, they have not opened the loop wide enough to permit true dialog among competing and ambiguous interpretations.

Lunar habitat design: An exploratory domain

The research being reported in this paper is an attempt to go beyond expert systems and expert critiquing systems to develop an approach to computer software design which can support the design process as described above, including the ambiguity of competing interpretations. This work was initiated at the request of a design firm that, among other things, contracts with NASA to do lunar habitat design. As it turns out, the domain of lunar habitat layout is a particularly rich one to investigate from the perspective of providing computer support and findings in this very specific domain promise to have broad generality for design, particularly for high-tech architecture.

The need for computer support of lunar habitat design was originally suggested by the sheer volume (complexity) of knowledge required -- far more than people could maintain in their heads or even locate easily in manuals. In fact, the manuals themselves seem to suffer from a lack of computer-supported maintenance, raising serious questions of how to interpret official regulations consistently with each other. There are voluminous sets of NASA regulations for all Man-In-Space designs, ergonomic standards and specific project contractual obligations that must be adhered to by designs. Furthermore, there is a concept of traceability, meaning that there must be documentation tracing how the regulations are incorporated in the design.

But the complexity of lunar habitat design is not just a matter of the quantity of information. Requirements, components and rationale all have to be reinterpreted within the *Gestalt* of the evolving design. This is an application realm in which, for instance, most physical components require some amount of customization. One cannot simply select a stock sink or bed from a catalog, because of gravitational or volumetric considerations. Even pumps and fans have to be re-thought. Therefore, the idea of representing standard parts with schematic icons or fixed items from a palette is inadequate. One wants to start from existing components, but one then needs to be able to modify them freely to account for differences in the lunar setting. Furthermore, there are many design interactions among components that are placed close together -- partially because space is at a premium and because things must work together to form a coherent environment for habitation. This means that design of a given part is very much situated in its context, in terms of neighboring components (e.g., buffers for sounds), design concerns (privacy) and projected usage issues (traffic flow). The computer representation of the design must function as the unique world in which situated design can take place effectively. The notion of a programmer defining in advance a formal language of terms and graphic primitives representing design concerns and physical components is out of the question.

Elements of lunar habitats should be similar to familiar products to facilitate manufacture and to give astronauts a sense of being at home, but they must also be different to meet the severe constraints of their context. This means that models and rules of thumb must be searched for in many other domains (houses, submarines, Antarctic labs) and then applied to the lunar setting. Such application is not a mechanical process; it must be done by the creative and synthetic minds of humans, with computer systems merely presenting the relevant elements. Even the determination of what might be relevant must involve the human designer, for this is also very much a matter of interpretation based on a deep understanding of the semantics involved. To support the subtlety of the communication between the computer system and its users, the users must be able to develop a language that operationalizes their evolving interpretations in ways that can be used by the software.

At the same time, the development of such a language can provide a basis for shared understanding among groups of designers, whether or not they are working together physically or temporally. For instance, a designer who is considering an old design for adaptation into a new project can learn about the old design through the language that was developed with it -- including the formulations of critics specific to that design. Aspects of this approach related to supporting collaborative work among groups are particularly critical in this domain because each successful design must undergo the scrutiny of many teams. Generally, the only communication between these teams is the design document itself. Thus, it is important that the design include effective documentation of the rationale and interpretive stance behind it.

A high-tech design goes through many stages of development, involving different design teams. Architects, designers, a variety of engineers and administrators all work on the designs from their own viewpoints. Successful designs are sent to other contractors around the country for detailing, mock-up, testing and construction. At each stage, the design is modified, based on people's understanding of the design and its rationale. If a creative design concept is to survive this argumentative process, with tight cost, weight and volume constraints at every stage, strong rationale must be communicated; a schematic or a pretty picture will not suffice. In fact, a typical product of lunar habitat design consists of a small booklet predominated by textual explanations of rationale, rather than simply detailed drawings.

Because designers do not have personal experience with life in lunar habitats, knowledge stored in previous related designs (including Skylab, the Shuttle, previous trips to the moon) is invaluable. Old designs are re-used extensively. To the extent that design rationale of the old designs has been captured, it is vitally important. Consequently, it is likely that design rationale will increasingly become an integral part of design. This should add tremendous power to practitioners who take it seriously and those who use computer tools that support rationale capture. Such a development represents a significant break with the tradition of CAD programs, which are purely graphical and embody very little semantics. However, it has impressive precedence in other fields like science, mathematics and philosophy, where written theories, proofs and arguments were refined through processes of public critique and grew into extensive bases of shared knowledge impossible in non-literate cultures.

Lunar habitat design is not a field in which one could expect to interview an expert and come up with a set of formal rules and elements to define a comprehensive system of knowledge. Workers in this field are attempting to explore a new domain and to begin to map out the potential problem space. A goal of researchers is to sketch in parametric curves that would indicate how designs have to change depending on such parameters as number of astronauts, length of mission duration or payload delivery capacity. (Cf., e.g., Design Edge, 1990; Moore, et.al., 1991; Kazmierski, et al, 1992) But even the most important parameters remain undefined and open to interpretation and debate. For instance, no NASA guidelines cover privacy issues, but this is an increasing concern of thoughtful designers and a topic for vigorous political debate and even power struggles within NASA. (Compton, et al, 1983)

In the lunar habitat design sessions studied for the current research, privacy issues were in fact the first real concerns to surface. They structured how the designers constructed their task. Related questions of social interaction dominated questions of physical layout, indicating that social planning was necessarily a significant aspect of the designing. When the geopolitics (or solar system politics) of NASA's goals are reflected in the deliberations, the result is truly a wicked problem in Rittel's full sense.

In relatively unexplored domains such as lunar habitat design, the purpose of design attempts is not to find optimal solutions within a known problem space, but to begin to create a solution space in the first place. The most important role of computer support for such domains may be to capture the ideas that are being generated. Terms and critics which are formulated on the spot during this design exploration process are expressions of what a designer may want to pay attention to. So, for instance, the important criteria for the critics is not the rigor of their computations in the sense of some rationalist engineering ideal, but their ability to capture the designer's interpretive intent. The computer system as a whole should not primarily be an autonomous equation solver, but a powerful medium of external memory to empower people's creativity. An appropriate software environment for this domain would be one designed to capture new and evolving knowledge, rather than one that simply incorporates predefined knowledge representations and systems of production rules.

Hermeneutic Software Design

A system for interpretation in design

The computer software for lunar habitat design is part of an effort to define an alternative to knowledge-based expert systems. The new approach is called "hermeneutic" software design because it is interpretation-based. It proposes a model of the computer as a medium within which designers can construct, interpret, converse with and communicate about design artifacts. The system does not claim to incorporate extensive knowledge of the domain in the sense of an expert system's elaborate set of universally-valid production rules or an expert critiquing system's battery of objective critics. Rather, the system provides an environment in which people can view evolving designs from perspectives that are important to them.

Interpretation-based systems are still domain-specific like expert systems in certain ways. First, the structure, implementation and interface of the designing environment are crafted in response to the nature of the domain. For instance, the system for lunar habitat design, which is named **Hermes**, adopts a different approach to providing a palette of building components than a corresponding system for kitchen design would, due to a difference in the domains. Kitchen appliances are stock items which are installed as they come out of the box, whereas lunar habitat components must generally be modified or even redesigned to work properly in the habitat.

Another domain-specific aspect of an interpretation-based environment is that it is always already seeded with a considerable amount of information about the domain, primarily in the form of examples of interpreted designs. There are also a variety of useful terms, critics and queries that have been defined in advance. From a theoretical viewpoint, their "seed" embodies a form of history: we always interpret from the background of past experiences and interpretive traditions, which we initially accept uncritically. In practical terms, it is much easier to design and create new perspectives by starting from and then modifying existing ideas and expressions.

A knowledge-based system would typically be seeded with information that purports to capture an objective understanding of the domain. For instance, it might contain an issue base that contains the primary issues of design in the domain along with the standard options for resolving the issues, a palette of the basic primitive components and a catalog of prototypical solutions. By contrast, an interpretation-based seed would provide tools for building interpretive perspectives of domain artifacts; it would include issues, palette items and artifacts that have been constructed under different interpretations in past design projects. The **Hermes** seed, for example, consists of such information from a series of lunar habitat design sessions that were captured on videotape during preliminary research on the domain and then modeled in the **Hermes** system. Additional examples were added from published designs of lunar habitats. Then, an issue-base was constructed to provide a structure to the complex of inter-related rationale issues.

Because lunar habitat design is an exploratory domain, there is no such thing as a comprehensive or objective view of the field. Case studies from particular interpretive perspectives provide the only base on which new design efforts can be built. Although it is often possible to systematize the information in a seed or in a system that has accumulated more designs through use, the result of this kind of "re-seeding" can make no claim to objectivity or comprehensiveness. The act of reorganizing itself proceeds under a certain interpretation or mixture of interpretations of the field and interesting future designs will focus on new approaches and concerns that were not previously thought of.

Hermes includes a language in which designers can express their concerns. There is also a system of interpretive contexts that can be used for grouping together a set of definitions in the language. Together, these features support the creation and sharing of interpretive perspectives on design artifacts in the computer system.

A language for disclosure and computation

Language is the ultimate medium for interpretation. Our ability to use language is what allows us to disclose things *as* certain kinds of things and thereby to comprehend them. This is what Gadamer has in mind when he claims, "being, which can be understood, is language" (Gadamer, 1960). As noted above, it is in the reflective conversation with the materials of the design situation that the artifact and the designer are both disclosed *as* what or who they are. This happens in the process of explication in which what was tacitly anticipated becomes expressed in language.

A primary stage of language use is naming. Accordingly, the **Hermes** system allows all objects in the design environment to be named by the system user. Graphical objects in a drawing, textual statements in the rationale, critics, etc. can all be named. This gives the user the ability to refer to them in other statements, such as critics and queries and to access annotations attached to them.

Perhaps the next most basic use of language is for categorization. For instance, statements in the **Hermes** issue base (or any other objects in the system) can be categorized by the user when they are created. The links connecting them are also given a type. Thus, an "answer" might be related to an "argument" via a "justification" relationship. Then one can request a display of all the "argument" statements that are related by "justification" links to "answer" statements of a given "issue" statement. Queries like this are fundamental to the ability of **Hermes** to support interpretation. Of course, the types themselves are created by users as are all its terms and constructs (predicates, conditional phrases, filtering clauses, interpretation expressions, critics, queries, etc.).

Because **Hermes** needs to display information in accordance with interpretations that are not pre-defined but are defined by the user, all displays must be computed dynamically. This is done with queries as opposed to the page-based approach of many hypertext systems. In a system like HyperCard, a presentation of design rationale might contain a page full of issues. Embedded with an issue would be a button for its justification. Clicking on that button would bring up another page of text presenting the justification. In **Hermes**, however, the justification must be recomputed based on the current interpretation. This is done by executing a query based on the information desired (e.g., justifications of an answer to a certain issue) and based on the definition of the current interpretation. The results of the query are then displayed, in place of a pre-formatted page.

The **Hermes** Disclosure Language defines all displays of information in the system. In a sense, it is a query language that searches through the database of design drawings and textual rationale to select and format data for displays. The language is specifically defined to correspond to the representation of information in the system. Furthermore, it is designed to be as English-like as possible, to make it easy for users to interpret. At the same time, it must be structured for the computer software to operate upon it and to do so in an efficient manner. So the language is itself a computer representation of user intentions.

The disclosure language is integral to **Hermes**. Computations can be defined by users in the language. For instance, a calculation of total private space in a lunar habitat could be expressed using a predicate for privacy, some measurements of graphical objects in the drawing and arithmetic operations. Critics are also defined in the language, as are display queries. The language allows critics and queries to be built up modularly from component definitions of predicates, filtering clauses, etc. So, the calculation of total private space could be named and referred to in a critic which checked that the result of that computation was at least a certain amount per astronaut. A query could request that all private spaces in the drawing be displayed, highlighted or shown in red. (Cf. Stahl, 1991, for a detailed discussion of the language.) These definitions can be modified in different interpretive contexts, changing the effects of calculations, queries and critics in those contexts.

Interpretive contexts for shared perspectives

Hermes allows its users to define contexts and switch between them. These contexts provide a system for establishing organizing and sharing interpretation. A given context might contain an inter-related set of language constructs (types, predicates, expressions, critics, queries) that articulate an individual's or group's perspective on design.

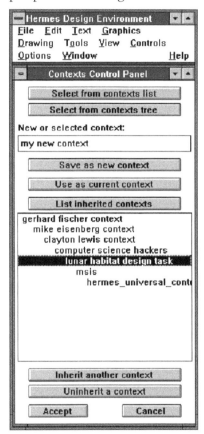

Figure 1. Creating a new context.

A context simply consists of a name for the context and a list of old contexts that are inherited by the new one. This creates a hierarchy of contexts. In Figure 1, for instance, a new context is being created which will inherit from the context named "Gerhard Fischer". Since Fischer's context inherits from Eisenberg's, which inherits from Lewis' and others', the new context will automatically have access to any information in these other perspectives.

Suppose that Lewis defined a clause in the language for entering or displaying "deliberation" as a tree of issues with their answers with their argumentation. Then this definition would be active in the new context as well. However, Eisenberg or Fischer could have redefined this definition in their context. That would not change the definition for Lewis, but it would affect the definition inherited by the new context. Of course, the new context could redefine the term again. In this way, contexts can share definitions. They can also make modifications that do not affect the original definitions that they share. However, if the definition that is inherited is at some point changed, for instance by Lewis, then that change is carried through to the new context.

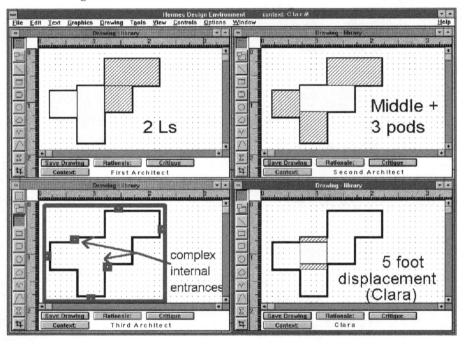

Figure 2. Four interpretations of the library.

Here is an example of contexts being used for different interpretations. In Schoen's experiment with architects designing a library from a given footprint, each of the subjects saw the building space differently and therefore defined the design task differently. Figure 2 shows how the space might be graphically represented in **Hermes** in the four cases reported by Schoen. If the four architects had defined their own contexts and inherited a context that contained the original sketch of the building footprint, then they could have modified the sketch in their own context. If one then asked the system to disclose the sketch of the library, it would appear as appropriate for whichever context one was in. The different graphic representations would form the basis for the development of different terms for discussing the design and for formulating different rationale.

Figures 3 and 4 both show displays of the same information, but from different perspectives: those of Lewis and Eisenberg, respectively. The Design Rationale window shows the results of the query, discussion of node issue 6.6.2.4. That issue read, "What are the design considerations for the sleeping area?" Lewis had answered the third question, "What should be the arrangement of the bunks?" He gave two answers, along with some arguments for these answers.

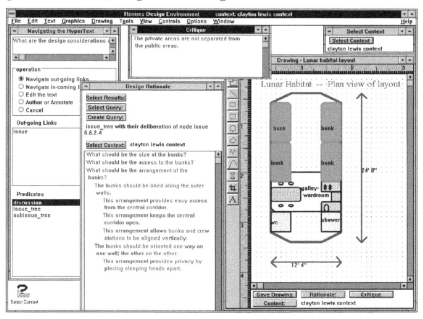

Figure 3. Lewis' interpretation of the lunar habitat design.

Eisenberg modified the answers and arguments in his context. By selecting a different context, we disclose a different display in response to the same query. From the rationale given, we might infer that Lewis is designing from an interpretive perspective primarily concerned with traffic flow and only secondarily with privacy issues. Eisenberg is particularly concerned with establishing a separation of public and private areas and also with minimizing the considerable amount of space taken up by the bunks.

The graphic representation of the lunar habitat has also changed from Figure 3 to Figure 4. The bunks have been rotated and rearranged. An additional area of stowage has been added. (It is not clear from the floor plans shown, but the bunks and stowage are at loft level, above the normal work area and corridor.) Although they look like two different designs, they are really just two views of one object, the lunar habitat design that is being worked on jointly and viewed in two different contexts.

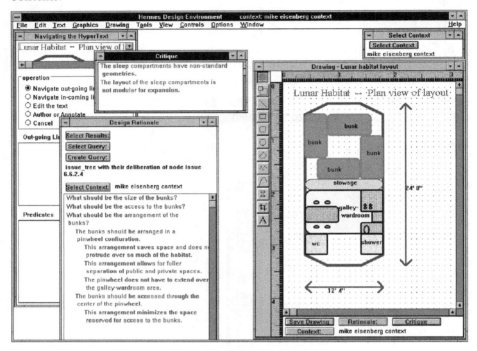

Figure 4. Eisenberg's interpretation of the lunar habitat design.

These figures also illustrate how interpretive critics can work. Assume that Lewis has finished his design. Then Eisenberg comes along with his concern for the separation of public and private spaces. He defines a critic that tests for the separation of these spaces and displays the message that appears in the Critique window of Figure 3. At that point, Eisenberg decides to create his own context and to inherit in it the work of Lewis' context. He then makes the changes to the drawing and rationale and tests his new version with the critic. Now the critic responds with, "No problems were found for this design," as in Figure 4. Eisenberg now has a new critic, which he can use to test other drawings that may be in the database to see how they hold up under his interpretational perspective.

Inheritance of contexts is a powerful mechanism for a couple of reasons. First, a new context can easily and instantly acquire definitions of terms in the disclosure language, textual contents in the issue base and graphical figures of designs from as many other contexts as it wants. This is done using techniques of virtual copying that require no overhead of time or computer memory. Second, procedures of the disclosure language and data in displays are computed dynamically. That means that queries that display information always use the definition of the procedures and data that correspond to the currently active context. So, if Fischer is interested in viewing design rationale with a different interpretation of deliberation, he can modify the definition and then all displays whose query uses that term at some level will be changed to correspond to the new interpretation.

Hypermedia for representation and integration

Modern scientific knowledge has been made practical by the medium of written language. (Donald, 1991; Norman, 1993) Writing provided an external memory for people, overcoming the limitations of human memory, especially short-term working memory. It let them put down their ideas where they and other people could view them, criticize them and refine them. It facilitated the communication of ideas and the evolution of shared perspectives. The **Hermes** design environment -- named after the wing-footed Greek messenger god credited with discovering both spoken and written language -- aims to extend the medium of external memory from static paper to a highly computational medium. The idea is to represent design ideas, graphical concepts, rationale and interpretive perspectives in a system that can dynamically make use of these representations to produce displays that disclose new views of the design situation for people to react to.

Traditional AI always sought clever representation schemes that allowed an automated system to solve the problems of well-known and narrowly defined domains. The perspective on design methodology presented in the first part of this paper argues for a more flexible representation style that empowers the intuitive skills of humans rather than trying to replace them with algorithmic computations. An English-like language in which all terms are defined by the users is one way to do this. A system of personal and shared interpretive contexts in which people can collect drawings, argumentation and language expressions which correspond to their unique interpretive concerns is a second way. In **Hermes**, the disclosure language and the interpretive context mechanisms are used to define an extended form of hypermedia, in which data of any medium and their associated procedural methods can be unified in one representation system.

In a hypermedia system, various kinds of media like text, line drawings, pictures, numbers, conditional propositions, sounds, video clips and animations can be stored as nodes within one database. Each medium has methods associated with it. For instance, each medium would have its own display method, so that text would be displayed as lines of characters in a certain font and size, which wraps to the next line when it reaches the right margin; numbers would be displayed in a certain decimal format; drawings would be displayed graphically. In **Hermes**, the types of nodes (e.g., "issue") and the components of the language (e.g., "deliberation") are also stored in nodes.

Hypermedia consists of these nodes and links between pairs of nodes. The links can have types just like the nodes. By means of the links, nodes can be attached to each other. Thus, in **Hermes**, any node can have textual annotation attached to it. It could also be linked to the name of its creator and the date it was last modified. Various procedures are available to the user of hypermedia to navigate through it. In **Hermes**, viewing of information in the system is controlled primarily by means of the disclosure language and always takes into account the active context. Through the language and context mechanisms, **Hermes** gives its users extensive access to all the information and control over its presentation.

Hermes' extended form of hypermedia provides an integrated representation for the various kinds of data and procedures that are needed to support design. This representation unifies all the information in a single medium that facilitates complex inter-relationships, is computationally active, supports shared interpretive contexts and promotes control by human users. Thereby, **Hermes** can support creativity in design, rather than trying to automate or rigidify the design process. With its disclosure language and its interpretive contexts, **Hermes** illustrates the approach of hermeneutic software design based on principles of design methodology and on the nature of human interpretation.

Acknowledgments

The perspective on design methodology and the approach to computer support for design presented here grew out of ideas of Ray McCall of the School of Environmental Design, Gerhard Fischer of the Department of Computer Science and other members of the Human-Computer Communication research group at the University of Colorado at Boulder. The hermeneutic approach stems from Hans-Georg Gadamer's classes at the University of Heidelberg in 1967/68.

The research in providing computer support for the domain of lunar habitat design was supported in part by a grant to Ray McCall from the Colorado Advanced Software Institute (CASI) for 1991-92 in collaboration with Johnson Engineering, Inc. of Boulder. CASI is sponsored in part by the Colorado Advanced Technology Institute (CATI), an agency of the State of Colorado. CATI promotes advanced technology education and research at universities in Colorado for the purpose of economic development.

This research was also supported by the National Science Foundation under grant No. IRI-9015441.

References

Alexander C (1964) Notes on the Synthesis of Form. Cambridge: Harvard University Press.

Compton WD, Benson CD (1983) Living and Working in Space: A History of Skylab. Washington, DC: NASA.

Conklin J, Begeman M (1988) gIBIS: A Hypertext Tool for Exploratory Policy Discussion. Proceedings of the Conference on Computer Supported Cooperative Work. New York: ACM. 140.

Design Edge (1990) Initial Lunar Habitat Construction Shack. Design control specification. Houston, TX.

Donald M (1991) Origins of the Modern Mind: Three Stages in the Evolution of Culture and Cognition. Cambridge: Harvard University Press.

Fischer G, Lemke A (1988) Construction Kits and Design Environments: Steps Toward Human Problem-Domain Communication. Human-Computer Interaction, 3, 3, 179.

Gadamer H-G (1960) Wahrheit und Method [Truth and Method]. Tuebingen: Mohr.

Heidegger M (1927) Sein und Zeit [Being and Time]. Tuebingen: Niemeyer.

Kazmierski M, Spangler D (1992) Lunatechs II: A Kit of Parts for Lunar Habitat Design. Unpublished project report, College of Environmental Design, University of Colorado at Boulder.

McCall R, Bennett P, d'Oronzio P, Ostwald J, Shipman F, Wallace N (1990) Phidias: A PHI-based Design Environment Integrating CAD Graphics into Dynamic Hypertext. Proceedings of the European Conference on Hypertext (ECHT '90).

Moore GT, Fieber JP, Moths JH, Paruleski KL (1991) Genesis Advanced Lunar Outpost II: A Progress Report. In Blackledge RC Redfield CL Seida SB (Eds.), Space -- A Call for Action: Proceedings of the Tenth Annual International Space Development Conference. San Diego, CA: Univelt, 55.

Norman D (1993) Things That Make Us Smart. Reading, MA: Addison-Wesley.

Rittel H, Webber M (1972) Dilemmas in a General Theory of Planning. Working Paper No. 194. University of California at Berkeley.

Schoen D (1983) The Reflective Practitioner. New York: Basic Books.

Schoen D (1992) Designing as Reflective Conversation with the Materials of a Design Situation. Knowledge-Based Systems, 5, 3.

Silverman B (1992) Survey of Expert Critiquing Systems: Practical an Theoretical Frontiers. Communications of the ACM, 35, 4, 106.

Simon H (1973) The Structure of Ill-structured Problems. Artificial Intelligence, 4, 181.

Simon H (1981) The Sciences of the Artificial. Cambridge: MIT Press.

Snodgrass A, Coyne R (1990) Is Designing Hermeneutical? Working paper. Faculty of Architecture, University of Sydney.

Stahl G (1991) A Hypermedia Inference Language as an Alternative to Rule-Based Expert Systems. Technical Report CU-CS-557-91. Computer Science Department, University of Colorado at Boulder.

3.   Toward a Theory of Hermeneutic Software Design

This paper proposes dissertation research on a new paradigm of software design based on theories of human interpretation. It is argued that computer-supported design environments in certain domains should leave all matters of interpretation to the human user and should try to support the user's interpretation, exploration and development of designs by providing a computationally powerful medium of external memory for storing the evolving design artifact and related knowledge. Hermes, a prototype software environment for the design of lunar habitats, is based on a unified hypermedia knowledge representation system incorporating group and personal perspectives as well as an end-user disclosure language for articulating interpretations of design elements.

Introduction

Prior to the days of professional architects, knowledge of building design could be retained in the heads of individuals, passed down by apprenticeship and tradition, modified by trial and error. In modern times, such knowledge has required supports external to the individual mind: increasingly complex drawings; textbooks of examples, rules and data; formal methods of computation. Today, high-tech design projects -- like the development of lunar habitats for astronauts -- call for computer support to help manage the extensive required knowledge.

The challenge for systems to support designers is to facilitate creativity and to enhance control by the users. Hermeneutic software design seeks to achieve this by understanding the process of design with the help of concepts from the philosophy of Martin Heidegger. In particular, four successive stages of human cognition (including design work) are distinguished: *disclosing* the world in which one is situated; being able to *use* things in the world tacitly; *discussing* or reflecting upon or explicitly interpreting something in a particular way; and *analyzing* things theoretically in accordance with formal methods. Each of these stages can be supported by a software system: a *model* of an imagined world can be created with computer graphics; the user can directly *manipulate* representations in this world with a mouse; a simple *language* can be defined for describing represented objects; and a variety of *methods* of computation can be provided for the user.

The process of design can be further conceptualized by extending Heidegger's analysis of the work of art as the opening up of a world in which truth is set to work. This characterization may apply to buildings, at least to great architectural works like the Greek temple in Paestum, but not yet to evolving designs. Rather, design is the tentative, risky process in which one struggles to bring a work into existence. Gradually, the designer creates a new world, explores its possibilities, resolves its conflicts, aligns its constraints, interprets its significances.

A computer system made to support this explorative process can provide an active, multi-media form of external memory for a design team. A graphics component can bring in design elements from catalogs of past designs and palettes of already designed components, as well as presenting the evolving design artifact itself. Textual comments and discussion associated with these graphical objects can communicate design rationale, project requirements, critiquing considerations. Design variations can be maintained for individuals, specific teams or the general public, to facilitate and help structure communication among people involved with a design over a period of time. Formal methods can be provided for computing volumes, costs, topological features or other concerns. Designers can then use these interlocking tools to vary, test and synthesize elements creatively.

Hermes is a prototype computer system for supporting architectural design. It was devised by studying the process of designing lunar habitats. Using this domain as an illustration, it demonstrates how the variety of forms of knowledge mentioned above can be captured within one representation system, which can then be used to support and integrate a broad range of cognitive functions. The knowledge representation system is a sophisticated form of hypermedia that maintains perspectives and incorporates an end-user interpretation language. This provides the technical basis for promoting designer creativity and control, while facilitating communication among team members.

Scenarios

Let us look at how **Hermes** supports the work of design teams.

1. Here is a view of the **Hermes** interface, with most of its tools represented across the bottom of the window by icons that can be opened into control windows or dialogues. The Graphic Design window shown is a graphics editor, which allows the designer to construct a scale drawing to any level of detail. Typically, components of a drawing will be designed separately or copied from previous designs and modified. Then they will be assembled into a composite drawing.

Here, a freezer is being roughed-in for the galley of a lunar habitat. Construction can take place top-down or bottom-up; components can be successively refined or modified; designs are developed through arbitrary iteration. Any object (graphic primitive, design component, top-level design, rationale issue, language predicate, critic, query, etc.) can be named by the user. Any object can have comments and argumentation attached to it. In the Rationale window, the issues which form the basis for the freezer's design rationale are displayed in preparation for review or modification of the discussion. A critic related to freezers is displayed in the Critic Editor window; it can be used to have **Hermes** critique a design.

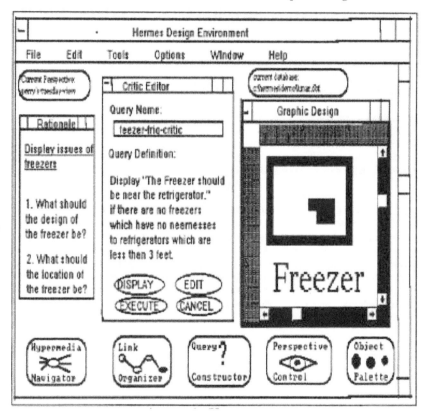

Figure 1. Designing a freezer in **Hermes**.

2. This is a browser of perspectives of current interest. Three uses of the perspectives mechanism of virtual copies are illustrated here:

a. Most noticeably, there is a hierarchy of public, group and personal perspectives, so the *sharing* of graphic and linguistic designs can be controlled by the users.

b. Toward the bottom, one sees instances of versioning, so *alternative* design choices can be explored in parallel.

c. The three beds in the upper right represent a graphical hierarchy in which a single sleep compartment design is viewed three times, with different spatial transformations and other modifications in each instance. The efficiency of *re-use* does not limit user flexibility in customizing each instance.

New perspectives can be created easily and a user can view from within other perspectives (assuming permissions are granted).

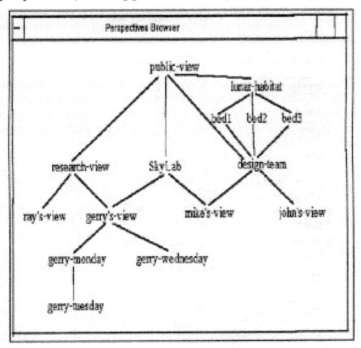

Figure 2. Browser for perspectives.

3. In this scenario, a formal (numeric) computation is defined using the predicate "private-spaces" in a shared perspective. The predicate is in turn modified in two other perspectives. Each perspective defines its own *interpretation* of private space. This means that the result of the computation will be different depending upon the current perspective. Note how the interpretations can be made available for inspection and public discussion by attaching rationale to the definitions.

```
current perspecuve = research-view

privacy-critic = Display "There is little private space in this design."
if the total of measures of private-spaces is less than 4 sq meters
multiplied by the number of astronauts.

private-spaces = sleep-compartments.

argument = This is where an astronaut can go to get away.
```

```
current perspective = ray's-view

private-spaces = sleep-compartments and personal-stowages.

argument = This storage is for the astronaut's private belongings.
```

```
current perspective = gerry's-view

private-spaces = sleep-compartments and work-stations.

argument = The work stations are assigned to individuals and can be
```

Figure 3. Defining a predicate in 3 perspectives.

4. This query shows how the very general interpretation language can be used to perform system functions, like checking for recent modifications. By default, all objects are time-stamped with hypertext links to creator, date, etc.

This query will produce a multi-media display. The application of a simple query to all forms of knowledge in the system is facilitated by an integrated architecture based on a single knowledge representation structure: hypermedia incorporating the interpretation language and the perspectives mechanism.

```
Display all items which have
authors which equal gerry
and which also have creation
-dates which are greater than
2/1/92.

comment = This will display
all graphics, argumentation,
queries, predicates, etc.
which I recently created in
the current perspective.
```

Figure 4. Querying for revisions.

5. The final example shows how the user has quite flexible control over system displays. This is critical to the creativity of the design process, because the displays are the shared external memory. They are the design artifact itself-- "the object to think with" -- that the designers must interpret, explore, synthesize and evolve.

Figure 5. User control over displays.

Central Thesis

The preceding examples illustrate the approach of hermeneutic software: The role of the computer system is to support human designers in their task of interpreting exploring and evolving designs.

Hermes is based on a cognitive theory of the process of architectural design; it provides an external memory for the design team, including graphic representations and design rationale as defined from multiple perspectives. Integrated with this computationally rich form of memory are a variety of tools to aid manipulation and interpretation, including a special language. This approach incorporates several considerations:

1.   Hermeneutic software design defines an open-ended and user-centered approach that contrasts with expert systems based on rationalist models of thought (reliant upon well-defined domain models, explicit computations and minimal involvement of the user).

2.   Design environments can support multiple levels of human cognition: case-based memory, tacit know-how, explicit articulation and methodological calculation (by providing graphic representation, direct manipulation, interpretive language, computation methods).

3.   Language is necessary for the development of powerful interpretations, so the user should be given a linguistic facility for control of and interaction with the domain model (especially to name objects, define predicates, formulate views).

4.   Shared communication should be supported with a mechanism for distinguishing perspectives providing personal/group/public versions of knowledge, language, designs).

5.   Hermeneutic software can promote designer creativity and user control (with personal perspectives, generative language for interpretation, linguistic control over views). Systems for domain professionals should respect the skills of the users and allow them the option of maximum control, even at the cost of unavoidable conceptual complexities that require learning.

6.   An integrated knowledge representation stored in a custom hypermedia system incorporating an interpretation language and a perspectives feature simplifies system architecture (allowing language, perspectives, computational mechanisms to apply to all knowledge, to interrelate it and to help it evolve) and unifies user interaction (helping the user to feel at home with the system and to synthesize various forms of knowledge represented in it).

The Domain and its Needs

The **Hermes** system is being developed through a process of participatory design in cooperation with an engineering firm that does design work under contract with NASA, including designs for lunar habitats. **Hermes** has grown in response to the needs of this kind of work and a study of traditional methods used. The domain of lunar habitat layout is a particularly rich one to investigate and findings in this very specific domain are likely to have broad generality for design, particularly for high-tech architecture.

The need for computer support of lunar habitat design was originally suggested by the sheer volume of knowledge required -- far more than people could maintain in their heads or even locate easily in manuals. In fact, the manuals themselves seem to suffer from a lack of computer-supported maintenance, raising serious questions of how to interpret official regulations consistently with each other. There are voluminous sets of NASA regulations for all Man-In-Space designs, ergonomic standards and specific project contractual obligations that must be adhered to by designs. Furthermore, there is a concept of traceability, meaning that there must be documentation tracing how the regulations are incorporated in the design.

A high-tech design goes through many stages of development, involving different design teams. Architects, designers, a variety of engineers and administrators all work on the designs from their own viewpoints. Successful designs are sent to other contractors around the country for detailing, mock-up, testing and construction. The design documents are the only form of communication among these many teams. At each stage, the design is modified, based on people's understanding of the design and its rationale. If a creative design concept is to survive this process, with tight cost, weight and volume constraints at every stage, strong rationale must be communicated; a schematic or a pretty picture will not suffice.

Because designers do not have personal experience with life in lunar habitats, knowledge stored in previous related designs (including Skylab, the Shuttle, past trips to the moon) is precious. Old designs are re-used extensively. To the extent that design rationale of the old designs has been captured, it is vitally important. Consequently, it is likely that design rationale will increasingly become an integral part of design. This should add tremendous power to practitioners who take it seriously and those who use computer tools that support rationale capture. Such a development represents a significant break with the tradition of CAD programs, which are purely graphical and embody very little semantics. However, it has impressive precedence in other fields like science, mathematics and philosophy, where written theories, proofs and arguments were refined through processes of public critique and evolved into extensive bases of knowledge impossible in non-literate cultures.

There are many other features of the domain of lunar habitat design which influence the functionality of **Hermes**. For one, it is a form of design in which most components require some amount of customization. One cannot just take a stock sink or bed from a catalog, because of gravitational or volumetric considerations. Even pumps and fans have to be re-thought. So the idea of representing things with schematic rectangles or even with fixed items from a palette is inadequate. One wants to start from existing components, but one then needs to be able to modify them freely to account for differences in the lunar setting. Furthermore, there are many design interactions among components that are placed close together -- partially because space is at a premium and because things must work together to form a coherent environment for habitation. This means that design of a given component is very much situated in its context, in terms of neighboring components (e.g., buffering sounds), design concerns privacy) and projected usage issues (traffic flow). The computer representation of the design must function as the unique world in which situated design can take place effectively.

Theoretical Context

The approach of **Hermes** -- and particularly its emphasis on language -- grows out of philosophic theory as well as out of design practice. In the most general terms, hermeneutic software design is an attempt to begin to define a human sciences approach to human-computer-communications, in contrast to the natural sciences paradigm of traditional artificial intelligence theory. Philosophically, the twentieth century has witnessed the debate between two general camps. The first is the rationalism which derives from Plato, Descartes and the neo-Kantians, takes credit for the successes of the physical sciences and is to blame for the excesses of positivism and behaviorism. The other is a tradition that insists that human sciences (like anthropology) require human understanding and the interpretation of subjective meanings, rather than just objective explanations. The rationalist position seems to be fighting an increasingly futile defensive battle in recent years, having received its most thoroughgoing (though little-understood) philosophical critique from Heidegger. Within computer science, this can perhaps best be seen in the increasing number of influential statements of situated cognition.

Schoen (1983), for instance, contrasts the situated seeing-as and doing-as of knowing-in-action with the explicit, theoretical propositions of technical rationality. For him, the designer constructs and manipulates virtual worlds; in making sense of a unique situation, the designer sees it as something else that is familiar and places it within familiar, named categories. This is a theory of interpretation, as opposed to a rationalist theory of propositional goals. Unfortunately, Schoen does not draw the implications of this theory for programming.

Dreyfus (1991) does argue directly against Minsky (1985) as a model of human cognition, providing an influential commentary on Heidegger (1927). But there are several shortcomings of this attempt: Dreyfus' readings of being as social practices and of breakdowns as the mechanism causing explication are idiosyncratic and limited; his argument does not include Heidegger's later thought; he proposes no alternative to the Minsky theory he dismisses.

Coyne (1991) explicitly views design as a process of interpretation and calls for hermeneutic programming based on Heidegger and Gadamer. But he too misses the power of Heidegger's later work and so his notion of "available architecture" is simplistic, ignoring how designs resolve constraints and how buildings work to define contexts for dwelling. His ideas for software point in the direction of **Hermes**, but are utterly vague.

Suchman (1987) emphasizes the contrast between rationalist plans and situated action. She also stresses the role of language in constituting human interpretation of situations. But she is concerned with human-computer-communication in which the computer must understand and act produce copies), rather than with the computer as external memory or as a medium for shared human cognition. Rather than proposing an alternative to rationalist programming, she fine-tunes traditional programs with more sensors of the human situation and with more situated testing of the communications.

Another clear critique of Minsky (1985) from a Heideggerian perspective is presented by Winograd and Flores (1986), who do call for a new approach to software design. They note that the computer is ultimately a structured dynamic communication medium and they stress the central role of language in coordinated action. They propose the Coordinator program as an example of new software as a medium for CSCW and note its limitation: "In many contexts this kind of explicitness is not called for and may even be detrimental" because language is ultimately an "open-ended domain of interpretation." Despite this recognition, they propose software that failed to be accepted in many social settings because it imposed a rigid, explicit, public structure where people often want to remain implicit and so it did not empower personal interpretations.

Participatory design, as described by Ehn (1988), is a method for developing software in partnership with the end-users, so it can be designed to support skillful work and democratic workplace relations, in contrast to traditional automation approaches. The idea is to design computer tools for experts that support and extend their skills, including their tacit know-how. As an example, the Utopia project pioneered a desktop publishing toolkit for graphic layout professionals, rather than the automated systems that were putting these experts out of work. This toolkit approach may have been innovative at the time, but is now standard.

Hermeneutic Theory

Hermeneutic software design revisits the philosophy of Heidegger -- which underlies the theories of situated cognition -- to develop a fuller foundation for a new paradigm of programming. It starts from the position that Searle (1980) opposed to "strong AI", namely that only humans (and not computers) have intentionality, that is the ability to *interpret* semantics. Given this in-principle limitation of computers, they need to concentrate on providing computationally active extended memory for people. Clearly, computers can be most useful in doing this if they present their stored knowledge in a format appropriate to human cognition. As Norman (1993) says, "Without someone to interpret them, cognitive artifacts have no function. That means that if they are to work properly, they must be designed with consideration of the workings of human cognition."

Human cognition is a complicated business. A recent analysis of its structure by Donald (1991) based on anthropological, neurological and linguistic evidence suggests four stages in its historical development (all of which remain still active): *episodic* (case-based), *mimetic* (tacit, gestural), *mythic* (linguistic) and *modern* (based on extended memory: pictures, writing, computers). Heidegger's (1927) philosophical analysis of the logical structure of human being-in-the-world can be comprehended as a parallel to this sequence: *understanding* (the world is disclosed to us as meaningful), *interpretation* (we can make things stand out as what they are), *assertion* (we can name and talk about things) and *theory* (we can state propositions using a formal method). Hermeneutic software design aims to support each of these modes of human cognition.

Heidegger goes on to discuss how we understand our situation, the things disclosed within it and ourselves. This part of his philosophy is called "hermeneutics", which builds on a tradition in the theory of interpretive human sciences and which was subsequently expounded by Gadamer (1960). Understanding is basically a synthesis which brings together our *background knowledge* (previous experience), *a preconception* (expectation, anticipation, tentative conceptual framework) and *foresight* (perspective, point of view). For Heidegger the synthesis is a temporal process that unifies our past (background), present (perspective) and future (projections). We always find ourselves already in a situation -- namely the result of our past interpretive activity. This can perhaps best be illustrated using Schoen's characterization of design: the designer draws upon past experience, tries interpretive moves and looks for consequences from the perspective of a set of concerns. The world is disclosed anew to us based on our interpretive synthesis; things are discovered in the world as what they are in the new interpretation; the world (in Schoen's phrase) "talks back" to the designer.

The notion that the world talks to us is reminiscent of Heidegger's later philosophy. In discussing art works, Heidegger (1950) talks about the work opening up a world in which truth or being is presented. If one extrapolates from his theory of finished art works (including architectural works), one can propose an ontology of designs as emergent works. In an evolving design, a world is partially, tentatively, progressively disclosed. This world does not have the unity, consistency, simplicity, beauty of a work of art. A bold stroke of the designer's pencil (or mouse) in a concept sketch may declare a new distinction, define a limit, juxtapose conflicting tendencies, reorganize relationships, catalyze the dialectic of part and gestalt. Each stroke threatens to either coalesce or shatter the unity of the nascent concept. If **Hermes** is to succeed according to this theory, it must act as the medium in which worlds can be set to work, explored and evaluated.

Comparison with Janus and Phidias

Hermes builds on research software models developed at the University of Colorado. It attempts to reinterpret and extend the **Janus** and **Phidias** systems within the paradigm of hermeneutic software design. **Janus** and **Phidias** are design environments that have both construction-kit palettes of graphic representations and issue-base textual argumentation. **Janus** provides a catalog of design cases and a critic mechanism. **Phidias** provides for authoring of issues, primitive graphics editing and issue-base querying tools.

Both systems suffer from a lack of integration of text and graphics (no unified knowledge representation) and from program design decisions that limit their ability to evolve into real-world systems. In particular, **Janus** provides little user control over graphics and none over the issue-base. Its computational power (e.g., inferencing capability, calculation of distances) is virtually inaccessible to the user. **Phidias'** graphics cannot easily be restructured once defined because of their reliance on the PHIGS hierarchy approach. Graphics and issues are only linked at certain fixed points in **Phidias**. There is no critic mechanism. The query language is limited: it does not support naming, interpretation, perspectives or queries over graphics. Generally, **Janus** and **Phidias** are still conceived on the expert system model, where the software works mainly behind the scenes and the computational power is not available to the user directly.

For instance, in **Janus** to add a freezer to a kitchen design (assuming the class of freezers has not been defined) requires following an explicit plan (vs. engaging in situated action). First define the freezer class: choose menu item "new object"; choose menu item "design unit class"; assign to class: attributes, descriptions, superclasses and other info used internally by system; assign to class every critic rule that should apply. The user may need to step back several levels to achieve subgoals: defining new critic rules, relations, global descriptions, inference rules, etc. Each subgoal involves understanding system concerns, menus, property sheets, internal workings and Lisp syntax. None of this is analogous to working in the domain. The plan followed must be one based on an understanding of how the program works internally -- user testing showed that users are forced to follow the plan conceived by the programmer. Furthermore, all the power of naming and inference that are available through Lisp are hidden from the user. The primitive uses of these capabilities that are passed on to the user require the navigation of many levels of menus. Symptomatically, although all of **Janus'** critics rely upon distance measures, there is no sense of scale apparent to the user in the graphic workspace.

As illustrated in the first scenario above, to add a freezer to a galley design in **Hermes** involves designing the freezer graphically and attaching argumentation, including critic statements formulated in the **Hermes** disclosure language. The freezer can then be named and saved as a palette item if desired. Rather than designing from scratch, a virtual copy could be made of a refrigerator with its attached argumentation and then modified. While this may or may not be easier in **Hermes** than in **Janus** for users of various backgrounds, at least in **Hermes** the user remains within the graphics and language of the domain world of design. The **Hermes** interpretation language and perspectives mechanism require no knowledge about the software implementation; once the user knows how to use them, all the power of **Hermes** is available for the user to modify, interpret, query, critique or display any combination of objects in the system.

Hermes Layered Architecture

To provide full user extensibility, all text, graphics and language constructs are stored as data. So, **Hermes** is fundamentally an object-oriented data-base system (optimized to be efficient and to scale up). All knowledge is represented in a custom hypermedia system that incorporates the interpretation language in nodes and the perspectives mechanism in links.

The perspectives mechanism is based on a virtual copying scheme like that in the NeXT operating System, which is designed to conserve computer memory. In **Hermes** this mechanism is re-worked to support human communication and shared understanding in cooperative work contexts.

Similarly, the interpretation language is based on a query language, inference language or end-user programming language approach. In **Hermes** it is developed into a tool for viewing data through an interpretation. Significantly, statements in the language (like previously defined critics, queries, predicate definitions, conditional clauses and display criteria) are readily interpretable by the user. All hypermedia navigation in **Hermes** is done by means of the language and perspectives, so that all operations and displays can be controlled (interpreted) by the user. The language syntax is quite expressive and capable of arbitrary complexity (nesting, macro expansion, recursion).

The **Hermes** database is built up in layers:

1. During creation of a new **Hermes** system, a number of data items (link types, predicates requiring special programming) are created.

2. Then the database is "seeded" by a team of domain experts and knowledge engineers. The seed includes media primitives for the domain (e.g., graphic attributes; sound volume, timbre, duration; video forward), useful predicates, standard critics, sample designs, common components and a structured issue

base for the domain. The seed might include supplementary hypertexts of argumentation, advice, regulations and information (such as ergonomic data or rules of thumb).

3. Through use, the database gains a rich history of data related to new design efforts.

4. Finally, a current project is developed which can draw upon knowledge stored at any of these layers.

The **Hermes** interface conforms to the MS-Windows standard. It is designed to shelter the naive user from the potential complexity and power of the system's user control. Methods of re-use and iterative construction are emphasized. The seed provides the language constructs most likely to be needed. Because they can be easily read and intuitively understood, these constructs can be readily explored, re-used and modified. The interface and the language also encourage modular and iterative building up of complex structures. Browsers provide quick access to previously defined objects. **Hermes** aims to support creative design by permitting arbitrarily innovative constructions of graphics and argumentation, while providing an intuitive and uniform interface that will not distract the user from domain concerns.

Work Plan

Tasks Done:

The goal of developing a new programming paradigm like hermeneutic software design is a "wicked problem" indeed. The general outlines of the project have now been defined and the remaining work is largely a matter of fleshing them out. The core philosophic issues have been identified and an initial review of the most important texts has suggested the tentative conceptual framework.

Close collaboration with experts in the domain of lunar habitat design has produced an initial understanding of their pressing needs and their traditional methods. About thirty hours of videotaped design sessions provides ample material for further study.

The primary software modules for **Hermes** have already been developed: the database system, hypermedia, perspectives, a preliminary version of the language and textual interfaces for testing.

Tasks To Do:

The hermeneutic philosophy and ontology of design must be developed through close textual reading and consideration of the design domain and the software prototype. This philosophy needs to be explicated and presented for a lay audience.

The videos have to be analyzed in detail to produce an inventory of what designers do and what supports or tools they need. Specifically, how do they use measurements, language, graphics? Any conclusions along these lines should be checked with the domain experts.

Before the code for the interpretation language is rewritten, a program walk-through of the language will be performed. The language will be revised according to the results of this and then implemented. Much work must be done on the windowing interface. While some initial concepts have been tried, it is likely that many iterations of design and testing will be necessary to achieve the required naturalness of feel, even for demo purposes.

Demos for the domain experts will start as soon as an initial version of the system is ready. This will require the definition and input of the seed data: issue-base, sample designs, predicates, critics, etc. The seed data will be derived from the videos. Full-blown scenarios in the domain will be defined and carried out. This will be an important learning experience about the limitations of **Hermes** and needed revisions. The scenarios will be carefully reviewed by the domain experts. They may be taped and circulated within NASA and Houston as well.

Finally, the dissertation will be written, explaining the project, expounding the theory, reviewing the participatory design process and describing the prototype software.

Post-Doc Tasks:

Part of the concept of **Hermes** is that it could become a real-world system, used by a team of environmental design students doing a lunar habitat project or even by a NASA design group. This would require considerable refinement of the software and the addition of more functionality. It would be nice to implement 3-D graphics, adjacency constraints and an inheritance mechanism, for instance. A cognitive walk-through, user testing and more demos would drive further interface development. Real-world testing would be an important step to take and one that would provide important insights into **Hermes** as a work-oriented tool or a medium of shared communication in a real situation. However, this is beyond the scope of the dissertation.

References

Adorno, T.W. (1964). *Jargon der Eigentlichkeit: Zur deutschen Ideologie* [The Jargon of Authenticity]. Frankfurt am Main: Suhrkamp.

Adorno, T.W. (1966). *Negative Dialektik* [Negative Dialectics]. Frankfurt am Main: Suhrkamp.

Alexander, C. (1964). *Notes on the Synthesis of Form* Cambridge: Harvard University Press.

Alexander, C., Ishikawa, S., Silverstein, M. (1977). *A Pattern Language*. New York: Oxford University Press.

Bell, B., Citrin, W., Lewis, C., Rieman, J., Weaver, R., Wilde, N., Zorn, B. (1992). *The Programming Walkthrough: A Structured Method for Assessing the Writability of Programming Languages*. Technical Report CU-CS-577-92. January 1992. University of Colorado.

Bush, V. *(1945,* June). As We May Think. *Atlantic Monthly,* 176 (1), 101-108. Reprinted in Greif (1988).

Carroll, J.M. & Kellogg, W.A. (1989). Artifact as theory- nexus: hermeneutics meets theory-based design, *Proceedings of the Conference of Human Factors in Computing Systems,* Austin, 7-14.

Coyne, R. (1991). Inconspicuous Architecture, *Gadamer Action & Reason: Conference Proceedings*. Australia: University of Sydney.

Donald, M. (1991). *Origins of the Modern Mind: Three Stages in the Evolution of Culture and Cognition*. Cambridge: Harvard University Press.

Dreyfus, H. *(1965). Alchemy and Artificial Intelligence*. The RAND Corporation.

Dreyfus, H. (1972). what *Computers Cannot Do*. New York: Harper and Row.

Dreyfus, H., ed., (1982). *Husserl, Intentionality and Cognitive Science*. Cambridge: MIT Press.

Dreyfus, H. & Dreyfus, S. (1986). *Mind Over Machine*. New York: The Free Press.

Dreyfus, H. *(1991). Being-in-the-Word: A Commentary on Heidegger's Being and Time, Division L* Cambridge: MIT Press.

Ehn, P. (1988). Work-Oriented Design of Computer Artifacts. Stockholm: Arbetslivscentrum.

Eisenberg, M. (1991). Programmable Applications: Interpreter Meets Interface.

Engelbart, D. (1963). A Conceptual Framework for the Augmentation of Man's Intellect. In P. Howerton (Ed.). (1963). *Vistas of Information Handling* (Vol.1). Washington, DC: Spartan Books. Reprinted in Greif (1988).

Ericsson, KA. & Simon, HA. (1984). *Protocol analysis: verbal reports as data*. Cambridge: MIT Press.

Fischer, G., McCall, R., & Morch, A. (1989, November). Janus: Integrating Hypertext with a Knowledge-based Design Environment, *Proc. of Hypertext '89,* Pittsburgh, PA: ACM, 105-117.

Fischer, G., Girgensohn, A. (1990). End-User Modifiability in Design
  Environments. *Human Factors in Computing Systems, CHI '90 Conference
  Proceedings (Seattle, WA).* New York: ACM.

Fischer, O., Grudin, J., Lemke, A., McCall, R., Ostwald, J., Reeves, B., Shipman,
  F. (1991). Supporting Indirect, Collaborative Design with Integrated
  Knowledge-Based Design Environments. Submitted to *Human- Computer
  Interaction.*

Gadamer, H. G. (1960). *Wahrheit und Methode* [Truth and Method]. Tuebingen:
  Mohr.

Gadamer, H. G. (1966). Die Universalitaet des hermeneutischen Problems [The
  universality of the hermeneutic problem]. In H. G. Gadamer (1967). *Kleine
  Schriften: Philosophie Heirneneutic.* Tuebingen: Mohr.

Greenbaum, J. & Kyng, M. (1991). *Design at Work: Cooperative Design of Computer
  Systems.* Hillsdale, NJ: Lawrence Erlbaum.

Greif, I. (Ed.) (1988). *Computer-Supported Cooperative Work.* San Mateo, CA:
  Morgan Kaufmann.

Habermas, J. (1968). *Erkenntnis und Interesse* [Knowledge and human interests].
  Franklurt a. M.: Suhrkamp Verlag.

Habermas, J. (1985). *Der philosophische Diskurs der Moderne: Zwoelf Vorlesungen* [The
  Philosophical Discourse of Modernity]. Frankfurt am Main: Suhrkamp.

Halasz, F.G. (1988). Reflections on Notecards: Seven Issues for the Next
  Generation of Hypermedia Systems. *Communications of the ACM,* Vol.31,
  No.7.

Heidegger, M. (1927). *Sein und Zeit* [Being and time]. Tuebingen: Niemeyer.

Heidegger, M. (1971). *Poetry, Language, Thought.* Trans A. Hofstadter. New York:
  Harper & Row.

Heidegger, M. (1975). *Der Grundproblerne der Phaenomenologie* [Basic problems of
  phenomenology]. Gesamtausgabe vol 24. Frankfurt am Main: Klostermann.

Heidegger, M. (1979). *Prolegomena zur Geschichte des Zeitbegriffs* [Introduction to the
  history of the concept of time]. Gesamtausgabe vol.20. Frankfurt am Main:
  Klostermann.

Heidegger, M. *(1950).* Ursprung des Kunstwerks [The origin of the work of art].
  In M. Heidegger *(1950). Holzwege.* Frankfurt am Main: Klostermann.

Heidegger, M. (1953). Wissenschalt und Besinnung [Science and reflection]. In
  M. Heidegger *(1954). Vortraege und Aufsaetze.* Pfulingen: Neske.

Hegel, G. W. F. (1833). *Grundlinien der Philosophie des Rechts* [Principles of the
  philosophy of right]. Leipzig.

Illich, I. (1973). *Tools for Conviviality.* New York: Harper & Row.

Kunz, W. & Rittel, H.W.J. (1970). *Issues as Elements of Information Systems.* Working
  paper 131. Center for Planning and Development Research, University of
  California, Berkeley.

Lakoff, G. (1987). *Women, Fire and Dangerous Things.* Chicago: Univ. of Chicago
  Press.

Lefebvre, H. (1991). *The Production of Space.* Oxford: Blackwell.

McCall, R. (1987). PHIBIS: Procedurally Hierarchical Issue-Based Information Systems. *Proceedings of the Conference on Architecture at the International Congress on Planning and Design Theory.* New York: American Society of Mechanical Engineers.

McCall, R. (1989). Mikroplis: A Hypertext System for Design. *Design Studies,* 10 (4), 228-238.

McCall, R., Bennett, P., d'Oronzio, P., Ostwald, J., Shipman, F., Wallace, N. (1990). Phidias: A PHI-based Design Environment Integrating CAD Graphics into Dynamic Hypertext. *Proceedings of the European Conference on Hypertext (ECHT '90).*

Minsky, M. (1985). *The Society of Mind.* New York: Simon and Schuster.

Nilson, N. (1980). *Principles of Artificial Intelligence.* Palo Alto: Morgan Kaufmann.

Norman, D. (in preparation). *Things That Make Us Smart.* Reading, MA: Addison-Wesley, expected publication early 1993.

Norman, D. & Draper, S. (1986). *User Centered System Design: New Perspectives on Human-Computer Interaction.* Hillsdale, NJ: Lawrence Erlbaum.

Palmer, R. (1969). *Hermeneutics: Interpretation Theory in Schliermacher, Dilthey, Heidegger and Gadamer.* Evanston: Northwestern University Press.

Polanyi, M. (1962). *Personal Knowledge.* London: Routledge & Kegan Paul.

Putnam, H. (1967). The Nature of Mental States. In N. Block (Ed.). (1980). *Readings in Philosophy of Psychology* (vol. 1). Cambridge: Harvard University Press. First published as Psychological Predicates. In W. H. Capitan & D. D. Merrill (Eds.). (1967). Art, *Mind and Religion.* Pittsburgh: University of Pittsburgh Press.

Putnam, H. (1988). *Representation and Reality.* Cambridge: MIT Press.

Richardson, J. (1991). *Existential Epistemology: A Heideggerian Critique of the Cartesian Project.* Oxford: Claredon Paperbacks.

Rittel, H. & Webber, M. (1973). Dilemmas in a general theory of planning. *Policy Studies,* 4, 155-69.

Rorty, R. (1977). *Philosophy and the Mirror of Nature.* Princeton: Princeton University Press.

Schoen, D. (1983). *The Reflective Practitioner.* New York: Basic Books.

Schutz, A. (1970). *Reflections on the Problem of Relevance.* New Haven: Yale University Press.

Searle, J. (1980). Minds, Brains and Programs. *The Behavioral and Brain Sciences,* vol.3.

Searle, J. (1983). *Intentionality: An Essay in the Philosophy of Mind.* Cambridge: Cambridge University Press.

Simon, H. (1973). The Structure of Ill-structured Problems. Artificial *Intelligence* 4, 181-200.

Simon, H. (1981). *The Sciences of the Artificial.* Cambridge: MIT Press.

Snodgrass, A., Coyne, R. (1990). Is Designing Hermeneutical? Working Paper. Faculty of Architecture, University of Sydney.

Stahl, G. (1975, Spring). Marxian Hermeneutics and Heideggerian Social Theory: Interpreting and Transforming Our World. Ph.D. Dissertation, Northwestern University.

Stahl, G. (1975, Winter). The Jargon of Authenticity: An Introduction to a Marxist Critique of Heidegger. Boundary 2, vol. III, no 2.

Stahl, G. (1976, Winter). Attuned to Being: Heideggerian Music in Technological Society. *Boundary 2*, vol. IV, no 2.

Stahl, G. (1989, February). *Philosophy of Metaphor: Implications of Philosophy for AI.* Presentation for Issues in Lexical Semantics course.

Stahl, G. (1989, *March*). *Arguments for Equality: Social Implications of the Euclid Argumentation Software.* Paper for Advanced AI Programming course.

Stahl, G. (1989, April). *Euclidean Reasoning versus Gentle Persuasion: a Matter of Semantics.* Paper for Issues in Lexical Semantics course.

Stahl, G. (1989, November). *The Proper Treatment of Representation.* Paper for Foundations of Cognitive Science course.

Stahl, G. (1991, January). *The Philosophical Context of AI and the Situated Cognition Paradigm Shift.* Presentation for Design Seminar.

Stahl, G. (1991, February). *The Relevance of Artificial Intelligence: what Relevant-knowledge-based Systems Could Do.* Paper for Design Seminar.

Stahl, G. (1991, March). *PhiQL: Formal Specification of a Query Language for HyperMedia.* Unpublished technical report.

Stahl, G. (1991, April). *Beyond Rational Design.* Presentation for Design Seminar.

Stahl, G. (1991, October). *Intelligent Hypertext* as an *Alternative to Expert Systems.* Presentation at Colorado Institute for Artificial Intelligence Research Symposium, Denver.

Stahl, G. (1992). *A Hypermedia Inference Language as an Alternative to Rule-Based Expert Systems.* Technical Report CU-CS-557-91. Computer Science Dept., University of Colorado a t Boulder.

Suchman, L. (1987). Plans and Situated Actions: The Problem of Human Machine Communication. Cambridge: Cambridge University Press.

Suchman, L. & Trigg, R. (1991). Understanding Practice: Video as a Medium for Reflection and Design. In Greenbaum & Kyng (1991).

Winograd, T. & Flores, F. (1986). Understanding Computers and Cognition: A New Foundation for Design. New York: Addison-Wesley.

Winston, P. H. (1981). *Artificial Intelligence.* Reading, MA: Addison-Wesley.

Wixon. D., Holzblatt, K. & Knox, S (1990, April). Contextual Design: An Emergent View of System Design. *CHI '90 Proceedings.*

Part II: Personalizable Software

4. Supporting Personalizable Learning

This paper outlines a research agenda for exploring computer-based approaches to rendering educational resources personalizable. Using proposed technologies, learners and their teachers can select exploratory activities as well as curriculum to support or guide these learning activities from digital libraries on the Internet and adapt the content and display of these materials to personal interests and local needs.

The paper begins by suggesting an initial testbed for personalizable learning software building upon the **Agentsheets** Remote Exploratorium (**are**) that is currently under construction at the University of Colorado. It then touches upon diverse pedagogical theories to underscore the importance of personalization to learning. Next, it presents a vision of a more comprehensive system of software for personalizing resources from global digital libraries, highlighting the general issues involved. This vision is grounded in two innovative software systems: a Teacher's Curriculum Assistant (**TCA**) and a Personalizable Learning Medium (**PLM**). Generalizing from these prototypes, it considers several issues for a theory of personalizable software.

Preface: In the Ideal World

In the ideal world of the future, you would receive this document in the form of personalizable hypertext. This Preface might query you:

[ ]   Which aspects of the following discussion are of most interest to you?

[ ]   What background do you already have in these matters?

[ ]   How much time do you want to spend going into details?

Of course, in the really ideal future, you would already have tailored your computational reading environment to your general preferences and you would just have to tune that embedded knowledge to your interests in this specific material. Then, rather than being a fixed presentation of text, this document would be tailored to your personal interests and it would allow you to explore its ideas in an open-ended format. The tailoring would be automated, using computational hypertext that restructures itself dynamically. You could delegate the personalizing and also make certain decisions yourself on what is presented. You could follow linkages among ideas at your discretion and expand materials to whatever levels of detail you desired.

We are not yet in that long anticipated future. As a default, the author has had to assume that you are too busy to study the details of the following argument and has attempted to present the main points as concisely as possible. Pointers to further motivational discussion and implementation technicalities are given at the end, since paper documents do not allow the active linkages of hypertext.

Section I. Personalizing Agentsheets and the Remote Exploratorium

Research at CU on human-computer communication and support of life-long learning has long recognized the need to make complex, poorly structured information spaces more personal (e.g., Fischer & Nieper, 1987; Fischer & Stevens, 1991). In the following pages, I propose a series of software systems to explore technologies for *personalizable software* to support *personalizable learning*. This research agenda largely applies approaches and functionality developed at CU— including in my dissertation (Stahl, 1993b)—to the needs of learners and their teachers.

During the past two years, I have designed two systems to support personalizable learning: a Teacher's Curriculum Assistant (TCA) and a Personalizable Learning Medium (PLM). The implementation of TCA and PLM would be a substantial undertaking involving several person-years of design, programming and testing. It involves creating a digital library of educational resources and curriculum, all structured in the correct hypertext format and properly indexed. It requires tools for authors to construct personalizable documents, for teachers to customize lesson plans and for learners to explore resources. The participation of teachers and learners is needed to ensure that the software is designed to fulfill real needs and to meet practical usage requirements.

An incremental approach to implementing the proposed approach to personalizable software is needed. The **Agentsheets Remote Exploratorium (ARE)** project at CU provides a potential testbed for doing this. **ARE** is a digital library of **Agentsheets** simulation titles (Ambach, Perrone & Repenning, 1995). Currently, the **ARE** library is centralized on a single Web server; there is little supporting information to guide or support the selection and use of the titles; only one version of each title is available; users cannot annotate or otherwise supplement the available information.

There is growing interest among students, teachers and researchers to see the ARE library grow and decentralize. ARE is now at a formative point in its development. The published library is still at a manageable size and its administration is still centralized so that new formats and standards can be introduced without causing problems for an installed base. This is a good time to explore how techniques of personalizable software could enhance the usability of ARE.

An incremental approach to developing personalizable software within the ARE project could proceed in several phases, such as:

- A personalizable User's Guide to Agentsheets and the Remote Exploratorium.

- Personalizable hypertext curriculum materials to suggest educational usages of Agentsheets simulations and to provide relevant background materials.

- A personalizable end-user language for manipulating the computational hypertext.

- Personalizable versions of Agentsheets titles, with their associated curriculum and commentaries.

- Personalizable tools for locating Agentsheets titles globally.

The following discussion of these phases is meant to be merely suggestive. The details would have to be worked out with the ARE developers and with typical potential users such as students and teachers.

Phase 1: A personal user's guide

Perhaps the most urgent need to support the wider use of Agentsheets is an adequate User's Guide. The current manual is too sketchy to meet this need. Without a more complete manual, the anticipated spread of Agentsheets use by researchers building new functionality, by university students developing sophisticated new titles and by public school teachers and students exploring titles in the classroom will continue to place a prohibitive burden on core ARE staff.

An Agentsheets User's Guide should be part of the Agentsheets environment, so that it can be incorporated into context-sensitive help to explain the features of Agentsheets within Agentsheets. This means adding a hypertext facility to Agentsheets. Giving people the ability to author commentary in the User's Guide, will allow developers at every level of Agentsheets (the substrate, the titles and the instances) to document their work in a centralized repository.

A hypertext extension to **Agentsheets** should include support for personal perspectives and a hypertext navigation language, even if these mechanisms are not fully implemented during this phase. With perspectives functionality, User's Guide contents can be entered within different perspectives, such as novice user, student, teacher, title developer and substrate builder. Then readers can select the appropriate perspective to display information about using **Agentsheets** at their personal level. Individual users and groups of developers can define their own perspectives and save annotations that are only relevant to them and that will not be displayed in other perspectives.

The addition of hypertext to **Agentsheets** will undoubtedly have uses that go far beyond the User's Guide and documentation and that cannot yet be foreseen. The power of computational hypertext will have strong synergies with the computational agency of the simulation environment. The User's Guide simply provides a practical artifact to experiment with in implementing the hypertext.

Phase 2: Personal curriculum

The next phase is to use the hypertext to develop personalizable educational curriculum to accompany the **Agentsheets** titles. This can include lesson plans such as those in **TCA** as well as textual (or multimedia) information for students exploring titles such as that in **PLM**. These curricular materials will be stored on the Web as part of **ARE**. All the techniques of **PLM** can be developed and tested in this context. Also, people using this personal curriculum can annotate it and modify it, creating their own new versions of documents.

Phase 3: A personal language in AgenTalk

Computational hypertext is driven by a navigational language. Queries are expressed in this language; among other things, these queries retrieve sets of linked nodes and display their proper versions for the user. This navigational language can be implemented in the new approach to **AgenTalk** currently under development. **AgenTalk** is the end-user programming language already used to define the behavior of agents in **Agentsheets**. The new approach provides a drop-and-drag visual programming interface that guides the user in constructing syntactically and semantically valid expressions. This interface would be very helpful and appropriate to the hypertext language.

The kernel of the navigational language is required to implement computational hypertext in Phase 1. However, once in place, it can be extended to serve as an end-user language for various functions, such as defining queries for searching the Web and defining critics for analyzing artifacts, including **Agentsheets** titles and curriculum lesson plans. Because the vocabulary of the language can be customized with personal extensions, people can define their personal queries, critics and displays by using the language.

Phase 4: Everything is personal

Ultimately, all aspects of the **ARE** can be made personalizable. Most of **Agentsheets** is already modularized or could be made so. This not only means that people can share pieces of their titles (like an agent behavior or appearance), but that titles can have multiple versions at any level. The Segregation simulation, for instance, could be posted on an **ARE** Web server with multiple versions of its parts embedded in it. Then a user (e.g., a teacher or a student) could select which of the available behavior versions a given agent should have. This choice could be made on an *ad hoc* basis in the interface for defining behaviors. However, it could also be made by choosing a perspective; the choice of perspective would make choices of versions throughout the title all at once, automatically and consistently. Associated hypertextual descriptions could guide the user in selecting which perspective to choose. Of course, once a narrow perspective was chosen, all commentary and User's Guide information would be specific (personalized) to the versions associated with that perspective unless one explicitly requested information from a broader perspective.

Phase 5: Personal retrieval

The **ARE** project is primarily concerned with making **Agentsheets** titles available over the Web. Enhancing the project with techniques of personalizable software would result in a globally distributed but locally personalizable web of **Agentsheets** versions, curriculum and commentary. That is, versions of title components, documentation and annotations would be distributed across multiple Web servers. The distributed nodes and links of the hypertext system would be located, retrieved, assembled and displayed by the computational hypertext system. In order to maintain acceptable levels of efficiency, all the relevant components would be downloaded to the user's computer and stored locally for a certain period. The algorithms for doing this would need to be worked out. The computational hypertext discussed here goes considerably beyond the HTML hypertext of the Web; it provides far more capabilities.

> *Computational hypermedia has been prototyped in a single-user system; the challenge is to adapt it to work across the Internet, extending the power an order of magnitude beyond HTML.*

It might be helpful to use some of the techniques from **TCA** to support the efficient finding of relevant titles and associated resources on the Web. These involve the indexing of all titles and documents at all sites and storing this meta-info at one or more central sites. Alternatively, it may be possible to automate some of this with Web search engines and other Internet daemons. It may also be useful to download the meta-info to local sites periodically to facilitate filtering and browsing of indexes in personally structured local search spaces.

In addition to posting **Agentsheets** titles, documentation and curriculum, the expanded system would allow users to post their new vocabulary for the hypertext language—their personal languages—including definitions of search queries and computational critics. They could also post the names of newly structured perspectives, along with documentation on the advantages of using those perspectives. The same language terms, queries and perspectives that are used for personalizing individual documents could then be used in searching the Web. In effect, the global **ARE** web would become a giant *personalizable* document.

Fulfilling the promise of the Web

The World Wide Web holds out the promise of providing a decentralized, public medium to meet people's information needs and interests. The proposed research agenda would create a web of information related to **Agentsheets** titles that could not only serve as a model for how to make information shareable and manageable, but would also show how to make the information personalizable. The **Agentsheets** Remote Exploratorium could provide an effective testbed in which to develop techniques for managing decentralized evolution of digital libraries with personalizable software.

Section II. Personalizable learning

Taylorizing the student *versus* tailoring by the learner

Learning in the future will not consist primarily of training based on Taylorized knowledge. With the term *Taylorizing* I refer to the industrial practice of rationalizing human activities popularized by Frederick Taylor in the early 1900's. This corresponds to the behaviorist movement in psychology, to instructionism in education and, more generally, to rationalism in philosophy. Following this worldview, one analyzes activities into elemental constituents of required skills, physical movements and intellectual efforts. Then one optimizes the process by removing unnecessary steps and often by separating the intellectual supervisory tasks (management, teachers) from the repetitive motions (workers, students). This approach drove the industrial revolution and the public education that schooled its work force.

The term *tailorable* (or personalizable) *learning* refers to an alternative approach needed for the info age. Rationalization provided an historically necessary service by making explicit the elements of work and learning that had traditionally been blended in amorphous, tacit, organic ways. But work and learning in today's world require reorganization and reintegration of those elements under the control of the individual worker or learner. There is too much innovation and info-overload now to rely on standard operating procedures. Many contemporary work and learning practices cannot be codified; to work in these domains is to negotiate new definitions of the domains with one's colleagues.

Since the beginnings of formal education, theorists have recognized the need to adapt teaching to the *personal situation* of the learner. Ironically, the rationalization process that led to standardization now makes personalizing feasible. By breaking education into instructional elements, it provides the raw materials for the computers of learners to re-synthesize these materials in ways suited to individual needs (e.g., to personal backgrounds or to an immediate task at hand). The computer provides a tool to assist in organizing enormous numbers of elements according to flexibly specified constraints. For instance, if this paper were analyzed into elemental ideas (say, roughly its paragraphs) and their interrelationships (their various types of linkages) in the form of computational hypertext, then the right software could allow you, the reader, to tailor the presentation of that material to your personal desires.

> *The promise of personal computers will finally be achieved when software makes information personalizable.*

Personal computers have always dangled a tempting promise in front of us: to grant us personal control over information. Too many systems make us adapt to the computer instead. The power of today's computers, the sophistication of available software techniques and the medium of the Internet combine to make feasible the fulfillment of that promise.

Supporting authentic exploration with personalized content

This paper proposes a research agenda to give learners—individually or in collaborations—control over the information they need for their *own* learning practices. Section II motivates the need for personalizing educational materials: both authentic projects for *constructivist* exploration and *instructional* curricular materials to support learning-on-demand using such projects. The two competing pedagogical approaches are here synthesized by making them both *personalizable* by the learner.

Pedagogical theories have long argued for a level of personalizing that has not been practical within traditional schooling contexts. New technologies promise to facilitate the sharing and personalizing of both constructivist activities and instructionist curriculum to support those activities. The following review of learning theories motivates the need for making educational resources personalizable by learners and their teachers.

Plato's concept of education

Plato presented his view of learning in the *Meno* dialog 2500 years ago. For him, education is a process of drawing knowledge out of the learner. This is accomplished by dialog with the learner, guiding the learner to construct an understanding of the idea being discussed, such as a theorem of geometry. The dialog format is a mechanism for situating teaching within the understanding of the learner and for basing the teaching on the learner's previous understanding. Unfortunately, this personalized approach to education was overshadowed by the idealistic strains that became dominant in the later Platonist heritage. The subsequent Western tradition—founded on Plato's vision of eternal ideas and culminating in rationalism—gives us little insight for understanding *evolving* knowledge. Plato himself could not account for new knowledge, hence his definition of education as a remembering of something once known but long since forgotten.

Rousseau's subtle role for the teacher or self-learner

In *The Education of Emile*, Rousseau, too, stresses the need to tune educational presentations to the personal interests and abilities of the learner. Rousseau thinks that new material can be learned if one properly prepares, motivates and situates the learner. The ideal is to lead the learner to construct his knowledge stage by stage, advancing over time to where he is prepared for learning more and more. In his labor-extensive economy, Rousseau recommends a private tutor who can adapt educational experiences to a learner's personal needs.

Vygotsky's zone of proximal development

Vygotsky (1934) clarifies the notion that learners can be ready to learn something they do not yet understand by defining that readiness as a zone ripe for development. His developmental psychology differs from Piaget's (1929), deriving from social communicative functions rather than primarily from an individualistic logic of development. For both Piaget and Vygotsky, formal education can only succeed when the student is developmentally prepared; for Vygotsky this is a function of the student's social context or community. That is, the ability to learn is dependent upon the social relations and situations in which the learner is active.

Lave's community of practice

Lave and Wenger (1991) present a theory of situated learning that focuses on an individual's gradually increasing participation in communities of practice. A learner moves from the periphery of a community inwards by learning the knowledge that defines that community. The acceptance of the newcomer into the community is a process of negotiation through which the knowledge base of the community evolves. This view of education applies not only to non-literate apprentice traditions like the midwives of Peru, but to socialization processes in public schools and within professions. Negotiations of knowledge are political processes in which traditions, factions and individuals vie for their rival interpretations of values and definitions from their varying perspectives, continually modifying the definition of domain knowledge in the process. In the theory of situated learning, learning takes place through social activity (practice or *praxis*). That activity constructs new domain knowledge—not just in the sense of constructing personally meaningful representations of the domain in the mind of the learner, but in the sense of the community reinterpreting its own definition of the socially constructed domain. Thus, the activity of learning transforms reality, truth and knowledge (Stahl, 1975).

The idea that communities of practice have fixed bodies of knowledge that can be identified and codified as domain rules provided a useful fiction for early attempts at knowledge-based computer support. However, the limits of this fiction were soon reached. The first problem is that domain knowledge is overwhelmingly tacit; it is learned through gradual participation in a community. Knowledge acquisition attempts via interviewing of experts confront a multitude of problems: there are no "experts" who know the whole field; it is hard for experts to formulate much of their wisdom outside of situated practice (e.g., when interviewed); terms and rules depend upon further tacit skills and knowledge for their meaning and applicability; different practitioners have wildly different perspectives on the same field; domains evolve over time; creative work reinvents the field continuously (Stahl, 1993b).

Learning as interpretation

The philosophy of interpretation—based on Heidegger's (1927) thought—explains how a prepared mind learns new domain knowledge, finally answering Plato's quandary of how one can learn what one does not already know. Interpretation is a process of making certain aspects of tacit previous understanding explicit in order to conceptualize and transform (reinterpret) the knowledge. When faced with a phenomenon that cannot be readily understood, one makes explicit one's relevant tacit understandings (from one's zone of proximal development) until one can extend previous knowledge sufficiently to embrace (*interpret*, comprehend) the new phenomenon. Afterwards, the new knowledge can revert to a tacit state for use in future situated practice. According to this philosophy, interpretation is situated, linguistic and perspectival. That is, it is based on previous understanding, current concerns and future goals; relies heavily on domain conceptualizations; and necessarily adopts a personal standpoint. Accordingly, computer support for interpretive processes should provide situational context, offer linguistic tools and be personalizable (Stahl, 1993a).

Hermeneutics (the philosophy of interpretation) provides a framework for relating and synthesizing competing theories of learning. According to hermeneutics, learning is an interpretive process and is therefore situated, linguistic and perspectival. *Situated* refers to the tacit dimension of background skills and knowledge and to the social context in which learning takes place. Constructivist attempts to create authentic projects try to create situations in which the learner has a personal concern for the activity and can bring a background of situated understanding to the learning experience. On the other hand, *linguistic* refers to the process of making knowledge explicit through conceptualization in language. This corresponds to the instructionist approach of providing abstract information about the topic being learned. Hermeneutics recognizes the value in both these approaches and assigns them to stages in the processes of interpretation, which take place within personal *perspectives*. Having a perspective means that the learner understands from within a context of personal concerns, background and goals that ground new knowledge in understood meanings (Stahl, 1992b).

Extending cognition to meet the challenges of the future

The challenges facing professionals today exceed the interpretive ability of unaided individuals. Often, the primary new skills needed are symbolic, representational, terminological. Extended memories (such as electronic media) are needed to keep track of overwhelming volumes of information, external representations are needed to structure it and computational tools are needed to process it. At the same time, such work cannot be simply automated; the tacit knowledge and the interpretive skills of experienced people are still absolutely central. As new challenges arise, we must extend our skills. Conversely, new skills allow us to project newer challenges that suddenly seem feasible within the proximal zone of our abilities. Through this dialectic, domains of practice evolve—for individuals and communities. The computer-based tools that are increasingly called for in this spiraling escalation of skill requirements must capture domain distinctions and innovations as they are created, must allow for the construction of new tools and must support creative personal perspectives on the domain. These are fundamental requirements for software to support learning throughout life (Stahl, 1992a).

To prepare people for the challenges of the future requires new pedagogical approaches and new supports. The best way to learn new practices is often to practice scaled-down versions of them, to join in a community of practice gradually from the periphery. Since skilled workers carry out collaborative projects involving analysis of data using multiple tools and representations, students should engage in similar but simpler open-ended projects. The skills that need to be learned are not well-defined, atomic facts but the ability to define problems, to evaluate approaches, to communicate issues, to use computational tools, to apply multiple representations, to delegate tasks, to negotiate team efforts, to plan and to report (NCTM, 1989). These skills are often best learned tacitly, through participation in projects. One must be prepared to learn (i.e., have a zone of proximal development already established) by having been involved in similar, if simpler efforts in the past. One must also be motivated and engaged in the new activities by being situated in personally authentic activities.

Need for curricular contexts of projects

The project-centered learning just described requires curriculum in two senses: guidance and content. Learners need to be guided through individual projects and from project to project to ensure that they are ready for the activities and can get the most out of them. They also need ready access to related information (Stahl, Sumner & Owen, 1995). Guidance might take the form of a teacher like Rousseau or it might be accomplished by social structures that guide newcomers into communities of practice. Often, skilled learners with access to stimulating ideas and engaging info sources can guide themselves by paying attention to their personal interests and abilities.

Written curriculum can suggest sequences of projects and can provide supplementary content to make the projects more effective learning experiences. Such content can include technical information needed to complete a project, explicit rules useful in the specific activities or general background information that makes the project more interesting and meaningful. Curriculum need not mean a detailed blueprint with all learning defined by explicit facts to be memorized and tested. Rather, it can provide material for learning-on-demand, giving flexible access to information in response to a learner's situated needs. The "situation" in this case includes not only the task at hand, the physical work environment and the social community of practice, but also the learner's personal background knowledge and skills. For this reason, information delivery should not only be relevant to the task, timely and culturally sensitive, but it should be presented in a personally meaningful and effective format for the learner (Stahl, Sumner & Repenning, 1995).

The problem and the promise

Education is in crisis. The challenges it is called upon to meet by our info society are daunting. Many bold actions are needed to reform education adequately. Once teachers, parents, students and administrators accept the constructionist approach in principle, the question of what is to replace the old textbooks, drill sheets and lesson plans poses an overwhelming practical obstacle. Here is where computer access to digital libraries on the Internet can help: by facilitating the sharing of well thought through educational activities and resources.

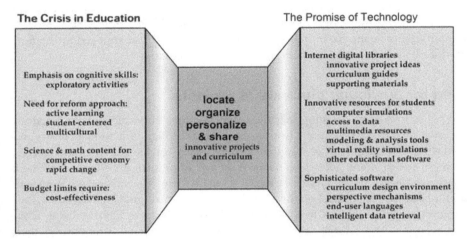

Figure 1. Software can bridge the gap between the crisis of education and the promise of technology by helping learners and their teachers to access project ideas and curriculum and to adapt them to personal needs.

The preceding paragraphs were intended to sketch a context for proposing how computers can support learning by making shared resources personal. Until now, educational software has generally pursued approaches (e.g., "drill and kill" or "edu-tainment") that missed the real potential of educational software: to present project situations and supporting information in formats that learners and their teachers can make personal. Sections III and IV will try to outline what such an approach might entail.

Section III. Teacher's Curriculum Assistant

Two sets of issues have already emerged through the effort to establish the **Agentsheets** Remote Exploratorium (**ARE**) on the World Wide Web (Stahl, Sumner & Repenning, 1995):

- *Curriculum support:* Simulations by themselves are not enough to ensure that learning will take place. There needs to be accompanying curriculum that (a) suggests ways for teachers to guide their students in integrating the creation and exploration of the simulations within broader learning contexts and (b) provides insightful and supportive background and related information.

- *Personalized access:* The possibility of **Agentsheets** users posting their creations on the Web via the **ARE** points to the need for software utilities to help other potential users to locate **ARE** sites, search through them for **Agentsheets** titles of interest, download and run selected titles, adapt the titles to their personal needs and share their creations or adaptations with other people through the Web.

The issues **ARE** raises are general problems for the use of educational digital libraries. An independent attempt to think through what kind of software is needed to address these issues resulted in two prototypes: a Teacher's Curriculum Assistant (**TCA**) to help teachers develop curriculum (Stahl, 1995b) and a Personal Learning Medium (**PLM**) to present textual materials to students (Stahl, 1995a). These two systems will be described in Sections III and IV. Then Section V will draw upon these examples to consider some general issues concerning software support for personalizable learning.

Need for computer support of curriculum development

Educational researchers are calling for constructivist reforms that require significant changes in curriculum (Greeno, 1993). Printed textbooks cannot keep pace with the necessary changes in approach, format or content required by these pedagogical approaches. Nor are textbooks readily adaptable to local conditions and individual learning styles. If schools are going to offer students opportunities to construct their own knowledge actively and interactively, then new educational materials are needed that foster exploration and that are tailored to local students and their situations.

Isolated ideas for classroom activities and individual resources like computer simulations, programming environments, CD-ROMs or video disks do not by themselves foster conceptual development. They need curricular contexts and related materials that supply motivation, background, goals and opportunities for reflection. They need to fit into developmentally appropriate, balanced structures that allow time on task/time off task, exploration/reflection, individual thought/group discussion, absorption/presentation. Classroom teachers have neither the time nor the resources to design this kind of subtle curriculum from scratch on their own.

Electronic repositories of curriculum are necessary to speed the pace of educational reform and to lower costs of innovative curriculum development. They must combine the latest educational resources with carefully crafted curriculum. Attempts to date to fill this need with scattered Internet postings or World Wide Web pages of fixed resources have proven to be too limited. They do not provide a complete solution to the needs of teachers who want to reform their classroom teaching. They lack supporting materials, suggested lesson plans or variations for different circumstances. Standard Internet browsers do not adequately support teacher needs: locating relevant resources, searching among them, selecting the best fit, adapting resources and curriculum to local needs, organizing curriculum into effective learning contexts and sharing results or experiences.

There is a need to: (i) reuse and adapt model curriculum and resources to local classroom situations, (ii) disseminate innovative classroom ideas and experiences globally, (iii) establish digital educational repositories to promote sharing of effective reform curriculum.

The TCA approach

The Teacher's Curriculum Assistant responds to the needs of teachers interested in implementing educational reform in their classrooms by exploring how best to make available to them model curriculum disseminated via the technology of digital libraries. It provides software tools to teachers for personalizing the curriculum to their students, their teaching styles and their local conditions.

TCA is an Internet-based curriculum development environment. It provides teachers with facilities to make effective use of educational resources available on the Internet. It allows providers of resources—such as publishers of textbooks, educational software or CD-ROMs—to index and publish their offerings where teachers can locate them. It manages the digital repositories so they can grow in an orderly way.

Acceptance of TCA by teachers, providers and repository managers entails agreement upon a set of standards for descriptive indexing of resources and for structuring of curriculum. For instance, a preliminary TCA prototype uses approximately 30 indexes for resources; it structures curriculum in a hierarchy of semester themes, weekly units and daily lesson plans composed of resources; and it adopts certain repository management policies. These standards are essential for providing computer support to teachers. With such standards, many techniques of artificial intelligence and information retrieval can be applied to the tasks of locating, searching, selecting, adapting, organizing and sharing resources and curricula. Without them, teachers will remain lost in the Web's immense hyperspace.

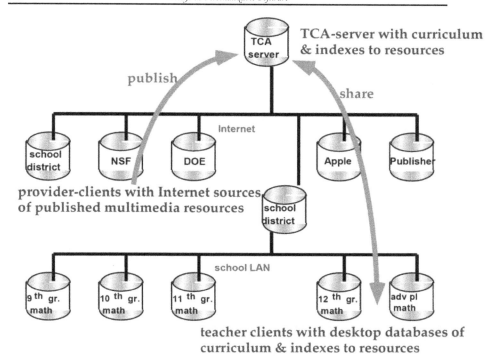

Figure 2. TCA network architecture. Large resources are stored on Internet servers, while summary information about these resources is copied to the desktop computers of teachers.

In TCA, the curriculum repository works as follows (figure 2): Curriculum providers post educational resources to their own servers on the Internet. They publish the addresses of these resources on a central TCA server. Along with the addresses, they also publish descriptions (indexes) of the resources and suggested curriculum for using the resources, adhering to TCA standards. Providers include educational software publishers, textbook publishers, educational research centers and other organizations interested in the development and dissemination of reform curriculum. Teachers have TCA client software on their desktop computers. This software maintains a database of resource indexes and curriculum that is periodically updated from the TCA Internet server via the school district. Teachers do their curriculum planning with the information on their own computers and then download resources they need from the Internet addresses stored there. This allows the latest educational resources to flow into the teacher's computer, where they are organized into meaningful curriculum to structure classroom activities.

A TCA prototype

TCA includes both client and server software for accessing and maintaining educational digital libraries on the Internet: (i) **teacher-client software** for teachers to make use of model curriculum and multimedia resources, (ii) **provider-client software** for organizations to publish educational resources on the Internet and (iii) TCA-**server software** to manage the digital repositories of curriculum.

Teacher-client software

The TCA approach begins with teachers and curriculum developers. It works with them to understand teachers' curriculum needs and the traditional curriculum usage process. It explores with teachers ways in which personal computers with access to educational resources and model curriculum can be used to meet their needs and to help them obtain and adopt useful curriculum in their classrooms.

When teachers try to use browsers like Netscape or Mosaic to take advantage of the educational ideas that are beginning to be posted to the Web, they meet with the following problems:

- there are no effective methods for **locating** relevant curriculum sites,

- it is too hard to **search** for items of interest,

- these is no choice of versions to **select** for different situations,

- there are no tools for **adapting** what is found to local needs,

- there is no support for **organizing** scattered ideas into workable curriculum,

- there are no ways for teachers to **share** their experiences.

These problems can be overcome with centralized repositories of carefully structured curriculum and indexed resources. The repositories should support two-way communication, so that teachers can share their experiences using materials in the repositories and can "grow" the repositories.

Based on preliminary study of these issues, a TCA prototype has been developed. Six interface screens have been designed for teacher support: **Profiler, Explorer, Versions, Editor, Planner, Networker**.

The Profiler, Explorer and Versions interfaces work together for information retrieval (figure 3). The Profiler helps teachers define classroom profiles and locates curriculum and resources that match the profile. The Explorer displays these items and allows the teacher to search through them to find related items. Versions then helps the teacher select from alternative versions that have been adapted by other teachers. Through these interfaces, teachers can locate the available materials that most closely match their personal needs; this makes it easier to tailor the materials to individual requirements.

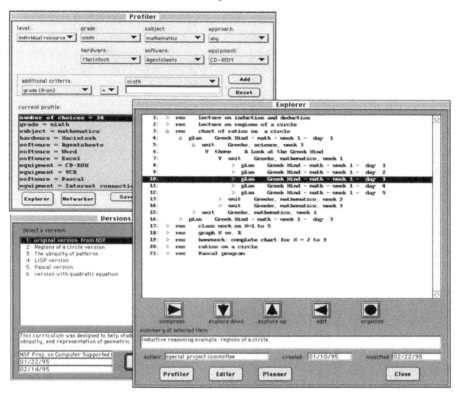

Figure 3. The teacher-client software interface for locating, searching and selecting resources and curriculum: the Profiler, Explorer and Versions.

The Planner, Editor and Networker help the teacher to prepare resources and curriculum for use and to share the results of classroom use (figure 4). The Planner is a design environment for reusing and reorganizing lesson plans. The Editor allows the teacher to modify and adapt resources. This is a primary means for personalizing the curriculum. Finally, the Networker supports interactions with the Internet, providing a two-way medium of communication with a global community of teachers. Using the Networker, a teacher can share personalized versions of standard curriculum with other teachers who might have similar needs.

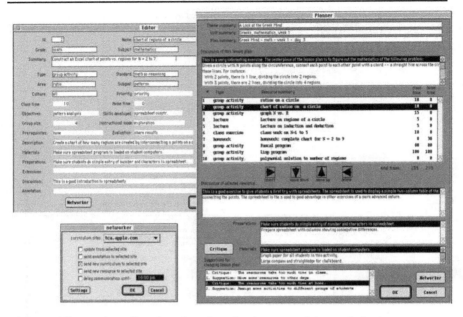

Figure 4. The teacher-client interface for adapting, organizing and sharing resources and curriculum: the Planner, Editor and Networker.

Provider-client software

For teachers to reuse and build upon model curriculum and innovative resources, they must have easy access to large repositories of materials that have been developed by provider organizations. It requires thoughtful design work, structuring and presentation to develop materials that can be personalized by many teachers with different needs. The TCA software supports this task. Provider-client software gives computer-based support to the providers of curriculum and resources in preparing their materials for the TCA Internet repository.

Digital libraries of model curriculum and related educational resources must be put on the Internet. Both units of curriculum and individual resources must be indexed with descriptors that correspond to teacher interests (e.g., educational standards) and to classroom profiles.

TCA includes software tools to facilitate the construction and inter-relating of curriculum items, the indexing of resources and the creation of alternative versions of both curriculum and resources. These tools are primarily for providers of curriculum. They can be used by NSF-funded projects submitting content to the repository, by school district staff and by publishers of educational software or textbooks.

Multimedia resources are maintained on servers distributed across the Internet. These are typically servers owned by the provider. The resources can include textual readings, evaluation materials, video clips or software such as simulations. That way, these large files do not take up room on the teachers' computers. This also allows the providers to update the materials whenever necessary.

A central **TCA** server maintains all the model curriculum associated with the resources as well as the descriptive indexes to the resources. Teachers have a copy of the indexes on their computers and can update their copies from the **TCA** server at will. The indexes allow teachers to search for interesting items without downloading the large resources. This means that teachers can do their curriculum planning and class preparation on their computer without connecting to the Internet. They only need to connect in order to download selected resources for adaptation and distribution to students. The Internet locations of the resources are included in the indexes. Downloading can be consolidated by a school district for all its teachers and done over night if Internet traffic is heavy during the school day.

Provider software incorporates the **TCA** index standards: what descriptors are required or optional, what values the descriptors may take and which descriptors may take user-defined values. These indexes are used to structure the curriculum items, the summary information for multimedia resources and the classroom profiles that teachers enter into their copies of **TCA**. This set of standards is what makes possible extensive software support for curriculum development in **TCA**.

TCA-server software

Acceptance of the proposed digital repository by a national community of teachers requires the collaboration of a number of organizations as well as the compilation of a critical mass of curriculum content. Management structures have to be agreed upon and standards need to be adopted for the formatting of content.

The organization and quality control of information in digital libraries is critical if they are to be useful and usable. There are two extreme models of how to build an effective library of personalizable materials: (i) provide a few very general materials that have been well thought out and carefully structured for adaptation to diverse needs or (ii) allow practitioners to contribute many versions of materials that have proven successful in classrooms. The need for control over contents must be balanced by the desirability of users being able to comment upon, modify and expand these contents. Digital repositories can be structured variously to adopt different management approaches. One repository could contain model mathematics curriculum developed by NSF-funded projects, be managed by a committee of NSF staff and grantees and allow no additions by teachers using the curriculum. A second repository could contain mathematics curriculum used by a local school district, be managed by curriculum staff and allow narrative annotations by teachers discussing their experiences using resources and curriculum. A third repository could be open for postings by teachers, be self-managed and allow teachers to add new ideas, innovative resources, adapted versions and annotations.

Section IV. Personalizable Learning Medium

Overview of PLM

While TCA is primarily intended to support teachers, PLM is designed for the individual learner; together, the two systems support personalizing of the whole classroom process of organizing learning activities and engaging in them. Once activities and curriculum are found in a digital library, they must be adapted to the needs and interests of individual learners and presented to them in personally meaningful formats. PLM is a systematic attempt to integrate a number of software techniques into a system to personalize educational materials and to present them in the most effective format for the individual learners. PLM incorporates some of the functionality from TCA within a system designed for learners to use themselves and then it adds personalizable display functions.

> PLM *(1) provides access to current educational materials on the Internet, (2) supports hypertext exploration, (3) incorporates multimedia simulations and (4) provides comprehensive personalizability.*

A personalized browser of digital libraries

It is not feasible to manually develop separate versions of curriculum for each type of learner and each set of student interests. However, it *is* technically feasible to store a single corpus of properly structured curriculum on the Internet, keep it up-to-date and automate its analysis into elemental units that can then be recombined in a large variety of ways to match the needs and desires of different audiences. Furthermore, this process of personalizing can be put under the control of the learner in ways that are not overly intrusive or demanding. PLM takes this approach. It provides a personalized browser of educational resources and related curriculum stored in digital libraries on the Internet. It then displays the material to the learner in a personalized presentation.

Computational hypermedia to customize HTML

Academic research in computer science suggests many promising applications of hypermedia to education, particularly if hypermedia is extended with techniques from artificial intelligence. Promising technologies for this include perspectives mechanisms and task-specific languages. Retrieval of hypermedia materials can use techniques of query reformulation, fuzzy logic and case-based reasoning (Stahl & Owen, 1995) to aid in the difficult task of making relevancy criteria explicit. The user interface to a hypermedia knowledge system can take the form of a design environment to help people construct useful presentations of information.

The technology underlying the PLM system is computational hypermedia. It is a fine-grained hypermedia approach that incorporates personal perspectives and a navigational language. This hypermedia differs from conventional approaches (like Hypercard) in that text is broken down into sentence or paragraph-length nodes rather than pages and eventually built back up through selection by labeled links. That is, sets of nodes are selected and organized based on choices of perspectives and formulations of queries in a task-specific end-user language. New labels for links can be defined by end-users; they extend the semantics of the navigation language. Alternative versions of nodes can be defined; they are displayed in different perspectives. Displays are defined by statements in the language and take into account the current perspective and the link labels (Stahl, 1991). These techniques facilitate the creation of hypermedia webs of information for learners to explore, where the presentation of displays and available paths are tuned to the learner's needs.

Multimedia incorporating active simulations

The multimedia available with PLM includes text formulated in versions of SGML (the Standard Generalized Mark-up Language for digital text), such as HTML (the hypertext mark-up language used by the Web). It also includes text formulated for Mathematica and other simulations. These alternative description systems are translated and integrated into the PLM hypermedia system. This way, resources posted to the Web or developed in applications like Mathematica can be seamlessly integrated. Someone reading a PLM document can click on a region to download another Web document or execute a Mathematica computation.

A comprehensive sequence of personalizing mechanisms

As currently conceived, information in PLM passes through eight stages in moving from an educational digital library on the Internet to a display on the learner's computer monitor. (The eight stages are detailed below.) During each transition there are mechanisms to tailor the information to the learner's needs. This provides a comprehensive process of customization. Although the mechanisms that control the personalizing at each stage can be accessed by the learner and adjusted as much as desired, most of them can operate automatically behind the scenes. Initial choices in specifying personal preferences can be made by the learner, a teacher or a software installer and then left alone. The learner can then simply select subject matter and options from menus.

Technologies for personalizing

Perhaps the most important advances in software in the next decade will come in technologies for personalizing information to individual users. A number of recent technological standards for hypertext set the stage for this advance. These standards include: the Dexter Hypertext Reference Model and SGML. They provide standard formats for hypertext that incorporate means for defining custom variations on the internal structure of the hypertext and on the display of hypertext documents. For instance, SGML specifies how to create Document Type Definitions (DTDs) that determine how various textual elements (titles, emphasized terms, embedded links) will appear in displays. World Wide Web documents conform to a specific SGML language, namely HTML.

Similar mark-up languages are used in software applications like **Mathematica**. **Mathematica** is a powerful program for the development of documents that include mathematical computations. Sections of the documents are labeled as titles, text, computation inputs, etc. One can, for instance, write the equations of a 3-D graphical object and then activate the document section to display the computed graphic. The **Mathematica** language allows a user to specify how the graphic should appear: 3-D perspective, scale, grid lines or axis labeling. A student reading a **Mathematica** document can edit the document to explore variations of the problem discussed and then decide how to display the result.

Until recently, most software was designed either for narrowly-defined tasks that required little effort by users but granted them little control (e.g., walk-up-and-use applications like ATM cash machines) or systems for dedicated specialists (like CAD programs for architectural drafting or professional programming environments) that require months or years to master. The high-functionality systems allow for open-ended expression, but at prohibitive cognitive costs. Personalizable software would be adjustable, so users could choose not only levels of power but which functions they want. These decisions could then be modified as user needs and experience evolve.

The next generation of software should empower users to personalize software and information displays without burdening them excessively.

Personalizable software should provide tools and mechanisms for users to structure information the way they want by indicating their desires in natural ways. PLM brings together a set of technologies that can work together to do this for learners accessing digital educational materials.

These technologies for providing user control of information were explored in Hermes, a system for NASA designers (Stahl, 1993b). The Hermes design environment was based on a philosophical analysis of human understanding and a theory of how best to provide computer support for designer's efforts to interpret new designs. The goal was to support personalized views of architectural drawings and of design rationale that corresponded to the designers' differing interpretive perspectives.

The system of hypermedia in Hermes incorporates fine-grained nodes and typed links, a perspectives mechanism and a navigational language. The Hermes project built on research into intelligent hypermedia, including Phidias (Stahl, McCall & Peper, 1992). It also incorporated the design environment approach of systems like Janus (Fischer, Nakakoji, Ostwald, Stahl & Sumner, 1993b). These technologies were developed for providing high-functionality, knowledge-based computer support to professionals working on complex tasks.

Computational hypermedia, as seen in the "Design Rationale" window of Figure 5, makes many decisions on the presentation of material dynamically (i.e., while the computer system is running), based on information that the user has specified. Here, the displays are assembled dynamically to meet the specified needs of the reader. The reader can then revise the criteria or make explicit decisions on what to see next.

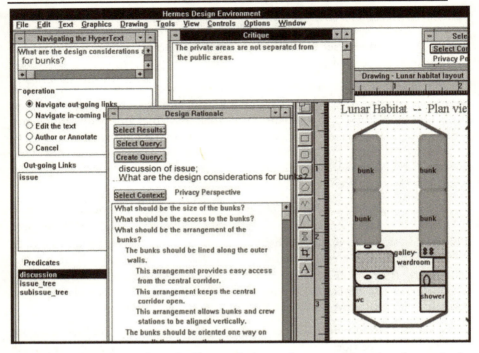

Figure 5. A screen image from the Hermes design environment. Note that the text in the central window has been dynamically assembled based on a statement in the end-user language (discussion of issue) and that a specific perspective has been selected (the privacy perspective). The text here is design rationale: a hierarchy of issues about the design of bunks, alternative answers to the issues and arguments for these answers. Each issue, answer and argument is stored as a separate node; labeled links store their interrelationships; they are consolidated into information displays by the execution of language statements within perspectives.

The sequence of personalizing in PLM

The technical approach to designing PLM *integrates customization ideas, mechanisms and industry standards from* TCA, Hermes *and SGML.*

Personalization in PLM takes place in eight sequential stages within the process of selecting materials from the digital library, analyzing them into hypertext nodes and links and synthesizing selected contents into a personalized display. The stages are represented in Figure 6 and discussed below:

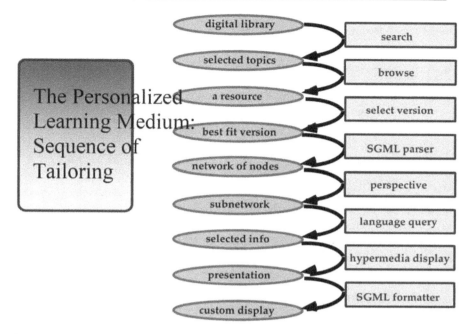

Figure 6. The sequence of personalizing mechanisms in PLM.

Stage 1. Searching for relevant materials.

The learner defines a *Profile* of the materials sought in the educational digital library. This profile includes characteristics of the learner as well; generally, the profile of the learner will not have to be altered frequently. For instance, the learner might request exercises involving the geometry of circles. The learner's profile might specify tenth grade mathematics ability, ninth grade reading level and a preference for visualizations. It might also indicate availability of specific computer hardware and software. The profile is used by PLM to formulate a query that retrieves a selection of materials from the library. The profile functions as a user model for the software, but one that is under the control of the user.

Stage 2. Browsing among related resources.

Descriptions of selected materials are displayed in an *Explorer* window. The learner uses this interface to browse among related library resources, such as curriculum guides, software tools, historical background, useful mathematical techniques, relevant video clips. By providing for browsing within the confines of the Profile search, PLM gives the learner freedom to explore without the danger of becoming lost. Figure 3 showed an implementation of this synthesis of search and browsing for teachers in TCA. Other browsing tools are possible, including graphical maps of hypertext associations among materials.

Stage 3. Selecting the best fit version.

The digital library may include multiple versions of a given resource. For instance, a geometry problem might be approached using 2-D constructions, equations or computer programming. The learner can select the most appealing approach. In Figure 3, a *Versions* selector was integrated with the Profile and the Explorer.

Stage 4. Parsing into nodes and links.

Documents are broken down into their elements (as hypertext nodes), connected by typed hypertext links. The link types are based on the element's SGML markup type (e.g., "title"). This is done automatically by PLM. Custom node and link types may be defined by learners—or by their teachers.

Stage 5. Viewing from a perspective.

The learner's profile defines a *perspective*. The currently active perspective selects which nodes and links can be viewed. This allows multiple, redundant forms of information to be present in resources in the library, of which all but one form will be filtered out. For instance, many people may have annotated a particular resource, but a learner may want to filter out all annotations except her own, her teacher's and her classmates'. Then she would define her own perspective and have it inherit from her teacher's and her class' in order to view what they view in their perspectives.

Stage 6. Querying with the language.

All PLM displays are created dynamically by queries in the hypermedia navigation language. Statements in the language in effect specify starting nodes and types of links to traverse. Execution of a statement takes place within a selected perspective and results in a collection of linked nodes. This collection is the material selected for display. The language can be extended by end-users and terms in the language can have different meanings in different perspectives. By judicious naming of terms, users can construct sets of language statements that read like natural expressions in the task domain of interest.

Stage 7. Synthesizing a display.

PLM constructs a document from the collection of nodes and links. The document is marked up using a version of SGML. At this stage, the information retrieved from the library has been personalized.

Stage 8. Formatting the presentation.

The final stage is to display the information. The display format can be personalized by adjusting the mark-up definitions. For instance, the hierarchical design rationale in Figure 5 was indented by level. Alternatively, different levels could be italicized or text size and color adjusted to individual preferences.

Through these eight stages, standardized materials are selected and displayed in a way that can be tuned extensively by individual learners to their needs. A thoughtfully prepared document in the digital library can be personalized differently by each learner in the world.

Section V. Personalizable software

Reflection upon the approach to personalizable software in TCA and PLM raises a number of general issues. Section V discusses several of these. It begins with the role of personal perspectives for organizing sets of choices made in personalizing information. Then it discusses the use of meta-info and meta-data for implementing functionality that empowers users with control over documents. It concludes by presenting a typology of approaches to personalizing, distinguishing the methods that have been used in different systems.

Personal perspectives on information

According to the philosophy of interpretation, everyone understands things from their own perspective. This perspective is based on their situation in history, in society, in their own life, in their work and in their general concerns: what they know, like and need; how they have been socialized; and how they interact with other people.

To be an effective learner is to be able to control information that one comes across and to personalize it within one's own perspective. Critical thinking—the hallmark of a sophisticated learner—consists in being able to uncover the perspectives that are implicit in information and to critique those perspective from one's own viewpoint. Ideology critique, for instance, lays bare the social mediations that have molded information so that one can evaluate the relevance of that information to one's own position and concerns.

Reality can only be viewed from perspectives; all knowledge is someone's interpretation.

There are several general implications of the perspectival character of information for the task of supporting education with software mechanisms: (i) information should be presented in ways that allow one to select different perspectives; (ii) one should be able to define and adjust one's own perspective; and (iii) one should be able to control definitions of perspectives. Control here means being able to make perspectives visible and changeable. For all perspectives, one should be able to see the definition of the perspective and to understand how it affects the display of information. For one's own perspective, one should also be able to modify its definition.

Such control over information has always been seen as desirable by visionaries of computer supported information exploration. In the inaugural discussion of the idea of hypertext libraries, Bush (1945) proposed that learners should be able to define their own paths through information. In the most recent vision of digital libraries, Negroponte (1995) emphasizes, "Being digital, whatever it means, means having your way." However, to date the need to personalize information sources has not received the attention it deserves in software system implementations.

One reason that systems to personalize information have not been pursued is that such control can be a double-edged sword. Most people do not have the time, skill or interest to organize the information that they use. Ideally, people want to delegate the organizing of most information, yet be in control of organizing very special elements. Delegation can take the form of trusting that some presumably reliable people have already organized the materials or, given software agent technology, it can take the form of instructing computers in how to automate the process of organizing the information.

In general, one probably wants different levels of control over information, accepting the perspectives in which much information is embodied and personalizing other information to one's own perspective. The implementation of such control may also take place on different levels. For instance, an author may structure some material, a teacher may adapt parts of it and a learner may personalize other sections. Each of these people may do some of this work manually, some of it using pre-programmed software mechanisms and some using mechanisms that they have tailored for specific tasks.

Implementing levels of control

Two programming principles are especially important for implementing computer support for levels of control:

- Provide information about information (meta-info).

- Migrate modifiable data up to levels of fixed program instructions (meta-data).

To empower users with control over information, provide them with access to meta-info and meta-data.

The following table illustrates these principles:

Table 1. The use of meta-info and meta-data in systems of hypertext, in Agentsheets and in PLM.

In table 1 three roles have been distinguished for people involved with each of three systems: hypertext, Agentsheets and PLM. Imagine the development and use of a hypertext document. Originally, an author (perhaps a textbook writer) enters information into the hyperdocument. Then someone (perhaps a teacher or curriculum specialist) performs a middle role, organizing the material by defining sections, giving them descriptive labels and linking them together in useful ways. This defines meta-info about the original material, making it more valuable by facilitating personalized use of the information. In the end, a reader (perhaps a student) blazes a personal path of exploration through the hyperdocument, using the meta-info to make informed choices about what to view.

Meta-info defines the linking that makes hypertext possible. But it also plays a role in prose. Note the extensive presence of meta-info in this paper to guide the reader through a dense argument: abstract, preface, reader's guide, table of contents, several layers of headings, figure text, cross-references, bibliographic references. There are also many implicit structural indicators, from grammatical ways of defining syntactic relationships to the repetition of names and terms that were discussed in previous sections. Many of these literary techniques of communicating meta-info to guide interpretation would be transformed in hypertext media. The danger in non-linear hypertext is that the reader will quickly become lost. Personalizing the hypertext can be used to re-impose structure—but this time under the reader's rather than the author's control.

Agentsheets was also developed with a three-level division of labor in mind. The program was created by a software developer to provide tools for simulation designers and behaviors for simulation viewers. The developer's product is a program. Periodically, he revises the program to meet new needs that title designers have reported. The designers build simulation titles within the Agentsheets environment. Their innovations do not change the Agentsheets program itself, but provide a level of meta-data that defines the look and behavior of components of the new simulation. For instance, the designer of the Segregation simulation defined ways of arranging houses and placing different sets of people in the houses with different rules about wanting to have neighbors who belong to their own set. These simulation titles are then shared across the Internet using **Are**. Finally, simulation players can use the titles to set up specific situations to simulate. For instance, students using Segregation can define three racial groups, each of which wants to have 50% of their immediate neighbors be of the same race. The students can arrange icons representing people of these three races in a simulated village and see how they move around. The definitions at this level are simply data (e.g., location coordinates of icons) to **Agentsheets**. The possibility of programming a general simulation environment like **Agentsheets** instead of having to program each title from scratch is a consequence of migrating much of the simulation functionality down to the level of meta-data. What would otherwise have been simply part of the program source code has been made into a layer of variable data that controls the end-user's data.

PLM incorporates both these strategies. It structures documents with layers of meta-info, such as labeled links. It also treats decisions about structuring, like choices of perspectives, as meta-data. These are built into the **PLM** program at the first level. The specific interface facilities enable people to either personalize information directly or else personalize the automated mechanisms that structure the presentations of information. This work can be done by the end users—the learners who read, create paths and annotate the hyperdocuments—or by people in intermediate roles (teachers, curriculum specialists or other super-users) who define the way information will be structured for the learners. Ideally, the work of controlling the presentation of information can be shared among authors, adapters, readers and the software support systems for each of them. This way the burden should not be too great on anyone, yet the level of control will be substantial and effective.

Levels of personalizing

There have been some initial efforts in commercial software relevant to the goal of making information personalizable, although most of the work remains to be done. (As Lanier (1995) points out, many current attempts to personalize software with agents and front-ends for novices insult the user's intelligence rather than augmenting it, as called for by Engelbart (1963).) Even the terminology to define this goal is yet to be worked out.

Various levels of personalizing can be distinguished. Different system approaches implement different forms of personalizability. These alternative forms represent specific trade-offs between what the user can do and what the system does automatically. Certain levels of personalizing are appropriate for specific domains, individual users and different use situations. It is useful to identify several categories or major forms that personalizing can take. In the following list, the labels are somewhat arbitrary because there has been no consistent distinction of these various forms in the literature. Each of the following levels is discussed below:

- *Specify:* adjust settings to select values of predefined parameters; e.g., a user expertise level may be specified on a scale between novice and expert.

- *Tune:* adjust display presentations; e.g., set second level headings to print in bold.

- *Customize:* extend list of options with new categories or objects; e.g., add a new icon to a palette of representations.

- *Personalize:* make choices that change the program's global set of settings; e.g., choose an overall viewing perspective.

- *Tailor:* change tool functionality; e.g., add a spelling checker or a spreadsheet to an existing application.

- *Program:* define arbitrary system behaviors; e.g., change the source code defining how something is computed.

Specification components and user models

Within the tradition of autonomous artificial intelligence, the common approach to personalizing the presentation of information is to include a user model, i.e., a description for the software of characteristics of the person using the software. For instance, many tutoring programs build up a model of the student being tutored based on the history of the student's behavior using the program (e.g., what sorts of errors that student typically commits). Due to the emphasis on implementing autonomous behavior by the software, these user models were generally not visible or modifiable by the students or their teachers.

The idea of a specification component is to allow users to define the computer's model of what the user wants (Fischer, Nakakoji, Ostwald, Stahl & Sumner, 1993b). For instance, a person using the software could specify a level of difficulty, particular topics of interest or other requirements. This is a mechanism for the sharing of meta-info between the computer and the user. Such shared information allows the software to draw more useful inferences. For instance, in TCA, the Profiler acts as a specification component allowing a teacher to define a user model relevant to the selection of curriculum. This is used by the TCA system not only to formulate search queries, but also to define critics for analyzing retrieved lesson plans. The critics are rules that compare meta-info in the indices of resources with meta-info in the user profile to determine whether particular resources are compatible with the needs of the teacher.

Display tuning

The display of information may be tuned to user preferences. The display of hypertext Web pages, for instance, is tuned by browsers like Netscape to the user's operating system: headings and other features look different on a Mac, on an ASCII (text only) terminal or in X-Windows. This is accomplished by encoding display information using the HTML standard, which is variously interpreted by the browsers. This technique is used extensively in PLM, although there the user has additional control over how the display is formatted, whereas Netscape does this tuning autonomously.

End-user customization

The list of features that can be specified and have their display tuned in a system like HTML is pre-defined and fixed. There are just so many levels of headings, etc. allowed. There is no way to define a new feature, like a call-out text.

End-user customization permits the definition of new features. For instance, in Hermes a user can add new names to the list of legal types of nodes and links. These names are also used in the navigation language, making the semantics of the language extensible. Similarly, the list of allowable perspectives can be extended, adding new perspectives (as meta-data) that may build on (inherit) existing perspectives. This kind of customization or extensibility is critical for knowledge-based systems because the definition of domains of knowledge is rarely fixed or independent of users and their innovative tasks (Stahl, 1995c).

Personalizable software

Users should be able to define how they want their software to behave for them. Personalizable software should request the name of the user and then reconfigure itself to do all the things that user specified in the past. If a user has entered a profile of specific interests, has tuned displays in certain ways, has customized lists of terms and has extended palettes to include new items, then all of this should be made automatically available to that user.

The personal perspectives mechanism provides a way of organizing this association of comprehensive changes with individual users. In a program like Hermes that incorporates perspectives, all work by a user is carried out in a perspective. Thus, everything created is associated with some perspective. In the simple case, users always use their own perspectives. Then, their changes are always available to them.

The perspective mechanism also allows for shared perspectives for collaboration. Here, several users can work in one perspective and share specifications, tunings or customizations made in that perspective. They can each also have their own perspectives with their private personalizations. Their private perspectives can inherit from their shared perspective, so that they can take advantage of group changes as well as their private ones. Inheritance of perspectives allows people to build up sets of personalizations by choosing among existing perspectives to inherit from and reuse. This means that one does not have to personalize a system from scratch, dramatically reducing the overhead otherwise involved in personalizable software.

Tailorable functionality

The trend in the next generation of commercial software is to support personalizing through component-ware. OpenDoc, OLE 2 and development environments like VisualBasic allow software functionality to be developed in independently compiled components. Users can then build their personal system by combining useful components. Everyone can have their own personal toolbelt of components—just like every carpenter meets his or her special needs with a unique toolbelt full of standardized tools. Unfortunately, the market is not yet ready for people to create their own software this way. When they do, the available components will still have to include mechanisms like specification components, display standards, perspectives and task-specific languages in order to support the forms of personalizability discussed above. It is not clear how independently developed components will be able to share meta-info and meta-data adequately to have these personalization components work effectively across them.

Programmability

There are many levels of programming: graphical direct manipulation, visual programming systems, task-specific end-user scripting languages and general purpose programming languages. Each has its advantages in power, disadvantages in cognitive load and appropriateness to specific uses. As a means to personalizing software, programmability probably serves best as a last resort. When specifying, tuning, customizing, personalizing and tailoring cannot accomplish what one wants then programming may be necessary. In many cases, a task-specific language can meet this need without imposing undue requirements on the user. Task-specific languages can use the visual conventions or textual terminology of the domain and can restrict the syntax through direct manipulation or predefined templates in order to minimize the cognitive load on the user.

Some general lessons concerning personalizable software

This paper has been concerned with computer support for learners and their teachers using resources from the Web. The systems that were described above,

TCA and PLM, illustrated a comprehensive approach to global sharing of educational resources combined with local personalizing of relevant materials. Computer support for this takes the form of personalizable software. A number of issues related to the design, implementation and use of personalizable software were discussed in this final Section. It is notable that many of the issues concerning software that personalizes documents apply to personalizing that software itself. Hence the productive ambiguity of the term *personalizable software*.

References

Ambach, J, Perrone, C, Repenning, A (1995) "Remote Exploratoriums: Combining Networking Media and Design Environments. *Computers and Education*. 24 (3) pp. 163-176.

Bush, V (1945) "As We May Think." *Atlantic Monthly*. 176 (1) pp. 101-108. Reprinted in (Greif, 1988).

Engelbart, D (1963) "A Conceptual Framework for the Augmentation of Man's Intellect." Reprinted in (Greif, 1988).

Fischer, G, Nakakoji, K, Ostwald, J, Stahl, G, Sumner, T (1993a) "Embedding Computer-Based Critics in the Contexts of Design." *Proceedings of InterCHI '93. Conference on Human Factors in Computing Systems*, Amsterdam, April 1993. pp. 157-164.

Fischer, G, Nakakoji, K, Ostwald, J, Stahl, G, Sumner, T (1993b) "Embedding Critics in Design Environments." *The Knowledge Engineering Review*, 4 (8), Dec. 93. pp. 285-307.

Fischer, G, Stevens, C (1991) "Information Access in Complex, Poorly Structured Information Spaces." *Proceedings of CHI '91. Conference on Human Factors in Computing Systems*, New York, April 1991. pp. 63-70.

Fischer, G, Nieper, H (1987) "Personalized Intelligent Information Systems." *Workshop Report, Breckenridge, CO*. Technical Report 87-9. Institute of Cognitive Science, University of Colorado at Boulder.

Greeno, J (1993) "For Research to Reform Education and Cognitive Science." In *The Challenge in Mathematics and Science Education: Psychology's Response*. Edited by Penner, L, Batsche, G, Knoff, H, Nelson, D. APA Press. 1993.

Greif, I (1988) *Computer-Supported Cooperative Work*. Morgan Kaufmann.

Heidegger, M (1927) *Being and Time*. Harper & Row. 1962.

Lanier, J (1995) "Agents of Alienation." *Interactions*. 2 (3) pp. 66-72.

Lave, J, Wenger, E (1991) *Situated Learning: Legitimate Peripheral Participation*. Cambridge University Press.

NCTM (1989) *Curriculum and Evaluation Standards for School Mathematics*. National Council of Teachers of Mathematics.

Negroponte, N (1995) *Being Digital*.

Piaget, J (1927) *The Language and Though of the Child*. Meridian Books. 1955.

Repenning, A, Sumner, T (1995) "**Agentsheets**: A Medium for Creating Domain-oriented Visual Programming Languages." *IEEE Computer*. March. pp. 17-25.

Stahl, G (1995a) *A Personalized Learning Medium*. Proposal to NSF/SBIR from Owen Research Inc. June 1995.

Stahl, G (1995b) *The Teacher's Curriculum Assistant: A Curriculum Repository and Development Environment to Support SMET Educational Reform*. Proposal to NSF/NIE from Owen Research Inc. April 1995.

Stahl, G (1995c) "Supporting Interpretation in Design." Submitted to *Design Studies*. Special issue on Design Cognition and Computation. 18 pages.

Stahl, G, Owen, R (1995) "Armchair Missions to Mars: Using Case-Based Reasoning and Fuzzy Logic to Simulate a Time Series Model of Astronaut Crews." Submitted to *Knowledge-Based Systems*. 10 pages.

Stahl, G, Sumner, T, Owen, R (1995) "Share Globally, Adapt Locally: Software to Create and Distribute Student-centered Curriculum." *Computers and Education*. Special issue on Education and the Internet. 24 (3) pp. 237-246.

Stahl, G, Sumner, T, Repenning, A (1995) "Internet Repositories for Collaborative Learning: Supporting Both Students and Teachers." Forthcoming in *Proceedings of Computer Support for Collaborative Learning*. October 17-20.

Stahl, G (1993a) "Supporting Situated Interpretation." *Proceedings of the Cognitive Science Society: A Multidisciplinary Conference on Cognition*. Boulder, 1993. pp. 965-970.

Stahl, G (1993b) *Interpretation in Design: The Problem of Tacit and Explicit Understanding in Computer Support of Cooperative Design*. Ph.D. dissertation. Department of Computer Science. University of Colorado at Boulder. Technical report CU-CS-688-93. UMI dissertation services, Ann Arbor, MI, order no. 9423544. 451 + xiv pages.

Stahl, G (1992a) *A Computational Medium for Supporting Interpretation in Design*. Technical Report CU-CS-598-92. Computer Science Department, University of Colorado at Boulder. 39 pages.

Stahl, G (1992b) *Toward a Theory of Hermeneutic Software Design*. Technical Report CU-CS-589-92. Computer Science Department, University of Colorado at Boulder. 16 pages.

Stahl, G, McCall, R, Peper, G (1992) "Extending Hypermedia with an Inference Language: an Alternative to Rule-Based Expert Systems." *Proceedings of the IBM ITL Conference: Expert Systems (October 19-21, 1992)*. pp. 160-167.

Stahl, G (1991) *A Hypermedia Inference Language as an Alternative to Rule-Based Expert Systems*. Technical Report CU-CS-557-91. Computer Science Department, University of Colorado at Boulder. 23 pages.

Stahl, G (1975) *Marxian Hermeneutics and Heideggerian Social Theory: Interpreting and Transforming Our World*. Ph.D. dissertation. Department of Philosophy,

Northwestern University. Evanston, IL. *Dissertation Abstracts* 36 (7) order no. 75-29,759. 372 pages.

Vygotsky, L (1936) *Thought and Language*. MIT Press. 1986.

5.   Personalizing the Web

The World Wide Web (the web) claims to address information needs of the whole world and therefore encourages knowledge to be expressed in universal formats. However, information is most meaningful and useful to people when it is adapted to their interests, backgrounds and situations. This paper presents a set of three mechanisms for adapting decontextualized information to personal needs: dynamic hypertext, personal perspectives and structural navigation. Five prototype systems illustrate how these mechanisms can be used in a variety of applications. Web browsers incorporating this approach make the web more interactive, adaptable and personal.

The Need for a Personal Interface to the Web

Excitement about the World Wide Web must be tempered by recognition of its unresolved contradictions. The new communication medium that strives to meet the future needs of the whole world fails to meet the needs of most people today. Security and censorship issues debated in the press and across the Internet point to conflicts concerning who should see what content in a medium designed to deliver everything to everyone.

If the medium is truly the message then we need to reflect on format as well as content. Should the web's world be one of homogeneous communication or should the world evolve into an arena where each person's individuality can shine forth and illuminate the perspectives of others? The military wars of today are being fought for the survival of anachronistic cultural differences. While ethnic groups desperately try to defend the existence of their traditional languages, the web irrepressibly promotes a simplified, universalized dialect of English as de rigueur. Ironically, the web's hegemonous technology may hold the key to a truly multi-personal world.

For information to be shared with everyone everywhere it must be represented in a highly decontextualized format, universally applicable. However, we know that information is the most interesting and useful when it corresponds in presentation style as closely as possible to our personal interests, conceptualizations, tasks and situations. When we are working on some problem, we want information that is directly applicable; when we are learning, we want information that matches our way of looking at things so that we can construct new understandings in our own ways.

The web poses an essential problem for computer-human interaction, not just superficial issues of user-friendliness. The computer wants computational (symbolic, universal) representations; people want personalized presentations. Web browsers and servers provide the software that mediates between data stored on the web and provide what web surfers need to resolve this conflict.

The current crop of web browsers let users customize only the frills, like colors of link indicators. This is because the web is based on a simplistic model of hypertext, embedding link information in blocks of text where it cannot be manipulated. The explosive growth of the web may actually be attributable to this imposed simplicity, which already strains most people's ability to share their thoughts over the web.

If the web is to become more interactive so that people can actively communicate as well as passively consume and more personal so that it serves the needs of readers as well as the agendas of publishers, then a new generation of web servers is needed. The model of hypertext underlying the web has to be extended and users have to be shielded from any consequent increase in complexity.

The following sections will first describe a set of three mechanisms to support the personalization of universalized information spaces: *dynamic hypertext, personal perspectives* and *structural navigation*. These mechanisms work together to make the web more interactive, adaptable and personal. Then applications of personalizable hypertext will be illustrated in a series of five prototypes we have designed. These systems include knowledge-based software environments for designers, teachers, students, workers and network managers. They show how the three basic mechanisms can be used to support a variety of human-computer interactions to recontextualize information stored in digital repositories.

Mechanism 1: Dynamic Webs

Comparisons of the web with other models of hypertext show several limitations of embedding links in static pages of text with HTML tags [2]:

- Readers cannot add annotations easily because they cannot modify the text in which they would have to add their comments or embed links to their pages.

- The links only point out from the text, so there is no way to avoid dangling references when target pages change.

- Contents cannot be restructured for different purposes because they are fixed pages – the linearity of large texts has only been broken down to the page level.

Web pages should be dynamic. Web browsers should adapt displays to users. This is accomplished by storing the content and its links in a database on the web server. When a browser requests a page, the web server assembles the page in real-time and sends that instead of sending the contents of a fixed file. The contents can be stored at a finer granularity (sentence or paragraph, rather than page), allowing selectivity in choice of content and linking, depending on the nature of the request to the server. This solves the problems that plague fixed web pages:

- Readers can annotate existing pages by adding supplementary contents or links to the database, to be included when the page is recreated by the server. (This process can be hidden behind natural seeming interactions and restricted under program control.)

- Since the database stores references to both ends of links, the server can check that references are valid and that their inclusion is relevant and authorized for a given request. (The server can also check for links to a page before deleting that page to prevent problems in advance.)

- Most importantly (from this paper's perspective), the server can assemble and display contents based on who wants to see what how.

Mechanism 2: Personal Perspectives on Universal Information

Perspectives are a way of determining what is displayed for whom. The mechanism we have explored for personal perspectives builds on the dynamic assembly of pages. Atoms of content (e.g., brief paragraphs or multimedia items) are assigned to primitive perspectives (such as `intermediate level electrical issues for residential house construction`) and this designation is stored in the links to those content nodes. Then a hierarchy of useful perspectives is built up by grouping primitive perspectives into higher-order perspectives. This is all done as part of the effort of seeding an information space with hypertext content organized into perspectives.

Individual information seekers can, in turn, define one or more personal perspectives reflecting their own interests. For instance, an architect might construct several distinct perspectives in order to view designs alternatively by `intermediate structural concerns, advanced aesthetic issues`, etc. Or a company can define perspectives for its employees, allowing each to view corporate documents that are appropriate to their status and roles in the organization, combining the perspectives of a work group in the perspective of the group's manager. Authorization of read, annotate and modify permissions can be defined through perspectives, facilitating a fine-grained security system without cumbersome passwords.

As people annotate and edit contents, the information space evolves in a controlled way. The perspectives mechanism incorporates the advantages of contexts [7], virtual copying [8] or transclusion [9]:

- Changes to contents only show up in the perspectives in which they were made or in perspectives that inherit from them; original contents are always available. Perspectives can therefore serve as a versioning and archiving system.

- The mechanism conserves memory space because only the brief elements actually modified have to be duplicated for different versions, not whole pages.

- If charges are levied on copywritten materials, the necessary information for this can be associated with elemental contents and preserved even in highly annotated or edited multi-source documents.

- The user's choice of perspective controls the adaptation of all information to the user. When a dynamic web page is assembled, only the versions of contents associated with the active perspective are displayed.

Mechanism 3: Navigating the Network

It is possible to create a nuanced information space in which detailed contents are inter-linked using a rich semantics. A structure-based query language provides power and generality in navigating this space to generate an unlimited variety of web presentations. For instance, in a design rationale repository one could display on a page all the issues added in the past year that have three or more answers with no justifications stated.

In our earlier systems we tried to incorporate common syntactic structures from English into our navigation language to make it readable [12]. It was like a combination of `Sql` and `HyperCard's HyperTalk`. The sample query of the previous paragraph looks like this in the language: `issues that have creation date after 1/1/96 and have more than 2 answers that have no justifications`. In our future systems we want to embed the language in a visual programming interface to allow users to construct and test queries using direct manipulation from graphical representations of syntax and content options.

A navigation language can be used internally to the web server software to assemble pages. It can also be used within the information space, e.g., to define virtual links that point to contents selected dynamically. The language can be arbitrarily powerful. The language we designed includes commands to create and manipulate lists of contents, to traverse combinations of associative links, to filter out various contents, to quantify and to perform arithmetic or logical computations.

While users of systems for professionals might want access to the full power of the navigation language to explore information spaces and to format reports, users of other applications might be thankful to have the language formulations hidden from them. In some of our systems, for instance, we have encapsulated useful standard queries behind buttons in the user interface or in special structured displays.

Prototype Systems

We have designed five applications that illustrate different approaches to and uses of personalizable information systems. The applications target different user communities as shown in Table1.

1. The three mechanisms described above were first developed for the **Hermes** system [10]. **Hermes** is a substrate for building domain-oriented design environments like **Janus** [5] and **Phidias** [7], desktop applications for designers to do their work with knowledge-based computational support. A design environment for lunar habitat designers at NASA was built on top of **Hermes**. It is still being developed to maintain design rationale at NASA.

2. The Teacher's Curriculum Assistant (**TCA**) was designed as a web browser for digital libraries of educational resources and curriculum [13]. **TCA**'s interface was prototyped to demonstrate how fine-grained hypertext stored in an indexed database could be assembled into curriculum tailored to the needs of classrooms [14].

		target users	system approach	focus for paper
1	**HERMES**	NASA designers	DODE substrate	assemble text
2	**TCA**	school teachers	digital library	curriculum planner
3	**PLM**	physics learners	personal medium	custom display
4	**CIE**	work groups	collabora-tion	merge versions
5	**WEBNET**	LAN managers	evolving info space	informatio n medium

Table 1. Five applications of personalized information delivery.

3. A Personalized Learner's Medium (**PLM**) was proposed for texts on high energy particle physics. The three mechanisms were combined with additional structuring techniques behind the scenes to present technical reading materials consistently at different levels of difficulty for different students.

4. The Collaborative Information Environment (**CIE**) was prototyped to help workgroups develop and maintain documents for ISO 9000 certification. It uses the three mechanisms to organize versions for individuals and groups and to enforce read, annotate and write permissions.

5. **WebNet** is our current effort to provide rich information sources on the web for LAN managers. It is starting to explore ways to use the three mechanisms and other techniques to support fluid evolution of information by communities of practice that need up-to-date information.

The following sections will review these five prototypes to illustrate how the mechanisms discussed in this paper can help to personalize the delivery of decontextualized information.

1. Hermes: Tailoring to the Task

The theory behind **Hermes** is based on hermeneutic philosophy, design methodology and observation of NASA lunar habitat designers [11]. It notes that professionals engaged in design tasks are continually interpreting their work while tacitly *situated* with the design artifact (e.g., a CAD drawing), viewing their problem from some particular personal *perspective* and articulating their interpretation in explicit *language*. The core technology was intended to support design by:

- providing a dynamic version of hypertext for representing the design *situation*,

- structuring the knowledge base into personal *perspectives* and

- providing a computational *language* for manipulating the represented artifacts, domain knowledge and design rationale.

Design rationale is accessible in **Hermes** as context-sensitive hypertext, but in a different sense from the usual help systems. That is, design knowledge is adapted to the current design task undertaken in the application's workspace. Typically, a designer is alerted to the need to review design rationale by an automated critic rule being triggered by the state of the design as it is developed in the CAD (Computer-Aided Design) component of the **Hermes** design environment. The CAD graphics is itself constructed from hypertext nodes and links so that the navigation language interpreter can analyze it. Critic agents defined in the language check the designs and provide feedback linked to domain knowledge and rationale. Information for delivery to the working designer is assembled from fine-grained textual elements linked together in accordance with the argumentation structure (e.g., design issues are linked to their alternative answers and subissues) [4].

The designer can navigate through the rationale using an interface that in effect builds queries whose results are assembled, formatted and displayed. There is always a personal perspective that is active; it determines what contents are filtered out and which are displayed. In **Hermes**, perspectives are used to differentiate different professional domains (life support; privacy concerns; noise and vibration; micro-gravity; electrical; etc.).

Note that the design rationale presented in the center of Figure 1 is displayed in a custom outline format, indenting alternative answers and their rationale under the issues. The dynamic approach to all displays of content from the hypertext database allows different materials to be arranged differently. The dialog to the left allows the designer to navigate links that have selected semantic simplicity using the language without having to program it explicitly. These are two examples of how the mechanisms (dynamic hypertext, structural navigation) can be hidden behind displays or controls that are natural and appropriate to a domain (e.g., design rationale).

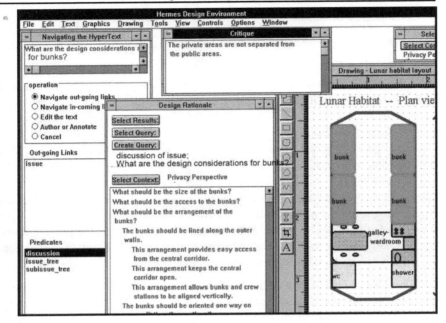

Figure 1. **Hermes**. From left to right the windows illustrate navigating the hypertext by choosing from a list of link types; a presentation of design rationale dynamically constructed from related texts by a query; an automated critique of the current design; the CAD workspace; a button for selecting a new perspective.

2. TCA: Customizing for the Classroom

The Teacher's Curriculum Assistant (TCA) was designed as a web browser for teachers to access digital libraries of constructivist curriculum. When teachers try to use browsers like Netscape Navigator to take advantage of the educational ideas that are beginning to be posted to the web, they meet with the following problems:

- There are no effective methods for locating relevant curriculum sites.

- It is too hard to search for items of interest.

- These is no choice of versions to select for different situations.

- There are no tools for adapting what is found to local needs.

- There is no support for organizing scattered ideas into workable curriculum.

- There are no ways for teachers to share their experiences.

These problems can be overcome with centralized repositories of carefully structured curriculum and indexed resources. The repositories should support two-way communication, so that teachers can share their experiences using materials in the repositories and can "grow" the repositories.

TCA's Profiler, Explorer and Versions components work together for information retrieval. The Profiler helps teachers define perspectives for a particular classroom and locates curriculum and resources that match the perspective. The Explorer displays these items and allows the teacher to search through them to find related items. The Explorer uses an interface similar to the Mac Finder or Win95 Explorer to navigate across links between a curriculum, its weekly units, their lesson plans and their individual resources. Versions then helps the teacher select from alternative versions that have been adapted by other teachers. Through these interfaces, teachers can locate the available materials that most closely match their personal needs; this makes it easier to customize the materials to classroom requirements.

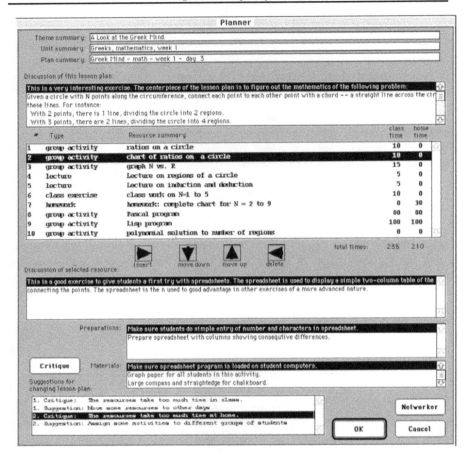

Figure 2. The TCA interface for the Planner.

TCA's Planner, Editor and Networker components help the teacher to prepare resources and curriculum for use and to share the results of classroom successes. The Planner (Figure 2) is a design environment for reusing and reorganizing lesson plans. Note that the Planner interface displays a variety of linked information in a useful format for teachers to study and manipulate. All the educational resources linked to a lesson plan are listed together where they can be rearranged or selectively deleted; their recommended classroom and homework times are added up as a guide; lists of required materials, prerequisites and preparation steps are compiled. In addition, a critiquing component displays suggestions and warnings within the plan. Here, relevant inter-related information is gathered together in a display that can print out the teacher's familiar lesson plan.

The Editor allows the teacher to modify and adapt individual resources (texts, spreadsheets, drawings, quizzes, collections of web pointers). This is a primary means for personalizing the curriculum. Finally, the Networker supports interactions with the Internet, providing a two-way medium of communication with a global community of teachers. Using the Networker, a teacher can share successfully customized versions of standard curriculum with other teachers who might have similar needs.

3. PLM: Readying for Readers

The **Personalized Learner's Medium** (PLM) illustrates how several mechanisms can be used synergistically to transform generalized information in an educational digital library on the Web into personalized information in a student's browser. The **PLM** technical approach integrates customization ideas, mechanisms and industry standards from **TCA, Hermes** and HTML. This approach can be applied to classroom applications or to learning-on-demand features in software for professionals, where information relevant to the current task is tailored to the person and to the task.

PLM was originally proposed for people learning high energy particle physics. This is a field where students have to go over the same material several times, at different levels of mathematical sophistication. There is little continuity in the available textbooks. To start, there are a number of popular books with no mathematics. Then there are some requiring substantial background in mathematical physics. Next, come highly technical texts and then the very specialized notation of the journals. The problem is that students come with different backgrounds and the texts use an assortment of seemingly incompatible formalisms.

The idea behind **PLM** is to provide one consistent and comprehensive hypertext source with paths through it at different levels. By specifying a perspective, a reader determines the level of material to be presented, including the amount of historical background, of mathematical elaboration or of experimental description. The hypertext format allows a reader to explore related material to supplement the perspectival path, e.g., to get a refresher on some forgotten mathematical formalism.

Personalization in **PLM** takes place in eight sequential stages within the process of selecting materials from the digital library, analyzing them into hypertext nodes and links and synthesizing selected contents into a personalized display. The stages typically take place automatically, but the user can intervene when desired.

Stage 1. Searching for relevant materials

The learner defines a Profile of the materials sought in an educational digital library. This profile includes characteristics of the learner as well. The profile is used by PLM to formulate a query that retrieves a selection of materials from the library. The profile functions as a user model for the software, but one that is under the control of the user.

Stage 2. Browsing among related resources

Descriptions of selected materials are displayed in an Explorer window. The learner uses this interface to browse among related library resources, such as textual selections, software tools, historical background, useful mathematical techniques, relevant video clips. By providing for browsing within the confines of the Profile search, PLM gives the learner freedom to explore without the danger of becoming lost.

Stage 3. Selecting the best fit version

The digital library may include multiple versions of a given resource. For instance, a physics problem might be approached using a graphical simulation, equations or computer programming. The learner can select the most appealing approach.

Stage 4. Parsing into nodes and links

Documents are broken down into their elements (as hypertext nodes), connected by typed hypertext links. The link types are based on the element's HTML markup type (e.g., `title`). This is done automatically by PLM. Custom node and link types may be defined by learners—or by their teachers.

Stage 5. Viewing from a perspective

The learner's profile defines a perspective. The currently active perspective selects which nodes and links can be viewed. This allows multiple, redundant forms of information to be present in resources in the library, of which all but one form will be filtered out. For instance, many people may have annotated a particular resource, but a learner may want to filter out all annotations except her own, her teacher's and her classmates'. Then she would define her own perspective and have it incorporate her teacher's and her class' in order to view what they view in their perspectives.

Stage 6. Querying with the language

All PLM displays are created dynamically by queries in the hypermedia navigation language. Statements in the language in effect specify starting nodes, types of links to traverse and characteristics of nodes to filter out. Execution of a statement takes place within a selected perspective and results in a collection of linked nodes. This collection is the material selected for display. The language can be extended by end-users and terms in the language can have different meanings in different perspectives. Readers, their classmates and their teachers can build up special queries to display materials of interest.

Stage 7. Synthesizing a display

PLM constructs a document from the collection of nodes and links. The document is marked up using a version of HTML. At this stage, the information retrieved from the library has been personalized.

Stage 8. Formatting the presentation

The final stage is to display the information. The display format can be personalized by adjusting the mark-up definitions. For instance, the hierarchical information can be indented by level. Alternatively, different levels could be italicized or text size and color adjusted to individual preferences.

Through these eight stages, standardized materials are selected and displayed in a way that can be tuned extensively by individual learners to their needs. A thoughtfully prepared document in the global library can be personalized differently by each learner in the world.

Ironically, the key to *individuating* the presentations of the materials is to exploit the *standardized* HTML structuring of documents to break them into semantically meaningful fine-grained hypertext that can then be re-assembled by software to adapt to personal preferences.

4. CIE: Coordinating Collaboration

The Collaborative Information Environment (CIE) is a tool for workgroups to collaboratively formulate policy and procedure documents in accordance with the Total Quality Management organizational style and ISO 9000 documentation standards. This groupware tool facilitates the development, review, critiquing, annotation, editing, versioning and auditing of shared documents. It supports efficient group communication about documents and sophisticated version control of them.

Each group member using CIE has a personal notebook that allows document versions to be viewed, annotated and edited in ways appropriate to the person's position in the organizational workflow. The notebook typically opens to the person's calendar. The Calendar lists documents with deadlines coming up soon. The user can then go to an Overview of the company's documents to begin reviewing one to work on. The Overview may display a variety of information about documents, such as how many comments or versions currently exist of each document, so that a manager can determine immediately where concerns lie and which documents are in need of revision. The Calendar and Overview contents are, of course, computed dynamically from an underlying hypertext, based upon options selected by the user, the user's perspective, queries defined by the user or by the system and the current information state.

The development of documents primarily involves people editing existing drafts and commenting on each other's proposed changes. CIE provides interfaces for viewing different versions by one's co-workers and comments that have been made to them, as well as means for easily adding one's own ideas. A number of features are also available for manipulating one or more versions. For instance, the chair of a workgroup might merge multiple versions together to arrive at a consensus document for the group. A CIE editor automatically merges versions, redlining terms deleted in each version and color-coding additions suggested in different versions.

Alternatively, one person's version can be promoted to the group's perspective. In CIE, perspectives enforce company security concerns and allow people to create and share personal versions of company documents without affecting other people's views of those documents. Permissions for reading, annotating and actually editing policies and procedures can be associated with individual perspectives.

Because perspectives inherit changes to documents from their ancestors, people can effectively be assigned perspectives that mirror their role in the organization chart. Assume my perspective inherits from the organization's and from my workgroup's, while my supervisor's perspective also inherits mine. Then my view of a company policy reflects any changes adopted by the company or by my workgroup. Moreover, my supervisor can view changes I propose and compare them to those of others in our workgroup. In this way, everyone can try out different ways of wording documents and then recommend adopting certain specific changes. This facilitates the coordination of collaborative document maintenance, which can otherwise raise a serious barrier to ISO 9000 level documentation in an organization.

5. WebNet: Enabling Evolution

At the Center for LifeLong Learning and Design we are interested in knowledge-based systems to support working and learning in professional domains. In our current **WebNet** project, we focus on supporting the *evolution* of domain-specific knowledge using *web-based* information repositories.

The view of the web as an information medium is often traced back to Vannevar Bush's vision [3]. At the close of the last world war, Bush emphasized the need to develop technology to support effective access to the burgeoning "record" of scientific knowledge. The web has not yet fulfilled Bush's vision; meanwhile the stakes have risen. We believe that:

- The web must be an interactive medium rather than the repository of a static record, so that knowledge in different domains will be "grown" by communities of practice interacting through the web, gradually overcoming the spotty coverage of information currently on the web.

- Knowledge on the web must be adapted to the work situations and learning perspectives of individuals so that decontextualized, explicit information can be meaningfully integrated into people's largely tacit understandings.

- People using the web, whether for information retrieval, knowledge evolution or collaborative communication must be empowered to control, adapt and extend the computational mechanisms of the web to serve their personal needs.

We are exploring the use of dynamic hypertext, personal perspectives, structural navigation and other approaches to achieve our extended vision of an evolving knowledge medium. One domain of knowledge we are trying to support is our own research "record": papers, slides, dissertations, proposals, work plans, email, glossaries, bibliographies, etc. Another is that of LAN designers and managers. The latter domain involves supporting a virtual community of practice that relies on knowledge of rapidly changing technology. **WebNet** has to allow for evolution at many levels: growth of content, restructuring of content, multiplicities of versions, proliferation of retrieval queries, diversification of information displays, changes in the domain and emergent system needs.

Conclusions

The prototype systems described above have shown that the model of dynamic hypertext with personal perspectives and structural navigation can mediate effectively between universal representations of knowledge and personalized presentations of relevant information. This approach has the potential to make the web significantly more interactive, adaptive and personal.

Our work is increasingly taking place within the context of rapidly changing web technologies. Advanced web servers like Hyper-G [1] and HyperNews [6] as well as intranet frontends to databases provide important functionality that needs to be integrated with our own mechanisms.

We are currently pursuing user-centered design efforts to fashion computer-human interactions to shield author/readers from the complexities of our approach:

- Authoring of comprehensive information spaces will require careful structuring of content nodes and their links to make information applicable to a wide range of applications; publishers of such information will need tools to support this work.

- We would like to automate some of the defining and refining of personal perspectives so that it happens behind the scenes, although we also want people to be able to knowingly review, modify and switch their computational perspectives.

- Finally, we want to expose the structure-based query language as an end-user scripting language with visual programming supports for power users who want to exceed the functionality of pre-programmed queries.

Although we do not believe that basic tools for professionals to use in exploring web resources will need to be walk-up-and-use in the future, we want to avoid cognitive burdens that distract from the immediate tasks of communicating, working and learning.

As the sources of our information become increasingly mediated by computers it becomes correspondingly important that people be able to maintain control over that manipulation when they want to. Web browsers that make the web empowering for personal expression and authentic knowledge construction can prevent the reduction of the web to a world wide digital mall of mass-produced information commodities.

Acknowledgments

The ideas and systems reported on came from collaborations with Ray McCall, Gerhard Fischer, Bob Owen, Doug Swartz, Tammy Sumner and Jonathan Ostwald. Hermes, the author's dissertation system, grew out of research on the Phidias system at CU's College of Environmental Design with support from CASI.

TCA was developed at Owen Research with support from NSF. PLM and CIE were designed at Personalizable Software, a consulting firm founded by the author. WebNet is a project of CU's Center for LifeLong Learning and Design under support from ARPA. Hermes ver 2 is © 1994 by Gerry Stahl; CIE is © 1996 by Personalizable Software.

References

Andrews, K., Kappe, F., Mauer, H. Hyper-G and Harmony: Towards the next generation of networked information technology. *Proc CHI '95 Companion*, 33-34.

Bieber, M., Vitali, F., Ashman, H., Balasubramanian, V., Oinas-Kukkonen, H. Fourth generation hypermedia: Some missing links for the World Wide Web. Submitted to *International Journal of Human-Computer Studies*. Special issue on HCI & the Web.

Bush, V. As we may think. *Atlantic Monthly*, *179*, 1 (1945), 101-108. Reprinted in *Interactions*, III, 2 (1996), 35-46. Available as <http:// www2.theAtlantic.com/ atlantic/ atlweb/ flashbks/ computer/tech.htm>

Fischer, G., Nakakoji, K., Ostwald, J., Stahl, G., Sumner, T. Embedding computer-based critics in the contexts of design. *Proc InterCHI '93*, 157-164.

Fischer, G., Nakakoji, K., Ostwald, J., Stahl, G., Sumner, T. Embedding critics in design environments. *The Knowledge Engineering Review*, 4, 8 (1993), 285-307.

LaLiberte, D. About HyperNews. Available as <http:// union.ncsa.uicu.edu/ HyperNews/ get/ hypernews/ about.html>

McCall, R., Bennett, P., d'Oronzio, P., Ostwald, J., Shipman, F., Wallace, N. Phidias: Integrating CAD graphics into dynamic hypertext. *Proc ECHT '90*, 152-165.

Mittal, S., Boborow, D., Kahn, K. Virtual copies: At the boundary between classes and instances. *Proc OOPSLA '86*, 159-166.

Nelson, T. H. The heart of connection: Hypermedia unified by transclusion. Available at <http:// www.cs.uct.ac.za/ Local/ CS300W/ HCI/ nelson.htm>.

Stahl, G. Supporting situated interpretation. *Proc Cognitive Science Society '93*, 965-970.

Stahl, G. *Interpretation in Design: The Problem of Tacit and Explicit Understanding in Computer Support of Cooperative Design*. Ph.D. dissertation (1993). Department of Computer Science. University of Colorado at Boulder.

Stahl, G., McCall, R., Peper, G. Extending hypermedia with an inference language: An alternative to rule-based expert systems. *Proc IBM ITL Conference: Expert Systems* (1992), 160-167.

Stahl, G., Sumner, T., Owen, R. Share globally, adapt locally: Software to create and distribute student-centered curriculum. *Computers and Education, 24,* 3 (1995), 237-246.

Stahl, G., Sumner, T., Repenning, A. Internet repositories for collaborative learning: Supporting both students and teachers. *Proc Computer Support for Collaborative Learning '95*, 321-328.

6.   Supporting Personalization and Reseeding-on-demand

Theory

To learn is to construct personal knowledge within a social context. As our social information space explodes globally, its computerized media must support personalization and restructuring on demand to help us make sense of its decontextualized content in our own terms.

Initial attempts to use the Internet to disseminate informational artifacts already demonstrate the need to develop computational supports for people to locate, use, adapt and share items of interest to them. Results of searches and browses that people undertake should coalesce into flexibly structured personal information space. When people adapt items from the universal space to their personal tasks and styles, they should be able to share their custom versions with communities of commonality.

System #1: Web-based Design Environment for LAN Maintenance (WebNet)

The central project of the L³D U&U group is **WebNet**, an effort to build a Web-based design environment. The idea is to allow LAN designers to communicate across the Internet by sharing designs, rationale, simulation artifacts, etc. The system will be optimized to support a rapidly changing technological context. Although the domain incorporates global standards, much of the shared knowledge will be contextualized by concrete designs.

Each community of designers (e.g., network managers at CU) will be encouraged to personalize their **WebNet** info space by tying in their own email repositories, importing CAD drawings of their buildings, capturing their current network topologies and defining their own terminologies in the end-user programming language. People can share their personal contributions by linking in Web pages with rationale of their reasons for their designs, their definitions of simulation behaviors in the language and their own sample designs. Other communities can construct versions of **WebNet** by selecting subsets of agents, rationale and language phrases that are relevant to their needs.

System #2: Teacher's Curriculum Assistant (TCA)

The L³D group has developed simulation environments for use in the classroom and begun to distribute them across the Internet. In particular, WebQuest is an environment in which kids make quest games that incorporate researching facts on the Web. Students play their classmate's games and critique their designs. Eventually, kids will share their creations with other schools across the Web. They will share characters and behavior-defining subroutines in the end-user programming language as well as entire quests. As the mass of sharable quests, agents and behaviors accumulates, computer supports for locating, selecting and using the most desirable ones will become critical.

Quests will need to be associated with curriculum and related classroom resources to be pedagogically useful to teachers. Some form of indexing will be necessary to help teachers or students find the quest that most closely matches their needs and capabilities. For instance, some quests might take advantage of special peripheral equipment or build on special background knowledge; one does not want to download multiple quests just to find out they are not useful. Most importantly, as kids modify quests that they find on the Web and then upload their versions, it will be necessary to differentiate the versions and allow potential users to select the version best for them. I prototyped a **Teacher's Curriculum Assistant** to explore mechanisms for supporting the locating, using, adapting and sharing of classroom resources in digital libraries.

System #3: Collaborative Info Environment (CIE)

We have been hampered in our attempts to build design rationale systems by the difficulty of getting people to make their reasoning explicit and to enter it in a computer. **GIMMe** captures email to avoid this problem, but ends up with an unsystematic body of documents with uneven coverage of the issues. The institutionalization of documentation standards like ISO 9000 -- especially when combined with a decentralized decision-making structure like Total Quality Management -- requires employees to formulate comprehensive statements of policies and procedures. It is still hard to get people and work groups to articulate their working knowledge and enter it into a corporate memory. However, computer supports can elicit explicit statements of tacit knowledge, can manage the group editing process and can deliver the shared information in personally relevant formats.

The **CIE** demo system I developed recently explores some mechanisms for supporting the construction and use of evolving organizational memories. The system is seeded with knowledge about the ISO 9000 requirements, including templates for typical documents. Two central processes for the asynchronous development of policy documents by committee are supported: commenting on shared drafts and editing new versions. There are mechanisms for viewing comments and versions created at different levels of the organization and for merging multiple versions or promoting selected personal versions to group consensual documents. This is a way of reseeding the memory as it grows. Computational indicators warn when versions of a particular document are proliferating and consolidation is warranted.

Corporations are complexly structured organizations and documents of their policies and procedures are sensitive assets. Individual employees are not interested in all of an organization's documents, but just in those that affect their own work -- and management does not want everyone editing every document. In CIE, security concerns merge with personalization features. A perspectives mechanism governs access to the organizational memory for each employee, manager and auditor based upon their position in the corporate work-flow. Employees have read, comment and edit permissions relative to their quality work circle, department, branch, peers or roles. Perspectives allow people and groups at different levels to experiment with and share tentative versions without interfering with the official drafts.

Mechanisms

The World Wide Web opens countless possibilities for global sharing of information to create and sustain knowledge-based communities. However, to be useful knowledge bases on the Web require sophisticated computational supports. As on-line memories grow and evolve, they need to be pruned and restructured to meet the needs of individuals with specific tasks and concerns. This cannot be done just at the global level -- although reseeding at this level is necessary as well (like Netscape frequently releasing new versions of its browser with new functionality). Everyone has their own interests and must be able to maintain their own personal information space as views onto rapidly evolving universal spaces.

The Web model of hypertext -- with simple links connecting static pages -- is too undifferentiated to support this. In my systems, I try to apply a model of computational hypertext to the Web. My Hermes substrate is based on:

- fine-granularity of text so that documents can be constructed dynamically,

- typing of links and nodes so that links and nodes can be displayed based on selective queries,

- hierarchies of perspectives so that displays are personalized to include appropriate domains of content,

- end-user extensibility of link/node types, the perspective hierarchy and the end-user language to support evolution.

These mechanisms allow for the generation of pages whose contents and links are dynamically personalized. Systems with such mechanisms let people construct their own knowledge by structuring personal information spaces that provide useful and usable access to virtually limitless, constantly evolving organizational and global repositories.

Part III: Software Perspectives

7.   Embedding Computer-Based Critics in the Contexts of Design

Gerhard Fischer, Kumiyo Nakakoji, Jonathan Ostwald, Gerry Stahl, Tamara Sumner

Computational critiquing mechanisms provide an effective form of computer-human interaction supporting the process of design. Critics embedded in domain-oriented design environments can take advantage of additional knowledge residing in these environments to provide less intrusive, more relevant critiques. Three classes of embedded critics have been designed, implemented and studied: *Generic critics* use domain knowledge to detect problematic situations in the design construction. *Specific critics* take advantage of additional knowledge in the partial specification to detect inconsistencies between the design construction and the design specification. *Interpretive critics* are tied to perspective mechanisms that support designers in examining their artifact from different viewpoints.

We view design as a process of successive refinement through trial, breakdown, interpretation and reflection [15, 16, 18, 21]. Critiquing - the communication of a reasoned opinion about an artifact or a design - plays a central role in the design process. Computational critic mechanisms provide an effective form of computer-human interaction supporting this important aspect of design. We have developed a series of design environments containing critiquing mechanisms to investigate how such environments can provide timely and relevant knowledge to designers.

Our research group's early work focused on building and evaluating stand-alone critiquing mechanisms. Critical analyses of these and other systems [7, 17], combined with empirical evaluations, led us to realize that the challenge in building critiquing systems is not simply to provide design feedback: the challenge is to say the "right" thing at the "right" time. We claim that embedding critics in domain-oriented design environments has provided an effective response to this challenge. Design environments are computer programs that support designers in concurrently specifying a problem, constructing a solution and interpreting an emerging design from alternative perspectives. Embedded critics can provide more focused, less intrusive critiques by taking advantage of knowledge of the contexts of design: the domain, the construction situation, the partial specification and interpretive perspectives.

While we have investigated critiquing in numerous domains such as computer network design [5] and lunar habitat design [19], the examples for this article will be based on floor plan design for kitchens [6]. This paper first describes the evaluations and theoretical motivations that led to the redesign and extensions of our critiquing mechanisms; we analyze early systems and empirical results that exposed the deficiencies of stand-alone critiquing mechanisms. Next, we present our redesign, three classes of embedded critics: generic, specific and interpretive critics. We conclude with a discussion of the benefits of this new approach.

ANALYSIS OF EARLY CRITIQUING SYSTEMS

Our analyses identified several shortcomings in early critiquing systems that hindered their ability to say the "right" thing at the "right" time:

- lack of domain orientation;

- insufficient facility for justifying critic suggestions;

- lack of an explicit representation of the user's goals;

- no support for different individual perspectives;

- timing problems with critic intervention strategies.

Saying the "right" thing...

LISP-CRITIC [3, 8, 12] allows programmers to request suggestions on how to improve their code. The system proposes transformations that make the code more cognitively efficient (i.e., easier to read and maintain) or more machine efficient (i.e., faster or smaller). However, lack of domain orientation limits the depth of critical analysis the critiquing system can provide. Without domain knowledge, critic rules cannot be tied to higher level concepts; LISP-CRITIC can answer questions such as whether the Lisp code can be written more efficiently, but it cannot assist users in deciding whether the code can solve their problem.

FRAMER [13] enables designers to develop window-based user interfaces on Symbolics Lisp machines. FRAMER's knowledge base contains design rules for evaluating the completeness and syntactic correctness of the design as well as its consistency with interface style guidelines. Evaluations of FRAMER showed that many users did not understand the consequences of following the critic's advice or why the advice was beneficial to solving their problem. We have observed that when users do not understand why a suggestion is made, they tend to follow the critic's advice whether or not it is appropriate to their situation. FRAMER [12] provided short explanations to address this problem. However, in design there are not always simple answers; access to argumentative discussions are necessary [15].

JANUS [6, 7] is a step towards addressing the previous shortcomings. JANUS allows designers to construct kitchen architectural floor plans. It contains two integrated subsystems: a domain-oriented kitchen construction kit and an issue-based hypermedia system containing design rationale. Critics respond to problems in the construction situation by displaying a message and providing access to appropriate issues. However, these critics often give spurious or irrelevant advice resulting from the lack of an explicit representation of the user's task. The only task goal built into JANUS is one of building a good kitchen. With an explicit model of the designer's intentions for a *particular* design, critics can be selectively enabled and provide less intrusive and more relevant advice.

It is not possible to anticipate all the knowledge necessary for a critiquing system to say the "right" thing in every design situation. Design domains are continually evolving as new knowledge is gained. JANUS-MODIFIER [10] was developed to respond to this problem by making the domain knowledge (including critics) end-user modifiable. But, being able to add new knowledge is not sufficient; different users must be able to organize and manage design knowledge and critics to reflect *their* perspectives on design. Design environments need to support interpreting a problem from many perspectives (technical, structural, functional, aesthetic, personal) and critiquing accordingly.

. . . at the "right" time

A number of systems [1, 8] investigated critic intervention strategies, i.e., strategies determining when and how a critic should signal a potential problem. This research focused on studying *active* versus *passive* intervention strategies. Active critics continually monitor user actions and make suggestions as soon as a problematic situation is detected. Passive critics are explicitly invoked by users to evaluate their partial design.

A protocol analysis study [12, 13] showed that passive critics were often not activated early enough in the design process to prevent designers from pursuing solutions known to be suboptimal. Often, subjects invoked the passive critiquing system only after they thought they had completed the design. By this time, the effort of repairing the situation was prohibitively expensive. In a subsequent study using the same design environment, an active critiquing strategy was shown to be more effective by detecting problematic situations early in the design process.

However, experience with our early critiquing systems showed that active critics are not a perfect solution either: they can disrupt the designer's concentration on the task at the wrong time and interfere with creative processes. Interruption becomes even more intrusive if the critics signal breakdowns at a different level of abstraction compared to the level of the task users are currently engaged in.

What is needed is a strategy that: (1) alerts designers to problematic solutions, (2) avoids unnecessary disruptions and (3) allows users to control the critic's intervention strategy. Embedding critics in design environments allows users to *control* critic intervention through interaction with the construction, specification and interpretation design contexts.

THEORETICAL MOTIVATION

Our evaluations of computer-based critiquing mechanisms show that while critics provide useful support for people engaged in design tasks, a number of problems arise if the critics are not adequately attuned to the task at hand. Design methodologists and proponents of situated cognition have argued that human critical reflection during designing is *situated* in various ways, suggesting that computational critics should be made similarly *context* dependent.

Suchman [20] argues that when pursuing a task people do not necessarily follow an explicit step-by-step plan they have mentally worked out ahead of time. Rather, they respond to their changing environment based on tacit skills. Schoen [16] describes design as a process of reflection-in-action where each design move creates a new situation, which may challenge the assumptions and strategies under which the designer is operating. These situations signal the designer of a need to reflect upon the design context and possibly to formulate new strategies.

Another approach is suggested by Rittel [15], who sees design as a process of argumentation. A domain like kitchen design consists of a variety of issues to be resolved in completing a task. Within the context of a specific design project, arguments for various answers to these issues can be debated from many perspectives. Solutions are not dependent only upon the unique task, but also upon the background, interests and commitments of the various stakeholders: i.e., the designers, their clients and the eventual users. More generally, Winograd and Flores [21] stress the role of interpretation in design. Designers interpret the task, the consequences of possible design decisions and competing design rationale from their shared or individual perspectives.

These theorists reject waterfall models of design according to which designers first derive an exhaustive specification of a task and then proceed to methodically implement the specification. Rather, design is viewed as an integrated process of problem framing (task specification), problem solving (design construction) and problem interpretation (interpretive perspectives).

These theoretical considerations suggest that critical reflection is most effective when seen as embedded in a number of inter-dependent contexts. Critiquing mechanisms need to be embedded in design environments in order to support critical reflection in design. Design environments represent a variety of design contexts. First, there is the context of knowledge of the *domain* itself. We represent this as an issue-base capturing the accepted wisdom of the field, a catalog of illustrative past designs and a palette of domain-oriented components. Unlike the rule-base of an expert system, the issue-base is neither complete nor consistent, but can evolve gradually, supporting design as an argumentative process by incorporating alternative and opposed viewpoints. Second, we represent the current state of *construction* in a graphical display. Third, the evolving partial *specification* is included to guide evaluation of the adequacy of design. Finally, support is provided for the definition of group and personal versions of domain knowledge that can represent critical *interpretations* [18]. By embedding critics in the contexts of the domain, construction, specification and interpretation, we overcome the problems of stand-alone critic systems.

EMBEDDING CRITICS IN DESIGN ENVIRONMENTS

In response to our evaluation of early critiquing mechanisms and to the theoretical arguments for contextualization, we have explored three types of mechanisms for embedding critics in computational design environments: *generic, specific and interpretive* critics. These mechanisms will be described below in a scenario involving **HYDRA** [4], a design environment that illustrates our multifaceted architecture.

Integrated Design Environments

Reflection on the shortcomings of JANUS [6] led us to extend it by incorporating representations of additional aspects of the design context. Like its predecessor JANUS, HYDRA contains both a construction and an argumentation component. HYDRA also supports a specification component [9] and a catalog of designs. The specification format is based on questionnaires used by professional kitchen designers to elicit their customers' requirements, such as the kitchen owner's cooking habits and family size. The catalog is a repository for past designs that are illustrative of the possible design space. Catalog entries support case-based reasoning and provide concrete design examples of issues discussed in the argumentation component. Perspective mechanisms allow the user to switch viewpoints corresponding to different interests or concerns [18]. These software components of the **HYDRA** system provide design creation tools and information repositories that reflect the real-world contexts of the design process.

Embedding critiquing systems in integrated design environments has several benefits. First, they have an increased level of critical analysis because critiquing mechanisms have been tied to the partial construction and the domain knowledge. The argumentation base and catalog of designs provide rich sources of domain knowledge that the critiquing mechanism can use in its explanation process. Second, the specification component provides an explicit representation of the designer's intentions for a specific design. The critiquing mechanism can take advantage of this information to enable sets of critics to evaluate the current design construction selectively for adherence to the designer's stated goals. Third, critiquing can be done from specific viewpoints, such as construction costs, resale value, plumbing concerns or work flow. Personal and group perspectives can also be developed to provide critiquing from different cultural, socio-economic or idiosyncratic viewpoints.

Scenario Illustrating Generic, Specific and Interpretive Critics

Bob has been asked to design a kitchen for the Smith family. Working with the Smiths, Bob enters the partial specification shown in Figure 1.

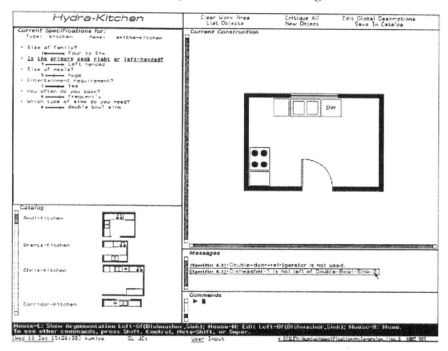

Figure 1. This figure shows a screen image of HYDRA. The "Current Specification" window shows a summary of currently selected answers using the specification component. An indicator attached to each of the selected answers allows users to assign weights of importance to the specified item in order to set priorities [9]. The "Catalog" window shows previous kitchen designs that can be examined or reused. The "Current Construction" window shows a partial construction being built using components

provided in a palette of kitchen design units (not shown). The "Messages" window is used to present critic notification messages. The number attached to the critic message is a weighted measure indicating the relevance of the fired critic.

Bob begins working on a floor plan in the HYDRA construction. He moves the dishwasher next to the cabinet. Bob's action triggers a *generic critic and* the message, "The dishwasher is too far from the sink," is displayed. Generic critics reflect knowledge that applies to all designs, such as accepted standards, building codes and domain knowledge based on physical principles. Often, this generic knowledge can be found in textbooks, training curricula or by interviewing domain practitioners. Bob highlights the critic's message and elects to see its associated argumentation. The argumentation explains that plumbing guidelines require the dishwasher to be within one meter of the sink. Bob follows the critic's suggestion and moves the dishwasher next to the right side of the sink.

This action triggers a *specific critic* with the rule, "If you are left-handed, the dishwasher should be on the left side of the sink." Specific critics reflect design knowledge that is tied to situation-specific physical characteristics and domain-specific concepts that not every design will share. These critics are constructed dynamically from the partial specification to reflect current design goals. This particular critic rule was activated because Bob specified that the primary cook is left-handed (see Figure 1). Bob examines the supporting argumentation, "Having the dishwasher to the left of the sink creates an efficient work flow for a left-handed person." Bob decides this is an important concern and puts the dishwasher on the left side of the sink.

Then Bob remembers that the Smiths are remodeling mainly to increase their property value in anticipation of selling in two years. So Bob decides to examine his design from a resale-value perspective. When Bob switches to the Resale-value Perspective, an *interpretive critic* is triggered with the rule, "The dishwasher should be on the right side of the sink." Interpretive critics support design as a interpretive process by allowing designers to interpret the design situation from different perspectives according to their interests. In this perspective, the critic about the dishwasher and sink has been redefined and its associated rationale has been modified. Now the argumentation says, "Optimizing your kitchen for left-handed cooks can adversely affect the house's resale value since most kitchen users are right-handed." Bob decides that enhancing the Smiths' resale value is the more important consideration and moves the dishwasher. As long as he remains in the Resale-value Perspective, Bob will be informed by the critics whenever they detect a feature negatively affecting resale value; access to argumentation concerning designing for resale practices will be provided.

Three Embedded Critiquing Mechanisms

Embedded critics increase the usefulness of design environments by making information structures more relevant to the task at hand [9]. The basic critiquing process consists of the following phases: (1) the set of appropriate critic rules to be enabled is identified; (2) the design construction is then analyzed for compliance with the currently enabled set of critic rules; (3) when a lack of compliance is detected, the critic signals a possible problem and provides entry into the exact place in the argumentative hypermedia system where the appropriate explanation is located; and (4) concrete catalog examples that illustrate the explanation given in the form of argumentation can optionally be delivered [7].

Generic critics

All three critic mechanisms - generic, specific and interpretive - use a production system style of knowledge representation and follow the basic critiquing process described above. Critic rules consist of condition and action clauses plus links into the argumentation context. The *condition* clause checks whether a certain situation exists in the current design construction and is defined in terms of spatial relations between design units, such as near, far, next-to, etc. The *action* clause notifies the designer that a particular situation has been detected.

Each critic rule is linked to a particular issue in the argumentation base. The designer can view the critic's associated argumentation by selecting the initial notification message to display an entry-point into the hypermedia issue-base. Such argumentative explanations help designers determine why the design situation identified by the critic message may be significant or problematic. Designers can optionally explore the issue-base or select an issue and an associated answer in the argumentation and request to see a positive example or a counter-example from the catalog of designs.

The three mechanisms for embedded critics differ from one another in how they determine which set of critic rules should be enabled. Generic critics provide the default set of enabled critics by evaluating the construction situation based on an assumption that a designer wants to design a "good" kitchen. "Good" in this sense refers to a kitchen that meets commonly accepted practices of most kitchen designers.

Specific Critics

Specific critics evaluate the construction situation for compliance with the partial specification. Specification-linking rules are used to dynamically identify the set of specific critics to be enabled [9].

A specification-linking rule represents a dependency between an issue/answer pair in the specification and associated pro and con arguments in the argumentation-base. As shown in Figure 2, a specification-linking rule connects the argumentation issue "Where should the dishwasher be placed?" with the specification item "Is the primary cook right or left-handed?" The shared domain distinction "left-handedness" is used to establish a dependency between this particular specification item and the argumentation issue.

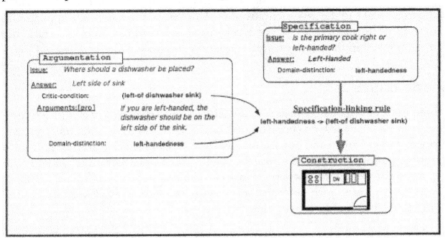

Figure 2. Illustration of a specification-linking rule that enables the "dishwasher should be on the left side of the sink" critic. The domain distinction associated with a specification item ("left-handedness") is paired with a matching pro or con argument in the argumentation (left-of dishwasher sink) to form a *specific critic rule*.

Each specification item has either an associated critic condition or an associated domain distinction. Domain distinctions are a vocabulary for expressing domain concepts, like left-handedness, safety and efficiency. Whenever the designer modifies the specification, the critiquing system recompiles the specification-linking rules to reflect the newly relevant domain distinctions. In this way, critiquing criteria are tied to a representation of the partially articulated goals of a specific design project.

Interpretive Critics

Interpretive critics [18, 19] provide support for design as a hermeneutic (interpretive) process. They allow designers to interpret the design situation according to their interests. Interpretive critics are associated with design *perspectives* rather than with partial specifications. Perspectives are a mechanism for creating, managing and selectively activating different sets of critics and design knowledge, such as spatial relations, domain distinctions, palette items and argumentation.

The perspectives mechanism organizes all the design knowledge in the system. It allows items of knowledge to be bundled into personal or topical groupings or versions. For instance, a Resale Perspective might include critics and design rationale pertinent to homeowners concerned about their home's resale appeal. Another perspective could be created for the Smith's kitchen; it might include considerations specific to the design of that kitchen.

The designer always works within a particular perspective. At any time, the designer can select a different perspective by name. New perspectives can also be created by assigning a name and selecting existing perspectives to be inherited. Bob, the designer working with the Smiths in the previous scenario, would create a Smith's Kitchen Perspective and select the Resale Perspective to be inherited by it.

Perspectives are connected in an inheritance network; a perspective can modify knowledge inherited from its parents or it can add new knowledge. Designers switch perspectives to examine a design from different viewpoints. Switching perspectives changes the currently effective definitions of critics, the terms used in these definitions and other domain knowledge Figure 3).

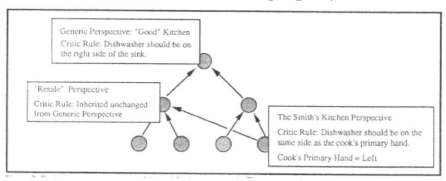

Figure 3. Design contexts are arranged in an inheritance network. Three perspectives - the generic, the resale and the Smith's - are shown. The preferred placement of the dishwasher depends on the perspective selected.

The organization of knowledge by perspectives encourages users to view the knowledge in terms of structured, meaningful categories that they can create and modify. It provides a structure of contexts that can correspond to categories meaningful in the design domain. This can ease the cognitive burden of manipulating large numbers of alternative versions of critics and other design knowledge.

DISCUSSION

Embedded critics represent another iteration cycle in our continuing research into computer-based design environments and critiquing systems. Embedded critics were designed and built in response to deficiencies uncovered in our early critiquing systems (LISP-CRITIC, FRAMER, JANUS), as well as insights gained from design theorists [2, 15, 16] and situated cognition researchers [11, 20, 21].

Recently, we have built design environments in a variety of domains including lunar habitat design [19], phone-based interface design [14], computer network design [5] and user interface design [12]. These design environments go beyond conventional CAD systems by modeling domain semantics in several design contexts and not just modeling geometric relationships. Though the knowledge bases of these research prototypes are not exhaustive, they exhibit a high degree of complexity with their many design units, catalog entries, critics and domain distinctions. Exploration of these environments has confirmed that simple browsing mechanisms are insufficient and that critiquing mechanisms capable of delivering the right information at the right time are desirable.

Design environments support designers in creating and modifying the problem framing throughout the design process, not just in the beginning. Problem framing in design environments is supported by the specification component, where designers articulate their goals and priorities for the design. The problem framing as represented in the partial specification does not serve as a rigid template for constructing a solution, but rather as a flexible framework in which to operate. Embedded critics support the integration of problem framing and problem solving [15] by making explicit relationships between the partial specification and the construction situation. Embedded critics evaluate the construction situation for compliance with the partial specifications, within a chosen perspective. When critics detect a conflict, the need to reflect-in-action [16] is signaled to the designer. Resolving the conflict might require a modification of (1) the specification by reframing the problem or (2) the construction by rearranging design units.

The three classes of critics we have explored correspond to three dimensions of embedding. Generic critics are embedded in the construction, because they are enabled by the placement of design units in the work area. Specific critics are embedded in the partial specification by being dynamically constructed from domain distinctions tied to specification items. Specific critics reduce the intrusiveness [13] of generic critics by narrowing the enabled critics to those that are relevant to the partially specified task at hand. Interpretive critics are embedded in the hierarchy of perspectives that supports the evolution of alternative viewpoints on designs. Using these critics, designers are able to consider their designs critically from multiple viewpoints.

Embedding critics in integrated design environments is an important step towards applying the critiquing paradigm to create more useful and usable knowledge-based computer systems. Embedded critics focus the attention of the system on the concerns of the designer in order to deliver the "right" thing at the "right" time. F uture research will focus on evaluating embedded critiquing systems in naturalistic settings, i.e., observing the systems in use by professional designers in their regular design activities.

ACKNOWLEDGMENTS

We thank the HCC group at the University of Colorado, who contributed to the conceptual framework and the systems discussed in this paper. The research was supported by: the National Science Foundation under grants No. IRI-9015441 and MDR-9253425; the Colorado Advanced Software Institute under grants in 1990/91, 1991/92, 1992/93; US West Advanced Technologies; NYNEX Science and Technology Center and by Software Research Associates, Inc. (Tokyo).

REFERENCES

1. R. Burton and J. S. Brown, "An Investigation of Computer Coaching for Informal Learning Activites," in *Intelligent Tutoring Systems*, D. Sleeman and S. Brown, Ed., London, Academic Press, 19g2, pp. 79-98.
2. P. Ehn, *Work-Oriented Design of Computer Artifacts*, arbetslivscentrum, Stockholm, 1989.
3. G. Fischer, "A Critic for LISP," *Proceedings of the 10th International Joint Conference on Artificial Intelligence*, Milan, Italy, 1987, pp.177-184.
4. G. Fischer, A. Girgensohn, K. Nakakoji and D. Redmiles, "Supporting Software Designers with Integrated, Domain-Oriented Design Environments,"*IEEE Transactions on Software Engineering, Special Issue on Knowledge Representation and Reasoning in Software Engineering*, Vol.18, pp.511-522, 1992.
5. G. Fischer, 3. Grudin, A. C. Lemke, R. McCall, 3. Ostwald, B. N. Reeves and F. Shipman, "Supporting Indirect, Collaborative Design with Integrated Knowledge-Based Design Environments," *HCI*. Vol. 7 (Special Issue on Computer Supported Cooperative Work), 1992.
6. G. Fischer, A. Lemke, T. Mastaglio and A. Morch, "Using Critics to Empower Users," *CHI '90*, Seattle, WA, 1990, pp.337-347.
7. G. Fischer, A. C. Lemke, T. Mastaglio and A. Morch, "The Role of Critiquing in Cooperative Problem Solving," *ACM Transactions on Information Systems*. Vol.9, pp.123-151, 1991.
8. G. Fischer, A. C. Lemke and T. Schwab, "Knowledge-Based Help Systems," *Human Factors in Computing Systems, CHI'8S Conference Proceedings (San Francisco. CA)*, pp.161-167, 1985.

9.   G. Fischer and K. Nakakoji, "Making Design Objects Relevant to the Task at Hand," *Proceedings of AAM Ninth National Conference on Artificial Intelligence,* pp.67-73, 1991.

10.   A. Girgensohn, "End-User Modifiability in Knowledge-Based Design Environments," Technical Report CU-CS-595-92, Department of Computer Science, University of Colorado at Boulder, 1992.

11.   J. Lave, *Cognition in Practice,* Cambridge University Press, Cambridge, UK, 1988.

12.   A. C. Lemke, "Design Environments for High-Functionality Computer Systems," Unpublished Ph.D. Dissertation, Department of Computer Science, University of Colorado at Boulder, 1989.

13.   A. C. Lemke, "Cooperative Problem Solving Systems Must Have Critics," *Proceedings of the* AAAI *Spring Symposium Workshop on Knowledge-Based Human Computer Communication,* pp.73-75,1990.

14.   A. Repenning and T. Sumner, "Using **Agentsheets** to Create a Voice Dialog Design Environment," *Symposium on Applied Computing (SAC '92),* Kansas City, MO., 1992, pp.1199-1207.

15.   H. Rittel and M. Webber, "Planning Problems are Wicked Problems," in *Developments in Design Methodology,* N. Cross, Ed., John Wiley & Sons, New York, 1984, pp.135-144.

16.   D. A. Schoen, *The Reflective Practitioner: How Professionals Think in Action,* Basic Books, New York, 1983.

17.   B. Silverman, "Survey of Expert Critiquing Systems: Practical and Theoretical Frontiers," *CACM,* Vol.35, pp.106-127, 1992.

18.   G. Stahl, "Toward a Theory of Hermeneutic Software Design," Technical Report CU-CS-589-92, Computer Science Department, University of Colorado at Boulder, 1992.

19.   G. Stahl, "Supporting Interpretation in Design," Accepted to *Journal of Architecture and Planning Research, Special Issue on Computational Representations of Knowledge,* Forthcoming in Summer 1993.

20.   L. Suchman, *Plans and Situated Actions: The Problem of Human-Machine Communication,* Cambridge University press, Cambridge, 1987.

21.   T. Winograd and F. Flores, *Understanding Computers and Cognition: A New Foundation for Design,* Addison-Wesley, Menlo Park, CA, 1986.

8.   Embedding Critics in Design Environments

Gerhard Fischer, Kumiyo Nakakoji, Jonathan Ostwald, Gerry Stahl, Tamara Sumner

Human understanding in design evolves through a process of critiquing existing knowledge and consequently expanding the store of design knowledge. Critiquing is a dialog in which the interjection of a reasoned opinion about a product or action triggers further reflection on or changes to the artifact being designed. Our work has focused on applying this successful human critiquing paradigm to human-computer interaction. We argue that computer-based critiquing systems are most effective when they are embedded in domain-oriented design environments, which are knowledge-based computer systems that support designers in specifying a problem and constructing a solution. Embedded critics play a number of important roles in such design environments: (1) they increase the designer's understanding of design situations by pointing out problematic situations early in the design process, (2) they support the integration of problem framing and problem solving by providing a linkage between the design specification and the design construction and (3) they help designers access relevant information in the large information spaces provided by the design environment. Three embedded critiquing mechanisms – generic, specific and interpretive critics – are presented and their complementary roles within the design environment architecture are described.

1.   Introduction

Human understanding in design evolves through a process of critiquing [Fischer, 1991 #74] existing knowledge and consequently expanding and refining the state of knowledge. Our work has focused on applying this human critiquing paradigm to human-computer interaction. Our experience with this approach is based on several years of system prototyping, the integration of cognitive and design theories and empirical evaluation of these systems. Based on these experiences, we conclude that computational critiquing systems are most effective at supporting human designers when embedded in domain-oriented design environments [Fischer, 1992 #238].

In Section 2, we explain why the critiquing paradigm is essential for supporting the complex activity of design. Using illustrations from critiquing systems we have built, we demonstrate in Section 3 how embedding in design environments enhances the computational critiquing process. Examples of our embedded critiquing system are drawn from HYDRA-kitchen, a residential kitchen design environment we have built. Section 4 explains three embedded critiquing mechanisms we have designed, implemented and studied, called generic, specific and interpretive critics. Finally, in Section 5 we assess some of the benefits of these embedded critiquing mechanisms.

2.   The Critiquing Approach

Critiquing is a dialog in which the interjection of a reasoned opinion about a product or action triggers further reflection on or changes to the artifact being designed. For example, a kitchen designer might critique a kitchen floor plan in terms of building code violations, efficiency, safety concerns or eventual resale value. An agent – human or machine – capable of critiquing in this sense is a *critic*. Computer-based critics are made up of sets of rules or procedures for evaluating different aspects of a product; sometimes each individual rule or procedure is referred to as a critic [Fischer, 1991 #74].

2.1.   Importance of Human Critiquing

Human critiquing plays an important role in design both in the growth of human knowledge and in terms of error elimination. By "human critiquing" we mean subjecting our designs and products to the scrutiny of other people, be they peers, domain specialists or society in general.

Complex design activities prohibit an individual from knowing everything that is relevant; in addition, expertise is frequently controversial. Complex design situations can therefore be characterized by a "symmetry of ignorance" [Rittel, 1984 #243] and the knowledge needed to solve a design problem is distributed among designers and their clients [Rittel, 1984 #71]. Critiquing is an important method for working within such a framework of distributed knowledge because it fosters a maximum of participation in order to activate as much of the distributed design knowledge as possible. In kitchen design, the designer and the homeowner take turns proposing ideas and criticizing each other's suggestions. In this way, the often tacit knowledge [Polanyi, 1966 #208] that each party has can come into play and complement the other's partial grasp of the design problem.

Critiquing is ubiquitous. It is, for example, at the heart of the scientific method. Popper [Popper, 1965 #62] theorized that science advances through a cycle of conjectures and refutations. Scientists formulate hypotheses and put forth these conjectures for scrutiny and refutation by the scientific community. Besides contributing to the growth of knowledge, this critiquing cycle of conjectures and refutations is essential for creating a shared understanding within the scientific community and providing a stable base for future growth in scientific knowledge.

Critics play an important role in making designers aware of breakdown situations [Fischer, 1993 #239]. Petroski [Petroski, 1985 #63] noted the importance of failure in the growth of engineering knowledge. For instance, when an airplane crashes, the Federal Aviation Administration sends a team of specialists to the site to determine the cause of the accident. In essence, these specialists are critiquing the plane's design and construction and current aviation practices. Over the years, this practice has contributed much to the growth of aviation knowledge in terms of both airplane design and improved safety regulations [Chambers, 1985 #237]. In turn, this growth in knowledge contributes toward future error elimination; that is, planes with the same defect are repaired and aviation regulations are improved to prevent similar crashes.

The activity of critiquing plays an important role in engineering, science and design in general. It produces many benefits, including the growth of knowledge, error elimination and the promotion of mutual understanding by all participants. Through the critiquing process, designers gain a better understanding of the design problem by hearing the different points of view of other design participants. In our work, we have taken this successful human critiquing paradigm and shown how it can be effectively applied to enhance human-computer interaction. In the remainder of this paper, the term "critiquing" will refer to computer-based critiquing systems.

2.2.   Applying Computer-Based Critiquing to Design

Our design environments are *cooperative problem-solving systems* [Fischer, 1990 #14] in which the computer system helps users design solutions themselves as opposed to having an expert system design solutions for them. As illustrated in Figure 1, critiquing is integral to cooperative problem-solving systems. The core task of critics is to recognize and communicate debatable issues concerning a product. Critics point out problematic situations that might otherwise remain unnoticed. Many critics also advise users on how to improve the product and explain their reasoning. Critics thus help designers avoid problems and learn different views and opinions. Critiquing systems *augment* the ability of human designers to evaluate their solutions; decisions concerning whether or not to follow the critic suggestions are left up to the designers.

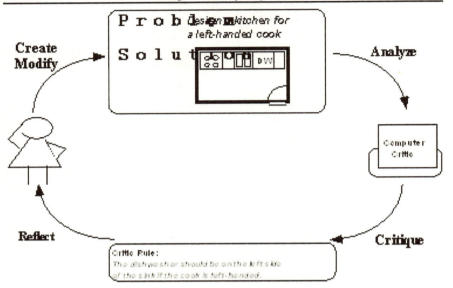

Figure 1. A cooperative problem-solving system has two agents – a human designer and a computer-based critic. Both agents contribute what they know about the domain to solving some problem. For the critiquing systems discussed in this paper, the human's primary role is to generate and modify solutions; the computer's role is to analyze these solutions and produce a critique for the human to consider in the next iteration of this process.

Critiquing systems are well suited for design tasks in complex problem domains in which the traditional expert systems or automated design approaches have proven inadequate. Such design tasks have the following characteristics: (a) knowledge about the design domain is *incomplete* and *evolving*, (b) the problem requirements can be specified only partially and (c) necessary design knowledge is *distributed* among many design participants.

a. Knowledge about the design domain is incomplete and evolving. Some domains, such as user interface design [Lemke, 1990 #91] and lunar habitat design [Stahl, 1993 #171], are not sufficiently understood; that is, creating a complete set of principles that exhaustively captures their domain knowledge is impossible. Complex problem domains are continually changing as new design knowledge is gained and old design knowledge becomes obsolete. For example, user interface design principles have certainly changed to accommodate the shift from primarily character-based user interfaces to sophisticated graphical user interfaces. Any system supporting design in complex domains must be able to evolve with the domain.

Expert systems and automated design approaches are infeasible in these complex situations in which all the potential relevant background knowledge cannot be articulated [Winograd, 1986 #213]. Because autonomous expert systems leave the human out of the decision process and all "intelligent" decisions are made by the computer, these systems require *a priori* a comprehensive knowledge base covering all aspects of the tasks being performed. Most expert systems also fail to adequately support the evolution of domain knowledge. First, expert systems typically do not support the addition of knowledge by domain experts and instead rely on knowledge engineers to acquire this knowledge from domain experts and subsequently codify it for the specific system. Second, expert systems have shown themselves to be brittle [Rittel, 1984 #71]; that is, a small shift in the problem domain can render an expert system's knowledge base obsolete and inoperative [Buchanan, 1984 #224].

An important aspect of embedded critiquing systems is their incremental nature; they do not need a large or comprehensive rule-base to be effective. Because critics are structured to be independent entities, adding or modifying a critic does not affect the behavior of the remaining critics. Parts of the critiquing system can remain operational and continue to support the design process while other parts undergo evolutionary change. In the HYDRA-Kitchen system we have prototyped a "generic" critiquing mechanism that is knowledgeable about commonly accepted design principles and standard design practices. These principles are found in textbooks and training programs and are recognized by professional kitchen designers as being important aspects of producing a "good" floor plan. Although this general knowledge base is insufficient for automating the design of kitchen floor plans or for making a detailed analysis of the appropriateness of the design for a particular client, the generic critiquing system provides designers with valuable feedback concerning their floor plan designs. One study involving both amateur and expert kitchen designers showed that HYDRA'S generic critics helped both categories of designers even though its rule-base contained only 24 critic rules [Fischer, 1989 #152].

b. The problem requirements can be specified only partially. Design problems are ill-defined: they cannot be precisely specified before attempting a solution [Rittel, 1984 #71]. Problem specifications reflect the designer's understanding of the problem framing and the problem solution. Researchers in situated cognition [Lave, 1988 #95] and design [Schoen, 1983 #129] have shown that designers arrive at solutions by iteratively reframing the problem – adjusting and refining their understanding of the problem framing and problem solution to reflect decisions made, means that may be chosen, materials available and other changes in the context. Thus, problem specifications are not only incomplete, they are also dynamic in nature.

The expert system approach is based on the assumption that the problem to be solved can be fully articulated to the system *a priori*. The system can return a solution only if given a complete and accurate problem specification. Furthermore, changes in the problem specification can completely invalidate the expert system's proposed solution. Thus, expert systems are inadequate in ill-defined domains with partial and evolving problem specifications.

We have constructed a critiquing mechanism that supports design as a process of problem reframing. This "specific" critiquing mechanism enables only those critics pertinent to the current partial specification and as such embodies domain knowledge concerning situation-specific design characteristics that not every design will share. In kitchen design, professional designers elicit this situation-specific knowledge from their customers using predefined questionnaires; the answers to these questionnaires form part of the kitchen specification. In HYDRA-kitchen, as the designer changes the problem specification, the "specific" critiquing mechanism brings different sets of critics to bear upon the design. This mechanism supports the coevolution of problem framing and problem solving by making explicit the relationship between the partial problem specification and the current design solution.

c. Necessary design knowledge is distributed among many design participants. Design domains such as network design are so large and complicated and have so many subdomains that no single person can know all there is to know [Fischer, 1991 #72]. In such complex domains, the necessary design knowledge is distributed among many participants and most design work is done by teams whose members have differing areas of expertise [Hackman, 1974 #198]; [Johansen, 1988 #202]. When designing in ill-defined domains, there are no "optimal" solutions [Simon, 1981 #4]. Conflicts in opinion about how to proceed often arise due to differences in the designers' areas of expertise, their personal styles and their particular problem framing. Often, such conflicts are resolved and design proceeds after designers present reasoned arguments supporting their opinions for discussion and negotiation.

Our critiquing systems support design as a deliberative and interpretive process. Critiquing systems contain a collection of critics that embody different areas of domain expertise, different design styles and often diverging opinions. Our "interpretive" critiquing mechanism supports designers with varying interests and differing areas of expertise to work together by allowing design knowledge to be defined and bundled into personal or topical groupings. Using this mechanism, designers can examine their design from many different perspectives in which each perspective brings different design knowledge and critics to bear upon the current design.

All of our critiquing mechanisms – generic, specific and interpretive – support design as a deliberative process. Besides simply pointing out a potential flaw in the design, these critics offer a reasoned opinion as to why their suggestion should or should not be followed. This interaction style typifies cooperative problem-solving systems: it is the role of the critiquing system to bring relevant design knowledge to the designer's attention; it is the role of the designer to evaluate the trade-offs and make the final decisions.

3. Embedding Critics in Integrated Design Environments

Our early research focused on building and evaluating general purpose (i.e., not-domain-oriented) critiquing mechanisms [Fischer, 1991 #74]. During later work, we became interested in building domain-oriented design environments [Fischer, 1992 #238]. In the last few years, we have merged these two research interests by embedding critiquing mechanisms into domain-oriented design environments. This embedding enhances both the richness of the critiquing process and the ability of our design environments to support the complex activity of design. This section discusses early critiquing systems we have built and how they contributed to the development of the multifaceted architecture, HYDRA, for design environments. A scenario using HYDRA-Kitchen illustrates how the embedded critiquing mechanisms integrate the various components in the design environment.

3.1. Analyses of Early Critiquing Systems

Critical analyses of our early stand-alone critiquing systems [Fischer, 1991 #74] and systems built by others [Burton, 1982 #214]; [Silverman, 1992 #211], combined with empirical evaluations, led us to realize that the challenge in building critiquing systems is not simply to provide feedback: the challenge is to say *the right thing at the right time*. Our analyses identified several shortcomings in early critiquing systems that hindered their ability to say the "right" thing at the "right" time:

    a.   lack of domain orientation;

    b.   insufficient facilities for justifying critic suggestions;

    c.   lack of an explicit representation of the user's goals;

    d.   no support for different individual perspectives;

    e.   timing problems with critic intervention strategies.

a. Lack of domain orientation. Lisp-Critic [Fischer, 1987 #146] allows programmers to request suggestions on how to improve their code. The system proposes transformations that make the code more cognitively efficient (i.e., easier to read and maintain) or more machine efficient (i.e., faster or smaller). However, the lack of domain orientation limits the depth of critical analysis the critiquing system can provide. Without domain knowledge, critic rules cannot be tied to higher level concepts; Lisp-Critic can answer questions such as whether the Lisp code can be written more efficiently, but it cannot assist a user in deciding whether the code can solve a specific problem.

b. Insufficient facility for justifying critic suggestions. Framer [Lemke, 1990 #91] enables designers to develop window-based user interfaces on Symbolics Lisp machines. Framer's knowledge base contains design rules for evaluating the completeness and syntactic correctness of the design as well as its consistency with interface style guidelines. Evaluations of Framer showed (1) that many users did not understand the consequences of following the critic's advice or why the advice was beneficial to solving their problem and (2) that when users do not understand why a suggestion is made, they tend to blindly follow the critic's advice whether or not it is appropriate to their situation. Framer provided short explanations to address this problem. However, in design there are not always simple answers; access to argumentative discussions detailing the pros and cons of a particular suggestion are necessary [Rittel, 1984 #71].

c. Lack of an explicit representation of the user's goals. Janus [Fischer, 1989 #152] is a step toward addressing the previous shortcomings. Janus allows designers to construct kitchen architectural floor plans. It contains two integrated subsystems: a domain-oriented kitchen construction kit and an issue-based hypermedia system containing design rationale. Critics respond to problems in the construction situation by displaying a message and providing access to appropriate rationale in the hypermedia system. However, these critics often give spurious or irrelevant advice resulting from the lack of an explicit representation of the user's task. The only task goal built into Janus is one of building a "good" kitchen; that is, a kitchen that conforms to commonly accepted standards and design practices. With an explicit model of the designer's intentions for a *particular* design, critics can be selectively enabled based on this model and provide less intrusive and more relevant advice.

d. No support for different individual perspectives. It is not possible to anticipate all the knowledge necessary for a critiquing system to say the "right" thing in every design situation. Design domains are continually evolving as new knowledge is gained. Janus-Modifier [Fischer, 1990 #240] was developed to respond to this problem by making the domain knowledge (including critics) end-user modifiable. But being able to add new knowledge is not sufficient; different users must be able to organize and manage design knowledge and critics to reflect *their* perspectives on design. Design environments need to support interpretation of a problem from many perspectives (technical, structural, functional, aesthetic, personal) and critique accordingly.

e. Timing problems with critic intervention strategies. A number of systems [Fischer, 1985 #144]; [Burton, 1982 #214] investigated critic intervention strategies, which determine when and how a critic should signal a potential problem. This research focused on studying *active* versus *passive* intervention strategies. Active critics continually monitor user actions and make suggestions as soon as a problematic situation is detected. Passive critics are explicitly invoked by users to evaluate their partial design.

A protocol analysis study [Lemke, 1990 #91] showed that passive critics were often not activated early enough in the design process to prevent designers from pursuing solutions known to be suboptimal. Often, subjects invoked the passive critiquing system only after they thought they had completed the design. By this time, the effort of repairing the situation was expensive. In a subsequent study using the same design environment, an active critiquing strategy was shown to be more effective by detecting problematic situations early in the design process.

However, our interactions with professional designers showed that active critics are not a perfect solution either: they can disrupt the designer's concentration on the task at the wrong time and interfere with creative processes. Interruption becomes even more intrusive if the critics signal breakdowns at a different level of abstraction compared to the level in which the task users are currently engaged. For example, if the designer is currently concerned about where the refrigerator should be located in a kitchen floor plan, then a critic suggestion that a double-bowl sink is better than a single-bowl sink is probably inappropriate and distracting at this point in time.

What is needed is a critiquing system that: (1) alerts designers to problematic solutions, (2) avoids unnecessary disruptions and (3) allows users to control the critic's intervention strategy. Embedding critics in design environments allows users to *control* critic intervention through interaction with the construction, specification and perspective design components built into the design environment.

3.2.   HYDRA: A Multifaceted Architecture for Design Environments

Design environments are computer programs that support designers in concurrently specifying a problem and constructing a solution. Design environments provide information repositories to store domain knowledge and allow designers to accumulate additional domain-knowledge through interaction with the environment.

HYDRA (Figure 2 represents its components schematically; Figure 3 provides a screen image) contains design creation tools in the form of a construction component and a specification component. Design information repositories are provided in the form of argumentation and catalog knowledge bases. The architecture is *multifaceted* because these components provide multiple representations of both the current design and underlying domain knowledge. The critiquing mechanisms integrate these facets in the design environment architecture. The various representations are managed by the following four components:

- The *construction component* is the principal medium for modeling a design. It provides a palette of domain-oriented design units, which can be arranged in a work area using direct manipulation. Design units represent primitive elements in the construction of a design, such as sinks and stoves in the domain of kitchen design. Critics can be tied to these domain-oriented design units and to relationships between design units.

- The *specification component* allows designers to describe abstract characteristics of the design they have in mind. The specifications are expected to be modified and augmented during the design process, rather than to be fully articulated at the beginning. The specification provides the system with an explicit representation of the user's goals. This information can be used to tailor both the critic suggestions put forth and the accompanying explanations to the user's task at hand.

- The *argumentative hypermedia component* contains design rationale based on the procedural hierarchy of issues (PHI) structure (see Figure 5) [McCall, 1987 #209]; [Conklin, 1988 #153]. The PHI structure consists of issues, answers and arguments about decisions made during the course of design. Users can annotate and add argumentation as it emerges during the design process. Argumentation is a valuable component in a critic's explanation; it identifies the pros and cons of following a critic suggestion and helps the user to understand the consequences of following a suggestion.

- The *catalog component* provides a collection of previously constructed designs. These illustrate examples within the space of possible designs in the domain and support reuse [Prieto-Diaz, 1987 #226] and case-based reasoning [Kolodner, 1991 #225]. Catalog entries are also important components in a critic's explanation. Often a critic does not suggest a course of action but instead points out a deficiency in the current design; catalog entries can then be used as specific examples illustrating sample solutions that address a deficiency noted by a critic.

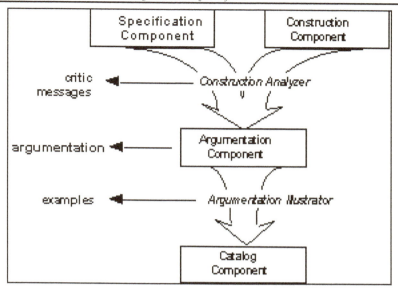

Figure 2. The critiquing process within Hydra. The links between the components – the CONSTRUCTION ANALYZER and the ARGUMENTATION ILLUSTRATOR – are crucial for exploiting the synergy of the integration.

This architecture derives its power from the *integration* of its components. When used in combination, each component augments the value of the others in a synergistic manner. The components of the architecture are integrated by two linking mechanisms (see Figure 2). Together, these linking mechanisms support the critiquing process by providing critic messages, explanatory argumentation and illustrative examples:

- The CONSTRUCTION ANALYZER is the core critiquing component in Hydra. This mechanism analyzes the design construction for compliance with the currently enabled set of critic rules. When a lack of compliance is detected, the critic signals a breakdown and provides entry into the exact place in the argumentative hypermedia component in which the appropriate explanation is located.

- The ARGUMENTATION ILLUSTRATOR can retrieve both positive and negative catalog examples to illustrate the problematic situation detected by the CONSTRUCTION ANALYZER. Providing specific examples is essential because the explanation given in the form of argumentation is often highly abstract and conceptual. Concrete design examples that match this explanation assist designers in understanding the potential problem, assessing the design situation and devising a solution.

In addition to the construction and argumentation components of its predecessor, **Janus, Hydra** supports a specification component [Fischer, 1991 #77] and a catalog of designs. The specification format is based on questionnaires used by professional kitchen designers to elicit their customers' requirements, such as the kitchen owner's cooking habits and family size. Each component in **Hydra** contains design knowledge that can be used by an embedded critiquing mechanism to overcome the deficiencies of the stand-alone systems previously described.

As mentioned in Section 2.2, we have studied three classes of embedded critiquing mechanisms: generic, specific and interpretive critics. These mechanisms embody different types of design knowledge and correspond to three dimensions of embedding. *Generic critics* are embedded in the construction and use domain knowledge concerning desirable spatial relationships between design units to detect problematic situations in the partial design construction. *Specific critics* are embedded in the partial specification and take advantage of additional knowledge in the partial specification to detect inconsistencies between the design construction and the design specification. *Interpretive critics* are embedded in a perspective mechanism that enables designers to create topical groupings of critics and design knowledge; such groupings support designers in examining their artifacts from different viewpoints. The argumentation and catalog components provide rich sources of domain knowledge that all three mechanisms use in their explanation process when communicating with the designer.

The following section provides a scenario depicting how kitchen designers work within the **HYDRA** environment. The scenario describes the three critiquing mechanisms and it illustrates the benefits derived from embedding these mechanisms in the multifaceted architecture.

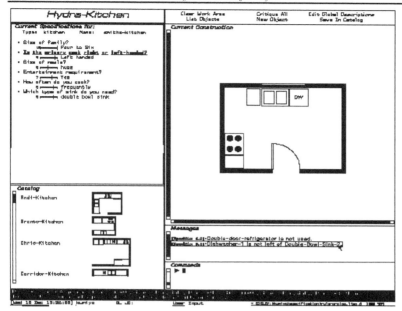

Figure 3. Screen image of HYDRA-KITCHEN. The "Current Specification" window shows a summary of currently selected answers using the specification component. An indicator attached to each of the selected answers allows users to assign weights of importance to the specified item in order to set priorities. The "Catalog" window shows previous kitchen designs that can be examined or reused. The "Current Construction" window shows a partial construction being built using components provided in a palette of kitchen design units (not shown). The "Messages" window is used to present critic notification messages. The number attached to the critic message is a weighted measure indicating the relevance of the fired critic.

3.3. Scenario Illustrating Generic, Specific and Interpretive Critics

Imagine that Bob, a professional kitchen designer, has been asked to design a kitchen for the Smith family. The partial specification of the Smith's kitchen is articulated using **Hydra**, as shown in Figure 3.

Bob begins working on a floor plan in the construction area. He moves the dishwasher next to the cabinet. Bob's action triggers a *generic critic* and the message, "The dishwasher is too far from the sink," is displayed. Generic critics reflect knowledge that applies to all designs, such as accepted standards, building codes and domain knowledge based on physical principles. Often, this generic knowledge can be found in textbooks, training curricula or by interviewing domain practitioners. Bob highlights the critic's message and elects to see its associated argumentation. The argumentation explains that plumbing guidelines require the dishwasher to be within one meter of the sink. Bob follows the critic's suggestion and moves the dishwasher next to the right side of the sink (for details, see Fischer, et al. [Fischer, 1991 #74]).

This action triggers a *specific critic* with the rule, "If you are left-handed, the dishwasher should be on the left side of the sink." Specific critics reflect design knowledge that is tied to situation-specific physical characteristics and domain-specific concepts that not every design will share. These critics are constructed dynamically from the partial specification to reflect current design goals. This particular critic rule was activated because Bob specified that the primary cook is left-handed (see Figure 3). Bob examines the supporting argumentation, "Having the dishwasher to the left of the sink creates an efficient work flow for a left-handed person." Bob decides this is an important concern and puts the dishwasher on the left side of the sink.

Then Bob remembers that the Smiths are remodeling mainly to increase their property value in anticipation of selling in two years. So, Bob decides to examine his design from a resale-value perspective. When Bob switches to the resale-value perspective, an *interpretive critic* is triggered with the rule, "The dishwasher should be on the right side of the sink." Interpretive critics support design as an interpretive process by allowing designers to interpret the design situation from different perspectives according to their interests. In this perspective, the critic about the dishwasher and sink has been redefined and its associated rationale has been modified. Now the argumentation says, "Optimizing your kitchen for left-handed cooks can adversely affect the house's resale value since most kitchen users are right-handed." Bob decides that enhancing the Smiths' resale value is the more important consideration and moves the dishwasher. As long as he remains in the resale-value perspective, Bob will be informed by the critics whenever they detect a feature negatively affecting resale value. Additionally, the critics will provide Bob access to argumentation concerning designing for resale.

4.   Three Embedded Critiquing Mechanisms

This section describes in detail three embedded critiquing mechanisms – *generic*, *specific* and *interpretive* critics. Examples of how these three critic styles are deployed was illustrated in the previous scenario. In all three mechanisms, critic knowledge is captured by rules with condition and action parts. The *condition* clause checks whether a certain situation exists in the current design construction. The *action* clause notifies the designer that a particular situation has been detected. Figure 4 illustrates a condition-action critic rule in which the condition checks if the stove is away from the window; the action part notifies the designer that "the stove is not away from the window."

For all three mechanisms, the basic critiquing process consists of the following phases: (1) the set of appropriate critic rules to be enabled is identified; (2) the design construction is then analyzed for compliance with the currently enabled set of critic rules; (3) when a lack of compliance is detected, the critic signals a possible problem and provides entry into the argumentative hypermedia component in which the appropriate explanation is located; and (4) concrete catalog examples that illustrate the explanation given in the form of argumentation can optionally be delivered [Fischer, 1991 #74]. As illustrated in Table 1, the three critic mechanisms differ mainly in terms of how they enable critic rules and in the types of design knowledge embodied in their rules.

Table 1. The three critic mechanisms – generic, specific and interpretive - differ in how they enable critic rules, the rules' scope of applicability and the types of design knowledge each mechanism is best suited to represent.

	How Enabled	Applicability	Design Knowledge	Example
Generic	Enabled by placing design units into the construction area	All designs	Standards Physical Principles	Cabinets should be 150 cm. above floor. Heat ignites flammable objects.
Specific	Enabled by the partial specification	Specific design	Situation Characteristics Abstract Domain Concepts	Cook is left-handed and 150cm. in height. Efficiency; safety.
Interpretive	Enabled by the currently active design perspective	Specific perspective	Multiple interpretations of domain concepts	Cabinet height: convenient for cook. Cabinet height: desirable for resale value.

Generic critics [Fischer, 1991 #74] are enabled by the placement of design units into the construction area. These critics apply to all designs containing the design unit to which the critics are attached. Generic critics reflect knowledge that is applicable to all designs, such as accepted standards or regulations or domain knowledge based on physical principles (see Table 1).

Specific critics [Nakakoji, 1993 #242] are constructed dynamically to reflect the designer's goals as they are stated explicitly in the specification component. These critics apply only to the design situation currently under consideration. Specific critics reflect design knowledge that is tied to situation-specific physical characteristics and domain-specific concepts that not every design will share.

Interpretive critics [Stahl, 1993 #171] provide a mechanism for supporting design as an interpretive process; that is, they are a response to the recognition that domain concepts such as "cabinet height" and "efficiency" can have more than one definition or interpretation depending upon the current situation and the designer. Interpretive critics allow designers to view their work from multiple perspectives by creating, managing and selectively activating different sets of design knowledge.

Specific examples illustrating each of these critic mechanisms will be discussed below. Generic critics will be used to discuss the basic critiquing process described at the beginning of this section. The three mechanisms for embedded critics differ from one another primarily in how they determine which set of critic rules should be enabled. The discussion of specific critics and interpretive critics will focus on how these mechanisms determine which critics are currently enabled.

4.1.   Generic Critics

Generic critics reflect knowledge that applies to all designs, such as accepted standards, building codes and domain knowledge based on physical principles. Often, this generic knowledge can be found in textbooks, training curricula or by interviewing domain practitioners. A generic critic representing an accepted kitchen design standard is the cabinet height critic. Kitchen designers agree that unless more specific information regarding the primary cook is known, the top cabinets should be placed 150 cm. above the floor. A generic critic reflecting domain knowledge based on safety principles is the "stove should be away from the window" rule shown in Figure 4. This rule reflects the principle that objects that generate heat (e.g., the stove) should not be placed under flammable objects (e.g., the curtains on the window).

Generic critics in **Hydra** are implemented as object-oriented methods of appliances and other design units in the design construction. When the design construction is altered, all design units implicated by the changes evaluate their critic methods. These methods are defined and parameterized by the information in property sheets such as those shown in Figure 4. For example, the rule box shown defines a generic critic for stoves. This method checks that the stove is "away from" all windows in the construction area.

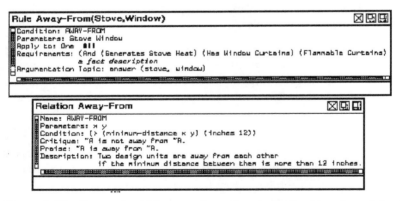

Figure 4. The "stove should be away from the window" critic rule and the definition of the "away-from" spatial relation.

The condition away-from is defined in the relation property sheet as taking two objects and evaluating whether or not the minimum distance between them is greater than 12 inches. The corresponding message for display if this condition is not met is the critique: the first object "is not away from" the second object.

The critic defined in the rule sheet applies this relation to the stove as the first parameter and sequentially to each window in the construction as the second parameter. The definition specifies that this rule shall be applied to all windows (Apply to: All) because stoves should be away from all windows to prevent fires. Other critic rules specify only that there should exist at least one object in the construction (Apply to: One) that matches the condition relation with the first parameter -- for example, the dishwasher should be near at least one sink.

Further requirements can be specified for the applicability of the critic rule. These applicability requirements make use of domain concepts like "generates heat," "has curtains," and "is flammable." In the example rule, a stove has to be away from a window only if the stove generates heat (e.g., it is not a microwave), if the window has curtains and if the curtains are flammable. Finally, the definition of the critic lists a topic in the argumentation issue-base that will be displayed if this critic fires and the user selects the critic message.

All generic critics in **Hydra** are defined through property sheets like these for rules and relations. Using these property sheets, designers are able to modify the definitions of existing critics and to create additional critics.

Critics inform designers of potentially problematic situations by using a three-tiered approach that involves simple notification, supporting argumentation and specific examples. First, the critic signals the designer of a potentially problematic situation with a simple initial notification message. The form of this initial notification message is defined by the critique phrase in the spatial relation definition. The critic shown in Figure 4 would display the message "Stove-1 is not away from Window-1." Variables in the notification string are resolved into specific design units by the critic rule using the spatial relation. Associating notification messages with the spatial relations allows these messages to be shared by many critic rules. The downside of this approach is that the notification message signals only that a spatial relation was detected and does not report why this is significant.

As discussed in Section 3.1, our work has shown that such "one-shot" notifications, which merely identify a situation, are inadequate. Critics that support design as an argumentative process [Rittel, 1984 #71] should be capable of presenting different alternatives and opinions and each alternative's corresponding advantages and disadvantages. The critiquing systems use the argumentation component of **Hydra** to provide the second tier of explanation, thereby "making argumentation serve design" [Fischer, 1991 #75].

Each critic rule has an associated link into the argumentation component where issues pertaining to the situation identified by the critic are discussed. For the critic in Figure 4, the associated link is found in the slot "Argumentation Topic: answer (stove, window)." The designer can view the critic's associated design rationale by selecting the initial notification message displayed in the Message area (Figure 3). Because design rationale contains design issues accompanied by positive and negative argumentation, critic explanations in this form help the designer understand why the current design situation may be significant or problematic.

Sometimes designers may not understand the arguments made in the design rationale or they may understand the arguments but not know what action to take. In these situations, providing designers with specific examples can be helpful. The third tier of critic explanation delivers specific examples upon request that illustrate the issue being discussed. Designers can select an issue in the argumentation and request to see a positive example or a counter example. As illustrated in Figure 4, critic conditions are associated with argumentation issues. When the designer requests to see an example of a specific issue, the **ARGUMENTATION ILLUSTRATOR** (see Figure 5) takes the critic condition associated with the selected argumentation issue and searches the catalog component for examples that fulfill the condition.

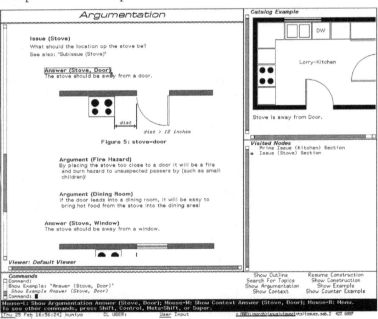

Figure 5. Argumentation consists of issues, answers and arguments supporting or refuting answers. The designer can view the stove-away-from-window critic's associated design rationale by selecting the initial notification message displayed in the Message area (e.g.

"Stove-1 is not away from Window-1") of Figure 3. The arguments shown explain why many kitchen designers believe windows and stoves should not be adjacent. Choosing the menu item "Show Example" causes example designs that illustrate the answer advocated in the argumentation to be delivered to the designer.

4.2. Specific Critics

In HYDRA, specification knowledge is related to: (1) situation-specific physical characteristics such as the size and shape of the kitchen or the owner's height, (2) specified requirements such as "a dishwasher should be included," and (3) abstract domain concepts such as safety and efficiency. The specification issues were derived from questionnaires used by professional kitchen designers [Nakakoji, 1993 #242].

Specific critics evaluate the construction situation for compliance with the partial specification. They reduce the intrusiveness of a critiquing system by narrowing the enabled critics to those that are relevant to the task at hand as determined from the partial specification. Specification-linking rules [Fischer, 1991 #77] are used to dynamically identify the set of specific critics to be enabled.

The specification consists of issue/answer pairs (see Figures 3 and 6). A specification-linking rule represents a dependency between an issue/answer pair in the specification and associated pro and con arguments in the argumentation component. As shown in Figure 6, a specification-linking rule connects the argumentation issue "Where should the stove be located?" with the specification item "Is safety important to you?" The shared domain distinction "safety" is used to establish a dependency between this particular specification item and the argumentation issue.

A critic condition is associated with each answer in the specification and a domain distinction is associated with each argument. Domain distinctions are a vocabulary for expressing domain concepts, such as safety or efficiency. Whenever the designer modifies the specification, the critiquing system recompiles the specification-linking rules to reflect the newly relevant domain distinctions. In this way, critiquing criteria are tied to a representation of the partially articulated goals of a specific design project.

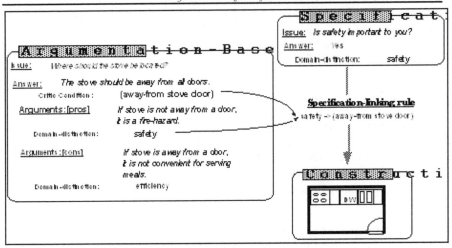

Figure 6. Derivation of the Specification-Linking Rules. The domain distinction associated with a specification item is paired with a matching pro or con argument in the hypermedia issue base. The critic condition associated with an answer is linked with the domain distinction to form a specific critic rule.

The operation of the specification-linking rules can best be conveyed with an example. Assume the designer knows that the kitchen owners have young children and he specifies that having a safe (child-proof) kitchen is very important (Figure 6). The domain distinction associated with this specification item is "safety." In the argumentation, answers (e.g., "the stove should be away from all doors") are associated with critic conditions (e.g., "away-from stove door"). Pro and con arguments are associated with domain distinctions. In Figure 6, the domain distinction "safety" is associated with the pro argument and the domain distinction "efficiency" is associated with the con argument.

Specification-linking rules link the domain distinctions activated in the specification with the appropriate critic condition. First, the argumentation is analyzed until the domain distinction activated in the specification (safety) is found. If the domain distinction is associated with a pro argument, then a specification-linking rule is created with the form: domain distinction implies critic condition. If the domain distinction is associated with a con argument, then a specification-linking rule is created with the form: domain distinction implies not critic condition. The specification-linking rules "safety implies stove away-from door" and "efficiency implies stove not away-from door" can be derived from the example in Figure 7. Whenever the designer modifies the specification, the critiquing system recomputes the specification-linking rules. For the partial specification shown in Figure 7, specification-linking rules supporting the notion of safety will be constructed. The right side of the specification rules are the enabled critic conditions used to evaluate the design construction for adherence to the current specification.

Often, conflicts between specific critics arise. The designer could have specified that he was concerned with both safety and efficiency. For example, having the stove to the left of the refrigerator may be efficient, but it may also be less safe if this places the stove next to a door. Using the specification component, the designer can not only state which concepts are of interest, he can also articulate his level of interest by weighting specification items. The critiquing system uses these weights to help prioritize critic activity. When a critic fires, it displays an importance weight next to the initial notification message that reflects the weights assigned to the specification items that enabled the particular critic rule (see Figure 3). The designer can then take these relative weights into account when deciding to respond to the critic messages.

4.3.   Interpretive Critics

Design can be viewed as an interpretive process [Stahl, 1993 #171]. Designers and their clients interpret the design situation according to personal backgrounds, experiences and concerns. This means that there cannot be a unique set of domain knowledge that is adequate for all people and all interests. We have prototyped a design environment [Stahl, 1992 #169] with *perspectives* [Bobrow, 1980 #236] to provide alternative views or approaches to given design situations. The perspectives mechanism organizes all the design knowledge in the system. It allows items of knowledge to be bundled into personal or topical groupings or versions. For instance, a resale-value perspective might include critics and design rationale pertinent to homeowners concerned about their home's resale appeal. A kitchen design environment might have perspectives for evaluating kitchens from the perspective of an electrician, a plumber, an interior designer, a realtor, a mortgage writer or a city inspector. Perspectives could also be defined for individuals who have special preferences or for specific kitchens. A perspective for the Smith's kitchen would include design rationale for its unique set of design decisions, so that any future modifications could be checked for consistency with those decisions.

The organization of knowledge by perspectives encourages users to view the knowledge in terms of structured, meaningful categories, which they can create and modify. It provides a structure of contexts that can correspond to categories meaningful in the design domain. This can ease the cognitive burden of manipulating large numbers of alternative versions of critics and other design knowledge.

Interpretive critics are the result of interactions between the perspectives structure and the critic mechanisms (Figure 7). Critics are associated with design perspectives. The perspectives provide a mechanism for creating, managing and selectively activating different sets of critics along with their related design knowledge, such as spatial relations, domain distinctions, palette items and argumentation. A perspective can incorporate critics from other perspectives, including generic and specific critics from the default perspective (see Figure 7). Additionally, a perspective may modify any inherited critics and define new ones.

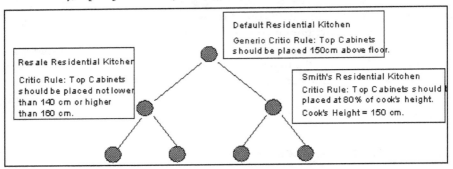

Figure 7. Perspectives are arranged in an inheritance network. Three perspectives – a "default kitchen," "Smith's kitchen," and a "resale kitchen" – are shown. The preferred placement of the top cabinets depends on the perspective selected. The critic rule analyzing the placement of the top cabinets is redefined within each of the three perspectives.

Designers switch perspectives to examine a design from different viewpoints. Switching perspectives changes the currently effective definitions of critics, the terms used in these definitions and other domain knowledge. As a result, the critics adapt to the different perspectives -- hence the term "interpretive" critics. The designer always works within a particular perspective. At any time, the designer can select a different perspective by name. New perspectives can also be created by assigning a name and selecting existing perspectives to be inherited. Bob, the designer working with the Smiths in the previous scenario, could create a Smith's kitchen perspective and select the resale perspective to be inherited by it.

Perspectives are connected in an inheritance network; a perspective can modify any knowledge inherited from its parents or it can add new knowledge. Consider the inheritance network shown in Figure 7. Suppose that in the default perspective there is a rule that checks "if the top cabinets are 150 cm above the floor." In the Smith's kitchen perspective the rule that determines cabinet height is based on the cook's height. This *same* critic rule will be evaluated differently in the three different perspectives because it is defined in terms of the spatial relationship whose definition varies. Similarly, either the rule or the spatial relationship in the rule could be defined indirectly in terms of something in the argumentation issue-base, such as the answer to an issue requesting the primary cook's height. Critics and the design knowledge on which they are based can be adapted to interpret designs differently in many ways: by inheritance, by modification of inherited objects or by addition of new objects into a perspective.

Interpretive critics based on perspectives provide a mechanism for refining the critiquing process that is orthogonal to the specific critics. Specific critics fine-tune the generic critics that embody general domain knowledge, relating them to the design choices specified for a given project. Whereas the set of generic and specific critics may be extensible in the sense that new critics can be added from time to time, the perspectives mechanism provides for multiple definitions of these sets to exist simultaneously so that individual designers can fluidly adopt varying viewpoints on designs. This provides a means for structuring new critics and other knowledge representations as they emerge during use of the design environment and systematically retaining this knowledge for use in future projects.

5.   Benefits of Embedding: Increasing the Shared Context

Computational media offer great capacity for storing large volumes of information and support for managing dynamic information spaces [Norman, 1993 #175]. Computational media can integrate diverse information sources such as reference materials, solutions to previous design problems and collections of design rationale. However, access to large information spaces creates a new problem for designers: information overload. In situations of information overload, the critical resource for designers is not information, but rather the attention with which to process information. Simon [1981 #4] argued with convincing examples that a design representation suitable for a world in which the scarce factor is information may be exactly the wrong one for a world in which the scarce factor is attention. When presenting people with information, the primary concern is to present items that are relevant to the task at hand [Fischer, 1991 #77]. Critics embedded in design environments exploit a rich notion of the designer's task at hand or context, to provide relevant information to designers.

Design environments support a cooperative problem-solving process in which the designer determines the context of design by manipulating interface objects (such as graphical objects and form-based objects) in the construction, specification and perspective components. Objects in the construction component define a construction context that provides generic critics with a representation for the task at hand. Values and priorities for specification objects define a specific context that allows specific critics to compute relevant information for the particular task as specified by the designer. The perspective mechanism determines an interpretive context that enables collections of critics and their associated argumentation.

The context defined by the construction, specification and perspective situations allows the system to provide information relevant to a dynamic representation of the task at hand that is shared by the designer and the design environment. This shared context enables precise intervention by critics, reduces annoying interruptions and increases the relevance of information delivered to designers. Critics embedded in design environments benefit the design process by increasing the designer's understanding of design situations, by pointing out significant design situations that might have been overlooked and by locating relevant information in very large information spaces.

5.1. Increasing the Designer's Understanding of Design Situations

The solution of a design problem necessarily involves coming to a deeper understanding of the problem through attempts to solve it. Design problems cannot be clearly defined "up front," before any attempt at a solution is made. New requirements emerge during the design process [Schoen, 1983 #129]; [Rittel, 1984 #243]; [Fischer, 1992 #83] that cannot be identified until portions of the artifact have been designed or implemented. These aspects of design create the following dilemma: (1) one cannot gather information meaningfully unless the problem is understood, (2) one cannot understand the problem without having a concept of the solution in mind and (3) one cannot understand the problem without information about it.

Problem framing and problem solving are *mutually enabling* design processes because each informs the other. Design methodologists such as Schoen [1983 #129] and Rittel [1984 #243] stress the strong interrelationship between problem framing and problem solving. They characterize design problems by the need for designers to impose a discipline or framing, on the problem in order to reduce the complexity of the situation to a manageable level. Problem framing is the process of determining the boundaries (or framework) of a problem, such as determining the "givens" of the problem, the assumptions under which the designer operates and the criteria for evaluating a solution. Each move toward a design solution tests the problem framing, potentially exposing conflicting or unrealistic goals. Critics embedded in design environments support designers in creating and modifying the problem framing throughout the design process – not just in the beginning. Critics support a design process where "understanding the problem is the problem."

In this view of design, in which problem framings and problem solutions coevolve, each action by the designer has the potential to alter the understanding of the problem, which in turn can influence subsequent actions. Our goal is to support design as a cooperative problem-solving dialog between the designer and the evolving design situation.

5.2. Pointing Out Significant Design Situations

By seeing design as a "reflective conversation with the situation" [Schoen, 1983 #129], action is governed by nonreflective thought processes and proceeds until it breaks down. A *breakdown* [Fischer, 1993 #239] occurs when the designer realizes that nonreflective action has resulted in unanticipated consequences – either good or bad. Schoen described this realization as ``the situation talks back." Reflection is used to repair the breakdown and then (nonreflective) situated action continues. The hallmark of reflection-in-action is that it takes place within the *action present* – within the time period during which the decision to act has been made but the final decision about how to act has not. This is the time period during which reflection can still make a difference in what action is taken.

Schoen's theory of design is based on designers interacting with traditional media and the "back-talk" from the situation is determined solely by the designer's skill, experience and attention. Computational technology, such as critics embedded in design environments, affords a new type of "back-talk" from the design situation. Computational design situations can actively point out breakdowns to designers. This active design support enables designers to hear the situation talk back in situations that might have remained mute in passive media.

Reflection-in-action, as supported by embedded critics, is an ongoing cycle of action, breakdown and reflection. Designers act when they shape the design situation. They establish a shared context with the design environment by manipulating interface objects in the construction, specification or perspective components. Breakdowns are triggered by critics embedded in the design environment that detect situations that indicate the designer might need to reflect. Based on the shared context, critics support reflection by delivering information relevant to the breakdown situation. Argumentative information helps designers understand the breakdown situation and the catalog contains design solutions that provide examples of how other designers have resolved similar problems.

The scenario illustrates how embedded critics support design as a reflective conversation with the situation. In the scenario, critics triggered two consecutive breakdowns. In the first, the construction situation talked back to Bob when his actions violated a generic kitchen design principle that "the dishwasher should not be too far from the sink." After some reflection, he moved the dishwasher nearer to the sink to comply with the critic. However, this action created a new breakdown situation. A specific critic signaled a breakdown to remind Bob that his actions were inconsistent with his partial specification; that is, his placement of the sink might not be optimal for left-handed cooks. This breakdown led him to reflect on his goals; instead of altering the design construction, Bob reformulated his partial specification.

5.3. Locating Relevant Information In Large Information Spaces

Making information relevant to the task at hand poses many challenges for the design of interactive computer systems, particularly for problems in which the need for information is critical and yet precise information needs cannot be known in advance of attempts to solve the problem. Our design environments that support design in complex domains are high-functionality computer systems; that is, they provide a large amount of functionality and are built on large information bases. Such systems provide more information and functionality than a single person can master [Draper, 1984 #85]. Two factors contribute to this behavior: (1) the effort of finding information often outweighs the perceived benefits of doing so and (2) users are not aware that the information even exists. Both factors can be related to the discrepancy between the designer's perception of an information space and the actual information contained in a high-functionality system (see Figure 8).

Designers are often unwilling to disrupt the design process to search for information in large information spaces, even if they know the information exists. In addition, designers may not know when they *need* information. Embedded critics save designers the trouble of explicitly querying the system for information. Critics notify designers of situations indicating the need to reflect (breakdowns) and provide access to information fueling reflection. The context of the breakdown situation serves as an implicit query that enables embedded critics to deliver relevant information. Designers benefit from needed information without having to explicitly ask for it.

Embedded critics can also deliver relevant information [Nakakoji, 1993 #242] about which designers were unaware (see Figure 8). Critics provide the designer with a pointer into part of the system's information space with which the designer needs to become aware. The designer can further browse the unfamiliar portion of the information space starting from the entry point provided by the critic.

Critics afford *learning on demand* [Fischer, 1991 #72] by letting designers access new knowledge in the context of actual problem situations; users are informed (1) when they are getting into trouble, (2) when they are missing important information and (3) when they come up with problematic solutions. Learning on demand is a promising approach for the following reasons: (1) it contextualizes learning by integrated it into work rather than relegating it to a separate design phase; (2) it lets designers see for themselves the usefulness of new knowledge for actual problem situations, thereby increasing the designers' understanding of their situations; and (3) it makes new information relevant to the task at hand, thereby leading to better decision making, better products and better performance.

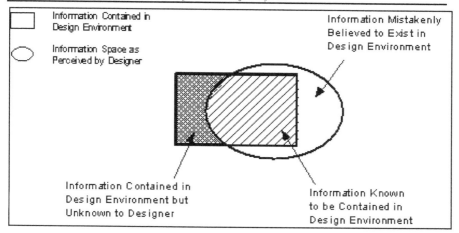

Figure 8. Large information spaces contain more information than a single person can know exists. The oval represents the information a designer perceives to be in the design environment. The square represents the information actually contained in the design environment. This figure illustrates that the designer's perception includes information that does not exist in the design environment and does not include some information that actually exists in the design environment.

Critics exploit the shared context of breakdown situations to compute what information is relevant to the task at hand. In the scenario, each critic's notification message was linked to information in the argumentation component. For the "dishwasher not too far from the sink" issue, the designer was reminded of plumbing requirements he might have known about but did not remember in the context of the design situation. The "left-handed" specific critic identified information the designer had previously been unaware of: that the recommended positions of the sink and dishwasher are dependent on whether the cook is right- or left-handed. The interpretive critic (enabled by adapting a Resale Perspective) informed Bob of additional information about which he had previously been unaware. Now that he is aware of this "resale" value concern, Bob could explore further implications of a resale perspective by browsing related information or by continuing his design process, where he will be informed on demand.

6.   The Dynamic Nature of Critiquing Knowledge

6.1 Supporting Designers in Adapting the Critiquing System

To be successful, embedded critiquing systems must adapt to reflect changes in the design domain. Two questions arise when considering system adaptation: will designers be *able* to adapt the system as required and will designers be *motivated* to adapt the system? End-user modifiability components and design environment "seeds" are important steps toward answering these questions.

Adapting the critiquing system involves modifying or adding critic rules, design units, design unit relations and critic explanations in the form of argumentation and catalog examples. Sometimes, adapting the system is as simple as changing parameters or filling out specialized forms. Girgensohn [Girgensohn, 1992 #172] explored end-user modifiability in domain-oriented design environments. His work showed that end-users without any formal training in computer science need considerable environmental support in the form of explanatory help, critics that support modification processes, task decomposition agendas and computer-supported object classification to effect significant system changes. Even with this extensive environmental support, none of the subjects in his user studies were able to complete the adaptations without intervention from the study supervisor. Girgensohn's research has demonstrated that enabling designers to adapt their systems is a very difficult problem that requires further research in the areas of demonstration components, domain-oriented knowledge representations and adaptive user modeling components. The **Hermes** project is exploring a different approach toward achieving end-user modifiability by building into the design environment an English-like end-user programming language [Stahl, 1992 #31].

6.2 "Seeding" the Critiquing System with Domain Knowledge

Whereas ongoing adaptation of embedded critiquing systems is in the hands of designers solving design problems, system builders must create the original conditions that enable and motivate this evolution process to occur. Specifically, system builders must provide initial environments in the form of a seed.

We cannot offer an easy-to-follow prescription for successful seed building. Seed building requires a deep understanding not only of the application domain, but also of the *practice* [Ehn, 1989 #2] of the people who will use the system. System builders cannot hope to attain such an understanding without, at least to some extent, becoming domain experts themselves. But this is generally infeasible. For useful seeds to be built, system-building must be based on a process of mutual education [Greenbaum, 1991 #241] between system builders, who know about building software design environments and domain designers, who understand the practice of design in the target application domain. The goal of this mutual education process is to establish a shared understanding of what domain knowledge a seed should contain so that it will immediately support the practice of designers within that domain.

6.3 Accumulating Design Knowledge Through Critics

Embedded critics play the crucial role of "knowledge attractors" in domain-oriented design environments. Design knowledge surfaces during reflection-in-action, when designers reflect upon the source of breakdowns and devise courses of action for resolving the breakdowns. User observations in using specific critics revealed that when designers were fired a critic rule, they often argued for or against the associated argument and were motivated to describe the reason by articulating pro or counter arguments to the argumentation [Nakakoji, 1993 #242]. The incomplete nature of design knowledge guarantees the argumentation is never complete. Designers who arrive at an innovative resolution to a breakdown may add their arguments to the existing rationale, enriching the information space contained in the design environment.

7.   Conclusions

Although this paper focuses primarily on a single design environment built for residential kitchen design, the **HYDRA-Kitchen** system, other ongoing research in our group has demonstrated that embedded critiquing systems have broad applicability to a variety of domains and that embedded critiquing systems can be applied to complex, new domains with few accepted design rules and practices and non-spatially-oriented domains.

The interpretive critiquing mechanism is being explored in the domain of lunar habitat design [Stahl, 1993 #171]. Unlike kitchen design, lunar habitat design is a completely new domain with few design rules and no standardized vocabulary. In domains with few standards, negotiation, argumentation and interpretation are increasingly important aspects of design. This aspect of the lunar habitat design domain led us to extend our critiquing systems to include interpretive mechanisms.

The **Voice Dialog Design Environment** tests the applicability of critiquing systems to non-spatial domains. The system supports the design and simulation of applications with phone-based interfaces [Repenning, 1992 #33]. In this domain, design units include audio prompts, voice menus and telephone touch-tone input. Relations between design units are temporal in nature; that is, design units occur before or after certain events in the execution sequence. This design environment is part of a joint research project between the University of Colorado and voice dialog application designers at US WEST Advanced Technologies [Sumner, 1991 #32].

We have demonstrated how embedding critic mechanisms in design environments overcomes many deficiencies found in stand-alone critiquing systems. The generic, specific and interpretive critics we have explored correspond to three dimensions of embedding. Generic critics are embedded in the construction context because they are enabled by the placement of design units in the work area. Specific critics are embedded in the partial specification by being dynamically constructed from domain distinctions tied to specification items; they reduce the intrusiveness of generic critics by narrowing the enabled critics to those that are relevant to the partially specified task at hand. Interpretive critics are embedded in the network of perspectives that supports the evolution of alternative viewpoints on designs; using these critics, designers are able to consider their designs critically from multiple perspectives. The beneficial role of human critiquing in science, design and engineering had been socially recognized long before the advent of computational critiquing systems. Our approach of embedding critics into integrated design environments is an important step toward applying the critiquing paradigm to create more useful and usable knowledge-based computer systems.

Acknowledgments

The authors thank the members of the Human-Computer Communication group at the University of Colorado, who contributed to the conceptual framework and the systems discussed in this paper. The research was supported by the National Science Foundation under grants No. IRI-8722792 and IRI-9015441, by the Colorado Advanced Software Institute, by US WEST Advanced Technologies, by the NYNEX Science and Technology Center and by Software Research Associates, Inc. (Tokyo, Japan). We especially wish to thank Barbara Gibson at Kitchen Connection in Boulder, Colorado, for sharing her expertise in kitchen design.

References

D. G. Bobrow, I. Goldstein, *Representing Design Alternatives*, In the Proceedings of AISB Conference, AISB, Amsterdam, 1980.

B. Buchanan, E. Shortliffe, *Human Engineering of Medical Expert Systems*, in B. Buchanan and E. Shortliffe (Eds.), Rule-Based Expert Systems: The MYCIN Experiments of the Stanford Heuristic Programming Project, Addison-Wesley, Reading, MA, 1984, pp. 599-612.

R. Burton, J. S. Brown, *An Investigation of Computer Coaching for Informal Learning Activites*, in D. Sleeman and J. S. Brown (Eds.), Intelligent Tutoring Systems, London, Academic Press, 1982, pp. 79-98.

A. B. Chambers, D. C. Nagel, *Pilots of the Future: Human or Computer?*, Communications of the ACM, Vol. 28, No. 11, 1985, pp. 1187-1199.

J. Conklin, M. Begeman, *gIBIS: A Hypertext Tool for Exploratory Policy Discussion*, Transactions of Office Information Systems, Vol. 6, No. 4, 1988, pp. 303-331.

S. W. Draper, *The Nature of Expertise in UNIX*, In the Proceedings of Proceedings of INTERACT'84, IFIP Conference on Human-Computer Interaction (Amsterdam), Elsevier Science Publishers, 1984, pp. 182-186.

P. Ehn, *Work-Oriented Design of Computer Artifacts*, (2nd ed.), Arbetslivscentrum, Stockholm, 1989.

G. Fischer, *A Critic for LISP*, In the Proceedings of Proceedings of the 10th International Joint Conference on Artificial Intelligence (Milan, Italy), Morgan Kaufmann Publishers, 1987, pp. 177-184.

G. Fischer, *Communication Requirements for Cooperative Problem Solving Systems*, Informations Systems, Vol. 15, No. 1, 1990, pp. 21-36.

G. Fischer, *Supporting Learning on Demand with Design Environments*, In the Proceedings of Proceedings of the International Conference on the Learning Sciences 1991 (Evanston, IL), 1991, pp. 165-172.

G. Fischer, *Domain-Oriented Design Environments*, In the Proceedings of 7th Annual Knowledge-Based Software Engineering (KBSE-92) Conference (MCLean, VA.), IEEE Computer Society Press, Los Alamitos, CA., 1992, pp. 204-213.

G. Fischer, *Turning Breakdowns into Opportunities for Creativity*, in E. Edmonds (Eds.), Creativity in Cognition, Penrose Press, (in press), 1993.

G. Fischer, A. Girgensohn, *End-User Modifiability in Design Environments*, In the Proceedings of CHI'90 (Seatle, WA.), ACM Press, 1990, pp. 183-191.

G. Fischer, J. Grudin, A. C. Lemke, R. McCall, J. Ostwald, B. N. Reeves, F. Shipman, *Supporting Indirect, Collaborative Design with Integrated Knowledge-Based Design Environments*, Human Computer Interaction (Special Issue on Computer Supported Cooperative Work), Vol. 7, No. 3, 1992.

G. Fischer, A. C. Lemke, T. Mastaglio, A. Morch, *The Role of Critiquing in Cooperative Problem Solving*, ACM Transactions on Information Systems, Vol. 9, No. 2, 1991, pp. 123-151.

G. Fischer, A. C. Lemke, R. McCall, A. Morch, *Making Argumentation Serve Design*, Human Computer Interaction, Vol. 6, No. 3-4, 1991, pp. 393-419.

G. Fischer, A. C. Lemke, T. Schwab, *Knowledge-Based Help Systems*, In the Proceedings of Human Factors in Computing Systems, CHI'85 Conference Proceedings (San Francisco, CA) (New York), 1985, pp. 161-167.

G. Fischer, R. McCall, A. Morch, *Design Environments for Constructive and Argumentative Design*, In the Proceedings of CHI '89 (Austin, Texas), ACM Press, New York, 1989, pp. 269-275.

G. Fischer, K. Nakakoji, *Making Design Objects Relevant to the Task at Hand*, In the Proceedings of AAAI-91, Ninth National Conference on Artificial Intelligence (Cambridge, MA), AAAI Press/The MIT Press, 1991, pp. 67-73.

A. Girgensohn, *End-User Modifiability in Knowledge-Based Design Environments*, Unpublished Ph.D. Dissertation, Department of Computer Science, University of Colorado at Boulder, 1992, Also available as TechReport CU-CS-595-92.

J. Greenbaum, M. Kyng, *Design at Work: Cooperative Design of Computer Systems*, Lawrence Erlbaum Associates, Hillsdale, NJ, 1991.

J. R. Hackman, R. E. Kaplan, *Interventions into group process: An approach to improving the effectiveness of groups*, Vol. 5, 1974, pp. 459-480.

R. Johansen, *Groupware: Computer Support for Business Teams*, Free Press, New York, 1988.

J. Kolodner, *Improving Human Decision Making through Case-Based Decision Aiding*, Vol. 12, No. 2, 1991, pp. 52-68.

J. Lave, *Cognition in Practice*, Cambridge University Press, Cambridge, UK, 1988.

A. C. Lemke, G. Fischer, *A Cooperative Problem Solving System for User Interface Design*, In the Proceedings of Proceedings of AAAI-90, Eighth National Conference on Artificial Intelligence, AAAI Press/The MIT Press, Cambridge, MA, 1990, pp. 479-484.

R. McCall, *PHIBIS: Procedurally Hierarchical Issue-Based Information Systems*, In the Proceedings of Proceedings of the Conference on Architecture at the International Congress on Planning and Design Theory (New York), American Society of Mechanical Engineers, 1987.

K. Nakakoji, *Increasing Shared Knowledge of Design Tasks Between Humans and Design Environments: The Role of a Specification Component*, PhD Dissertation Thesis, Department of Computer Science, University of Colorado at Boulder, Boulder, CO, 1993.

D. A. Norman, *Things That Make Us Smart*, Addison-Wesley Publishing Company, Reading, MA, 1993.

H. Petroski, *To Engineer Is Human: The Role of Failure in Successful Design*, St. Martin's Press, New York, 1985.

M. Polanyi, *The Tacit Dimension*, Doubleday, Garden City, NY, 1966.

K. R. Popper, *Conjectures and Refutations*, Harper & Row, New York, 1965.

R. Prieto-Diaz, P. Freeman, *Classifying Software for Reusability*, Vol. 4, No. 1, 1987, pp. 6-16.

A. Repenning, T. Sumner, *Using Agentsheets to Create a Voice Dialog Design Environment*, In the Proceedings of Symposium on Applied Computing (SAC '92) (Kansas City, MO), ACM Press, 1992, pp. 1199-1207.

H. Rittel, *Second Generation Design Methods*, in N. Cross (Eds.), Developments in Design Methodology, John Wiley & Sons, New York, 1984, pp. 317-327.

H. Rittel, M. M. Webber, *Planning Problems are Wicked Problems*, in N. Cross (Eds.), Developments in Design Methodology, John Wiley & Sons, New York, 1984, pp. 135-144.

D. A. Schoen, *The Reflective Practitioner: How Professionals Think in Action*, Basic Books, New York, 1983.

B. Silverman, *Survey of Expert Critiquing Systems: Practical and Theoretical Frontiers,* CACM, Vol. 35, No. 4 (April 92), 1992, pp. 106-127.

H. A. Simon, *The Sciences of the Artificial,* (second ed.), The MIT Press, Cambridge, MA, 1981.

G. Stahl, *Toward a Theory of Hermeneutic Software Design,* No. CU-CS-589-92, Computer Science Department, University of Colorado at Boulder, 1992.

G. Stahl, *Supporting Interpretation in Design,* Journal of Architecture and Planning Research (Special Issue on Computational Representations of Knowledge), 1993 (Forthcoming).

G. Stahl, R. McCall, G. Peper, *A Hypermedia Inference Language as an Alternative to Rule-based Expert Systems,* In the Proceedings of submitted to Expert Systems ITL Conference, 1992.

T. Sumner, S. Davies, A. C. Lemke, P. G. Polson, *Iterative Design of a Voice Dialog Design Environment,* Technical Report No. CU-CS-546-91, Department of Computer Science, University of Colorado at Boulder, 1991.

T. Winograd, F. Flores, *Understanding Computers and Cognition: A New Foundation for Design,* Addison-Wesley, Menlo Park, CA, 1986.

9.   POW! Perspectives On the Web

The perspectives mechanism described in this paper provides a flexible approach to organizing information in a shared repository for the use of individuals and groups engaged in collaboratively constructing knowledge. The perspectives approach builds on a long history of ideas for personalizing access to information within large hypertext spaces, but the POW! perspectives server is the first example of implementing this approach on the WorldWideWeb. After reviewing the concept of perspectives as a support mechanism for Web-based collaboration, this paper will present the main features of the approach and describe common functional types of perspectives. The POW! perspectives server is currently being used in two educational applications: one an environmental course in middle school and the other a graduate seminar in cognitive science. These two collaborative learning applications will be discussed briefly. At the WebNet '99 Conference, evaluation results from these two courses will also be presented.

1. Perspectives: A Collaboration Support Mechanism

The concept of perspectives comes from the hermeneutic philosophy of interpretation of Heidegger (1927) and Gadamer (1967). According to this philosophy, all understanding is situated within interpretive perspectives: knowledge is fundamentally perspectival. This is in accord with recent work in cognitive science that argues for theories of socially situated activity and collaborative learning (e.g., Lave & Wenger, 1991; Winograd & Flores, 1986).

Collaborative work typically involves both individual and group activities. Individuals engage in personal *perspective making* and also collaborate in *perspective-taking* (Boland et al., 1995). That is, people and communities construct not only elements of domain knowledge, but also their own "take" on the domain, a way of understanding the network of knowledge that makes up the domain. An essential aspect of making one's perspective on a domain of knowledge is to take on the perspectives of other people in the community. Learning to interpret the world through someone else's eyes and then adopting this view as part of one's own intellectual repertoire is a fundamental mechanism of learning. Collaborative learning can be viewed as a dialectic between these two processes of perspective making and perspective taking. This interaction takes place at both the individual and group levels of analysis – and it is a primary mode of interchange between the two levels.

While the Web provides an obvious medium for collaborative work, it provides no support for the interplay of individual and group understanding that drives collaboration. First, we need ways to find and work with information that matches our personal needs, interests and capabilities. Then we need means for bringing our individual knowledge together to build a shared understanding and collaborative products. Enhancing the Web with perspectives may be an effective way to accomplish this.

As a mechanism for computer-based information systems, the term *perspective* means that a particular, restricted segment of an information repository is being considered, stored, categorized and annotated. This segment consists of the information that is relevant to a particular person or group, possibly personalized in its display or organization to the needs and interests of that individual or team. Computer support for perspectives allows people in a group to interact with a shared community memory; everyone views and maintains their own perspective on the information without interfering with content displayed in the perspectives of other group members.

One problem that typically arises is that isolated perspectives of group members tend to diverge instead of converging as work proceeds. Structuring perspectives to encourage perspective taking, sharing and negotiation offers a solution to this by allowing members of a group to communicate about what information to include as mutually acceptable. The problem with negotiation is generally that it delays work on information while potentially lengthy negotiations are underway. Here, a careful structuring of perspectives provides a solution, allowing work to continue within personal perspectives while the contents of shared perspectives are being negotiated. We believe that perspectives structured for negotiation is an important approach that can provide powerful support for collaborative use of large information spaces on the Web.

The idea of Perspectives On the Web traces its lineage to ideas like "trail blazing" (Bush, 1950), "transclusion" (Nelson, 1981) and "virtual copies" (Mittal et al., 1986) – techniques for defining and sharing alternative views on large hypertext spaces. At the University of Colorado, we have been building desktop applications with perspectives for the past decade (McCall et al., 1990; Stahl, 1993a). With the implementation of the POW! perspectives server, we can now use perspectives on the Web.

2. Features of the Perspectives Mechanism

The perspectives mechanism that we have been exploring (Stahl, 1993b) incorporates the following features for a community of users:

- Individual community members have access to what appears to be their own information source. This is called their *personal perspective*. It consists of items from a shared central information repository that are tagged as being visible within that particular perspective (or in any perspective inherited by that perspective). This provides a workspace for perspective-making.

- Community member A can integrate an item from B's perspective into A's personal perspective by creating a *link* (or virtual copy) of the item. If B modifies the original item, then it changes in A's perspective as well. However, if A modifies the item, a new item is actually created for A with the modified content, so that B's perspective is not changed. This arrangement generally makes sense because A wants to view (or inherit) B's item, even if it evolves. However, B should not be affected by the actions of someone who copied one of B's items.

- Alternatively, A can *physically copy* the contents of an item from B's perspective. In this case, the copies are not linked to each other in any way. Since A and B are viewing physically distinct items now, either can make changes without affecting the other's perspective. Linking and copying notes from other perspectives allows perspective-taking to occur.

- When A creates a virtual copy of an item from B's perspective, A can decide if she will also get virtual copies of items related to that one or if she will create her own sub-network for her copy of that item. Arbitrarily large sub-networks of information can be inherited with no overhead using the linking and inheritance mechanisms.

- Items of information can be created, edited, rearranged, linked together or deleted by users within their personal perspective without affecting the work of others.

- There is an inheritance tree of perspectives; descendants inherit the contents of their ancestor perspectives. Changes (additions, edits, deletions) in the ancestor are seen in descendent perspectives, but not vice versa. (See Figure 1.)

- New perspectives can be created by users. Perspectives can inherit from one or more existing perspectives. Thus, a team perspective can be created that inherits all the content of the perspectives of the team's members. A hierarchy of team, sub-team and individual perspectives can be built to match the needs of a particular community.

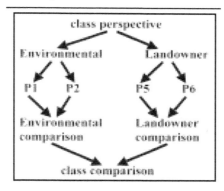

Figure 1. A typical inheritance hierarchy of perspectives. The comparison perspective includes all content from member perspectives. Results of negotiation can be added to class and team perspectives to be shared in all members' personal perspectives.

This model of perspectives has the important advantage of letting team members inherit the content of their team's perspective and other information sources without having to generate it from scratch. They can then experiment with this content on their own without worrying about affecting what others see. This is advantageous as long as one only wants to use someone else's information to develop one's own perspective.

However, if one wants to influence the content of team members' perspectives, then this approach is limited because one cannot change someone else's content directly. This limitation is overcome with the linking/copying functions and the definition of certain types of perspectives, as discussed below. It is of course important for supporting collaborative work that the perspectives maintain at least a partial overlap of their contents in order to reach successful mutual understanding and coordination. The underlying subjective opinions must be intertwined to establish intersubjective understanding (Tomaselo et al., 1993; Habermas, 1981). When we set up a new application using POW!, we structure an initial hierarchy of perspectives to support both divergent and convergent discourse among perspectives. The innovation in our collaboration applications – compared for instance to CSILE (Scardamalia & Bereiter, 1991) – is the flexible perspectives mechanism, in which content is automatically inherited down a hierarchy of perspectives and in which this hierarchy can itself evolve to meet changing user needs.

3. Types of Perspectives and Practices

A typical **POW!** application provides several functional types of perspectives within a multi-layered graph of perspective inheritance to help students compile their individual and joint research (Figure 1). Certain social practices for using the application are associated with these different types of perspectives:

- The *class perspective* is created by the teacher to start everyone off with some initial pointers and suggested topics. It typically establishes a structure for classroom activities and provides a space for collecting the products of collaborative intellectual work.

- *Team perspectives* contain items that have been accepted by the members of a team. This perspective is pivotal for collaboration; it gradually collects the products of a team's effort.

- A student's *personal perspective* is a private workspace for constructing the student's personalized perspective on the shared information. It inherits a view of everything in team perspectives of the teams to which the student belongs. Thus, it displays the owner's own work within the context of items proposed or negotiated by teams and the class – as modified by the student. Students can each modify (add, edit, delete, rearrange, link) their copies of team items in their personal perspectives. They can also create completely new material there.

- The *comparison perspective* combines all the personal perspectives of team members and the team perspective, so that anyone can compare all the work that is going on. It inherits from the personal, team and class perspectives. Students can go here to get ideas and copy items into their own personal perspective or propose items for a team perspective.

Students each enter notes in their personal perspective using information available to them: the Web, books, encyclopedia, CD-ROM, discussions or other sources. Students can review the notes in the class perspective, their team perspectives and the personal perspectives of their team mates. All of these contents are collected in comparison perspectives, where they are labeled by their perspective of origin. Students extract from any of these perspectives those items that are of interest to them. Then they organize and develop the data they have collected by categorizing, summarizing, labeling and annotating. The stages of investigating, collecting and editing can be repeated as many times as desired. Team members then negotiate which notes should be promoted to the team perspective to represent their collaborative product.

The class project ends with each team producing an organized perspective. This year's research products can be used to create next year's class perspective starting point, so new researchers can pick up where the previous generation left off – within a Web information space that will have evolved substantially in the meantime.

4. Negotiating Environmental Perspectives

This Fall we piloted the use of **POW!** in a classroom at the Logan School for Creative Learning in Denver, using both HTML and Java applet interfaces to the perspectives server. For the past five years, this class of middle school students has researched the environmental damage done to mountain streams by "acid mine drainage" from deserted gold mines in the Rocky Mountains above Denver. They actually solved the problem at the source of a stream coming into Boulder from a mine site by building a wetlands area to filter out heavy metals. This year they are investigating the broader ramifications of their past successes; they are looking at the issue of acid mine drainage from various alternative – and presumably conflicting – perspectives. The students interview adult mentors to get opinions from specific perspectives: environmental, governmental, mine-owner and local landowners.

The **POW!** application serves as a medium through which students collaboratively research these issues with their mentors and with each other. Each student and mentor has their personal perspective and these perspectives inherit from one of the content-based team perspectives (environmental protection, governmental regulation, etc.), depending upon which intellectual perspective they are working on constructing. Even email interactions happen through the application and are retained as notes in its perspectives.

A tree of discussion threads was "seeded" in the application with question categories, such as "Environmental Analysis Questions". Within these categories, the teacher posted specific questions for the students to explore, like, "Do you believe that acid mine drainage is a serious threat to the environment?" Students can send an email to one or more mentors asking for information related to this question. When replies are sent back, they will be automatically posted to the discussion thread under the original email. When someone clicks on a title in the discussion, the contents of that item are displayed in an HTML frame below the applet (Figure 2).

A student works in her personal perspective, which might inherit from the class, student team and landowner team perspectives. She can add, edit and delete ideas in her perspective, as well as sending email in it. Because she is a member of the landowner team and the student group as well as the class, she can browse ideas in the student team comparison, the landowner team comparison and the class comparison perspective.

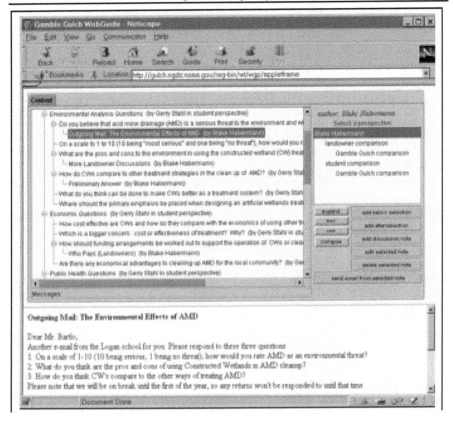

Figure 2. An interface to the POW! Perspectives server. A Java applet shows a student notes in his personal perspective. An HTML frame below displays the content of a selected note.

For this application, the teacher has decided that negotiation and perspective taking will take place in live classroom discussions, rather than within the Web application. After a team or the whole class reaches a consensus, the teacher will enter the statements that they have agreed to into the team or class perspective.

The goal of the yearlong course is not only to negotiate within teams to construct the various positions, but also to negotiate among the positions to reach consensus or to clarify differences. The teacher designed this class to teach students that knowledge is perspectival, that different people construct views, compilations of facts and arguments differently depending upon their social situation. He hopes that his students will not only learn to evaluate statements as deriving from different perspectives, but also learn to negotiate the intertwining of perspectives to the extent that this is possible.

As an initial field-testing of our system, this trial has resulted in valuable experience in the practicalities of deploying such a sophisticated program to young students over the Web. The students are enthusiastic users of the system and offer (through the application) many ideas for improvements to the interface and the functionality. Consequently, the software is benefiting from rapid cycles of participatory design. The differing viewpoints, expectations and realities of the software developers, teachers and students provide a dynamic field of constraints and tensions within which the software, its goals and the understanding of the different participants co-evolve within a complex structural coupling.

5. Constructing Perspectives on Computer Mediation

We have also recently begun an interdisciplinary graduate seminar on computer mediation of collaborative learning. The seminar uses a POW! application in several ways:

- *As the primary communication medium for their internal collaboration.* The seminar takes place largely on-line. Limited class time is used for people to get to know each other, to motivate the readings, to introduce themes that will be followed up on-line and to discuss how to use the software within the seminar.

- *As an example system of computer-mediated collaboration to analyze.* Highly theoretical readings on mediation and collaboration are made more concrete by discussing them in terms of what they mean in a system like ours. The advantage of using a locally-developed prototype as our example is that we not only know how it works in detail, but we can modify its functionality or appearance to try out suggestions that arise in the seminar.

- *As an electronic workspace for members to construct their individual and shared ideas.* Ideas entered into the system persist there, where they can be revisited and annotated at any time. Ideas that arise early in the seminar will still be available in full detail later so that they can be related to new readings and insights. The record of discussions over a semester or a year will document how perspectives developed and interacted.

- *As a glossary and reference library.* This application is seeded with a list of terms that are likely to prove important to the seminar and with a list of seminar readings. Seminar members can develop their own definitions of these terms, modifying them based on successive readings in which the terms recur in different contexts and based on definitions offered by other members. Similarly, the different readings can be discussed and interpreted on-line.

- *As a brainstorming arena for papers.* The application has already been seeded with themes that might make interesting research papers drawing on seminar readings and goals. It allows people to link notes from anywhere in the information environment to these themes and to organize notes under the themes. Thus, both individuals and groups can use this to compile, structure and refine ideas that may grow into publishable papers. Collaborative writing is a notoriously difficult process which generally ends up being dominated by one participant's perspective or being divided up into loosely connected sections, each representing a single perspective. Software with perspectives may facilitate a more truly collaborative approach to organizing ideas on a coherent theme.

- *As a bug report mechanism or feature request facility.* Seminar participants can communicate problems they find in the software as well as propose ideas they have for new features. By having these reports and proposals shared within the Web-based medium, they are communicated to other seminar participants, who can then be aware of the bugs (and their fixes) and can join the discussion of suggestions.

The seminar version of **POW!** incorporates a built-in permissions system that structures the social practices surrounding the use of the system. Seminar participants each have a home personal perspective in which they can manipulate notes however they like without affecting the views in other perspectives. They can add quick discussion notes or other kinds of statements. They can edit or delete anything within their home perspective. They can also make multiple copies or links from notes in their personal perspective to other notes there. Anyone is free to browse in any perspective. However, if one is not in one's own perspective then one cannot add, edit or delete notes there. To manipulate notes freely, one must first copy or link the note into one's own personal perspective. The copy or link can optionally include copying (or linking) all the notes below the selected note in the tree as well. These rules are enforced by the user interface, which checks whether or not someone is in their personal perspective and only allows the legal actions.

The fact that an individual note may have different edited versions and different linking structures in different perspectives, that notes may have multiple parents within a discussion thread, that new perspectives can be added dynamically and may inherit from multiple other perspectives sets our systems apart from simple threaded discussion media. It also makes the computations for displaying notes rather complex. This is a task that definitely requires computers. By relieving people of all this bookkeeping, computer support may help people to collaborate.

The seminar application emphasizes the use of perspectives for structuring collaborative efforts to build shared knowledge. The goal of the seminar is to evolve sophisticated theoretical views on computer mediation within a medium that supports the sharing of tentative positions and documents the development of ideas and collaboration over time. A major hypothesis to be explored by the course is that software environments with perspectives can provide powerful tools for coordinated intellectual work and collaborative learning. For instance, it will explore how the use of a shared persistent knowledge construction space can support more complex discussions than ephemeral face-to-face conversations. We will explore the effectiveness of this application as a computationally active tool to augment the knowledge construction work of a community and report our findings at WebNet '99 in the Fall.

Acknowledgments

The research on perspectives is a collaboration of the author with Rogerio dePaula, Thomas Herrmann and his students at Dortmund, Ted Habermann and his group at NOAA, Dan Kowal and his middle school students, the participants in the "Readings in Cognitive Science" seminar and the researchers in the "Articulate Learners" project. The work reported here was supported in part by grants from NSF IRI-9711951, the McDonnell Foundation and NSF EAR-9870934.

References

[Boland & Tenkasi 1995] Boland, R. J. Jr. & Tenkasi, R. V. (1995) Perspective making and perspective taking in communities of knowing. *Organization Science*. Vol. 6, No. 4, 350-372.

[Bush 1950] Bush, V. (1950) As we may think. *Atlantic Monthly*. Vol. 176, No. 1, 101-108.

[Gadamer 1967] Gadamer, H-G. (1967) *Truth and Method*. Crossroad Books.

[Habermas 1981] Habermas, J. (1981) *Theorie des kommunikativen Handelns. Band 1. Handlungsrationalität und gesellschaftliche Rationalisierung*. Suhrkamp Verlag.

[Heidegger 1927] Heidegger, M. (1927) *Being and Time*. Harper & Row.

[Lave & Wenger 1991] Lave, J. & Wenger, E. (1991) *Situated Learning: Legitimate Peripheral Participation*. Cambridge University Press.

[McCall et al. 1990] McCall, R., Bennett, P., d'Oronzio, P., Ostwald, J., Shipman, F., Wallace, N. (1990) Phidias: Integrating CAD graphics into dynamic hypermedia. *ECHT '90*. 152-165.

[Mittal et al. 1986] Mittal, S., Boborow, D., Kahn, K. (1986) Virtual copies at the boundary between classes and instances. *OOPSLA '86 Proceedings.* 159-166.

[Nelson 1981] Nelson, T. (1981) *Literary Machines.* Mindful Press.

[Scardamalia & Bereiter 1991] Scardamalia, M. & Bereiter, C. (1991) Higher levels of agency for children in knowledge building: A challenge for the design of new knowledge media. *Journal of the Learning Sciences,* 1, 37-68.

[Stahl 1993a] Stahl, G. (1993a) Supporting situated interpretation. *Proceedings of the Cognitive Science Society 1993.* 965-970.

[Stahl 1993b] Stahl, G. (1993b) *Interpretation in Design: The Problem of Tacit and Explicit Understanding in Computer Support of Cooperative Design.* Unpublished Ph.D. Dissertation. Department of Computer Science. University of Colorado at Boulder. Chapter 9 on "Interpretive perspectives for collaboration" available at http://www.cs.colorado.edu/~gerry/publications/dissertation/Ch09.html.

[Tomasello et al. 1993] Tomasello, M., Kruger, A. C. & Ratner, H. (1993) Cultural learning. *Behavioral and Brain Sciences.* 495-552.

[Winograd & Flores 1986] Winograd, T. & Flores, F. (1986) *Understanding Computers and Cognition.* Addison-Wesley.

10. Reflections on WebGuide: Seven Issues for the Next Generation of Collaborative Knowledge-Building Environments

A number of software environments have been developed as media to support collaborative knowledge building, typically featuring a Web-based threaded discussion facility. We have recently developed such a system, known as **WebGuide**. The distinctive feature of this system is support for structuring collaboration and knowledge construction with personal, group and comparison perspectives. While piloting **WebGuide** in a middle school classroom and a graduate seminar, we encountered a variety of issues related to both software design and classroom practices. Some of these issues are common to experiences with similar systems and some have to do specifically with support for perspectives. In this paper we review seven of the major issues encountered with an eye toward suggestions for future work.

There is a growing genre of software systems that I will refer to as *Knowledge-Building Environments* (KBEs). KBEs are intended to support collaboration processes in which, for instance, a classroom of students researches, discusses, critiques and articulates their own developing understanding of scientific phenomena. Perhaps first explicitly championed by Scardamalia and Bereiter (Scardamalia & Bereiter, 1991), KBEs have been implemented and assessed in the past decade by research centers at the universities of Toronto, Michigan, Berkeley, Northwestern, Colorado, Vanderbilt, Georgia Tech, Stanford and Swarthmore, among others.

I have argued elsewhere that understanding is perspectival and that computer environments should deliver information to people based on their preferred *perspectives* on the information (Stahl, 1993; Stahl, Sumner, & Owen, 1995). In particular, collaboration consists of processes of perspective-making and perspective-taking involving personal and group perspectives (Boland & Tenkasi, 1995). To explore the representation of perspectives within KBEs, we (see acknowledgments) developed a system called **WebGuide**. This year we piloted

WebGuide in a middle school environmental science classroom and in an interdisciplinary cognitive science graduate seminar. We ran into many of the same issues that have confronted other KBEs. Our perspectives-based software addresses or transforms some of the issues and raises others of its own.

This paper reflects on seven issues raised by our WebGuide experiences. We think these issues are critical to the ability to support collaborative learning with Web-based environments. The potential for computer mediation of collaboration seems extraordinary, but our experience warns us that the practical barriers are also enormous. The following issues for KBEs like WebGuide are not problems that we have solved, but rather foci for future work, in analogy with Halasz's (Halasz, 1988) issues for hypermedia.

This paper summarizes our understanding of the seven issues we identified for future work. That understanding is based on a synthesis of theory and reflection on our experiences with WebGuide. For background details, see: (Stahl, 2000) which presents a theory of collaborative learning and our approaches to computer support that led to WebGuide; (Stahl & Herrmann, 1999) which describes the technicalities of intertwining perspectives and negotiation to support group and individual learning and contrasts WebGuide's mechanisms to related work; (Stahl, 1999) which describes the software interface, its underlying cognitive theory and its trial application in two use situations.

Issue 1: Constructing perspectives on knowledge from threaded discussions

Most KBEs consist primarily of persistent discussion forums, with typed nodes and other supplementary software features and classroom practices to guide the discussion from personal opinions to collaborative knowledge. WebGuide is designed to go a bit further than most KBEs in supporting both knowledge construction and collaboration with a structure of personal and group perspectives. In order to support knowledge construction, it provides functionality for each student to process the ideas in the shared discussion: selecting, editing, arranging, linking and summarizing notes freely within one's own perspective without affecting the views in other people's perspectives (see the knowledge construction commands in Figure 1).

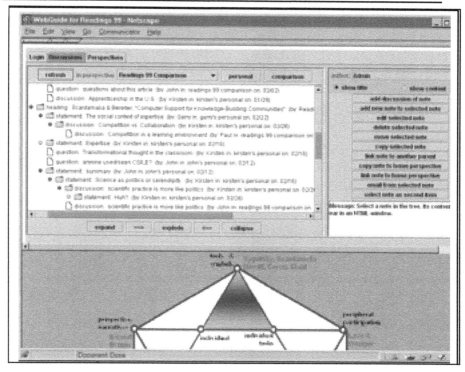

Figure 1. The WebGuide interface. Left: expandable outline of discussion viewed in the "Readings 99 comparison" perspective. Right: knowledge construction commands. Below: selecting a note title in the Java applet above displays its content in this HTML window.

Constructing knowledge involves tasks that are difficult for people to do individually, let alone collaboratively. Providing virtual workspaces for people to formulate their own perspectives and to view each other's ideas may simplify and clarify this process. WebGuide also provides group perspectives in which a team or the class as a whole can agree on expressions of negotiated knowledge. This is designed to structure and model the collaborative process, seen as an interplay among individuals and groups. In this way, WebGuide is intended to support collaboration.

The ability of students and groups to select subsets of the shared repository of discussion notes and to arrange them at will also addresses the problem of growth of the repository contents, which can otherwise lead to information over-load and chaos. Our theory of group memory evolution identifies phases of seeding (e.g., the teacher starts a project off with some ideas or background information), growth (the discussion takes place) and reseeding (somehow the repository must be weeded and reorganized) (Fischer *et al.*, 1993). In WebGuide, the reseeding process can take place continuously, simultaneously with the growth process. Individuals or groups can be responsible for organizing their own perspectives on knowledge.

Issue 2: Distinguishing learning tasks

In iterating the design of WebGuide it has become increasingly clear that there are significant differences between knowledge building and simple discussion. Students more readily engage in discussion, responding spontaneously to existing notes without taking time to appropriate the ideas in new syntheses. True construction of knowledge involves distinct tasks – including brainstorming, articulating, reacting organizing, analyzing and generalizing. Rather than trying to support all of these within a threaded discussion format, it may be more effective to provide specific components, such as an editing window to set down tentative ideas, a discussion area to respond fluently to a flow of interchanged ideas and a separate facility for making sense more reflectively of selected notes. (Buckingham Shum & Hammond, 1994) These different tasks require distinct skills, states of mind and supports.

Collaboration can facilitate knowledge building by bringing many minds (and perspectives) to the job and by practicing social processes that will later become internalized skills (Vygotsky, 1930/1978). But collaborative learning also introduces complexity. We should not expect novices in thinking, writing and researching (e.g., middle school students) to do what most experts cannot do – like write a truly collaborative paper – on their own without significant scaffolding. It will be important to develop new forms of functionality, structure and computer support to enable collaborative knowledge construction – and then to differentiate and integrate these various supports within KBEs.

Issue 3: Representing collaborative perspectives

In our classroom experiences, WebGuide provided three kinds of perspectives or views on the shared network of notes: group, personal and comparison perspectives (see Figure 2). The *group* perspectives were seeded by the teacher to suggest topics of research and discussion. All participants had their own *personal* perspectives, where they could create, modify, link and organize whatever notes they wanted to. Personal perspectives included or inherited all information that was in their group perspectives. The *comparison* perspectives included all information from a set of personal perspectives, so they could be browsed to see notes by everyone in the group. The goal of the class was to share ideas (perspective-taking) in the comparison perspectives, synthesize them (perspective-making) in personal perspectives and then agree to promote some of them (collaborate) to the group perspectives. Thus, the network of perspectives represents and supports the dynamics between individuals and groups that defines collaboration.

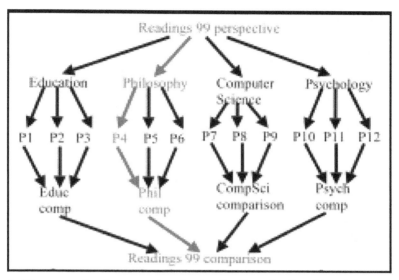

Figure 2. The network of perspectives in the Readings in Cognitive Science seminar. Arrows indicate inheritance of content from class to groups to personal perspectives to group comparison to class comparison. Red arrows indicate what personal perspective R4 displays and where its notes are inherited.

The fact that an individual note may have different edited versions and different linking structures in different perspectives, that notes may have multiple parents within the discussion threads, that new perspectives can be added dynamically and may inherit from multiple other perspectives sets **WebGuide** apart from simple threaded discussion media. It also makes the computations for displaying notes extremely complex. This is a task that definitely requires computers. Although the software now hides much of the complexity, it is not yet at the point where people can operate smoothly without confusion.

One problem is that people using **WebGuide** do not have a clear mental model of relationships of perspectives to each other. The current **WebGuide** interface of the perspective structure (see Figure 3) is inadequate. The expandable outline hierarchy, which is useful in other ways, cannot accurately represent the convergent structure of multiple inheritance (compare Figure 2). The comparison perspectives are listed multiple times, under each perspective that they aggregate.

A graphical representation is needed to show the structure of perspectives and also that of multiply-linked notes. Similarly, a graphical interface might be useful for manipulating and organizing notes within a perspective as well.

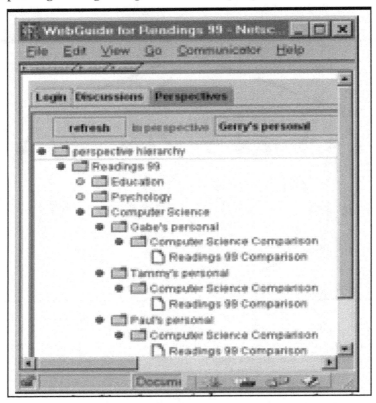

Figure 3. WebGuide's display of the network of perspectives. The hierarchical outline fails to faithfully represent the convergence of information in comparison perspectives, more clearly represented in Figure 2.

Issue 4: Converging ideas

In reviews of KBE experience, Hewitt (Hewitt, Scardamalia, & Webb, 1998) and dePaula (1998) identify divergence of ideas to be a common problem. They argue that the tree structure imposed by standard threaded discussion support is inadequate for collaboration. The idea of a threaded discussion is that one contribution or note leads to another. The result is that discussions proceed along ever diverging lines as they branch out and there is no systematic way to promote convergence (see Figure 4). It seems clear, however, that collaboration requires both divergence (e.g., during brainstorming) and convergence (e.g., during negotiation, synthesis, summary and consensus).

WebGuide addresses this structural problem at three levels:

- The note linking mechanism in WebGuide allows notes to be *linked* to multiple parents (Figure 4), so that they can act to bring together and summarize otherwise divergent ideas.

- Similarly, the graph of perspectives (Figure 2) allows for *multiple inheritance*, so that comparison perspectives aggregate or converge the contents of multiple perspectives.

- By introducing carefully conceived *headings* high in the perspective inheritance network, a teacher can define topics that will be inherited in all other perspectives, encouraging related ideas to be arranged together.

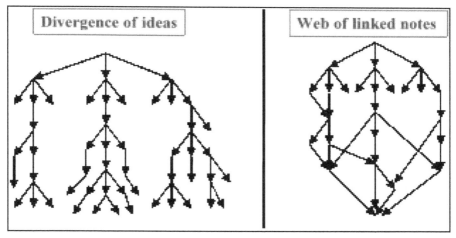

Figure 4. Divergent and convergent structures. Left: a simple threaded discussion cannot represent convergence. Right: Supplementary linking supports convergence.

Issue 5: Negotiating agreement

However, it is not enough that convergence is technically possible or that a teacher desires it. Students need opportunities and supports to bring ideas together and to agree on whose ideas will be accepted as group positions. WebGuide was originally designed to include a negotiation component to complement the perspectives mechanism. The idea is that individuals propose notes from their personal perspectives to be voted on. When enough votes are entered for a given proposal, that proposal is promoted to the group perspective. Communication on proposals proceeds asynchronously and is subject to threads of discussion.

A promoted note represents knowledge accepted by the group. As such, it is automatically inherited into the personal perspectives of all group members, where they incorporate it into their own knowledge organization. In this way, collaborative knowledge exceeds what any one member had expressed and it is always subject to interpretation by individuals. As in unsupported collaboration, individuals build upon knowledge they inherit from their social context and the relation of their understanding to the group interpretation is always tenuous.

In our classroom trials, negotiation had to proceed face-to-face or not at all. Clearly, the addition of software support for negotiation is a priority. The hard part is to make it an enjoyable social experience and a flexible, consensual process rather than a burden that discourages usage.

Issue 6: Encouraging system use

The clearest failure of KBEs is that people avoid using them. There are many explanations for this. *Media competition* poses a barrier to acceptance of new communication software. People are naturally hesitant to adopt yet another communication technology. They must calculate how much a burden the new medium will impose in terms of learning how to use it, acquiring the equipment, checking regularly for incoming messages and letting people know that they are communicating through it. Clearly, a *critical mass* of adoption by one's communication partners is necessary as well.

In a classroom context, some of these problems are minimized. Still, communication with classmates is much easier face-to-face then typing everything (knowing it may influence grading). Perhaps the integration of new capabilities and uses of KBEs can increase their practical value and spur increased usage, as long as confusions and conflicts are not introduced. For instance, providing facilities for people to maintain lists of annotated Web bookmarks, things-to-do, favorite references, up-coming deadlines, etc. within their personal perspectives might not only give them familiarity with using the system, but would also spur adoption. Gradually, they could start to construct their own knowledge in the KBE: personal diary, research notebook, inspirations for papers, theory insights. Then, the step to computer-mediated collaborative knowledge building would follow more naturally.

Issue 7: Scaffolding learning practices

We have argued based on previous experience that the crucial aspect of supporting collaborative learning has to do with structuring social practices (Koschmann, Ostwald, & Stahl, 1998). *Practice* is the set of generally tacit procedures that are culturally adopted by a community. In introducing WebGuide into its two user communities, we tried unsuccessfully to establish certain usage practices, both by instruction and by enforcement in the software (see Figure 5). In the middle school classroom it proved too confusing to allow students to work in every perspective, so the interface was changed to limit navigation to the student's personal perspective and their group and class comparison perspectives. This still left the problem that they preferred to work in the comparison perspectives where they could easily engage in threaded discussion.

For the graduate seminar, the interface was configured to let students navigate to any perspective but to limit what they could do in most perspectives. Most knowledge construction operations were allowed only in one's personal perspective and new options were added to permit copying or linking notes back to one's personal perspective from the other perspectives. This made discussing someone else's note awkward, so simple discussion notes were later allowed everywhere. But then one could not edit even typos that one made in fluent discussion. There seemed to be no satisfactory solution to these detail design decisions short of rethinking the larger issues raised in this paper. The problem of designing classroom practices and matching them with software supports will be with us for the long haul.

Powerful KBEs are not just a fulcrum for leveraging practices that are more student-centered; ideally, they facilitate new classes of practices that would not be feasible without such computer support. Nevertheless, such technologies can also be adapted to reinforce traditional teacher-centered approaches. As Scardamalia & Bereiter (Scardamalia & Bereiter, 1996) say, "Nobody wants to use technology to recreate education as it is, yet there is not much to distinguish what goes on in most computer-supported classrooms versus traditional classrooms" (p. 249). How can the use of KBEs be structured to provide students with a visionary model of collaborative learning? Such a model could prefigure a networked globe where individual competition is replaced by collaborative cognition, social division of manual and mental labor is superceded by equal intellectual access and private ownership of socially created ideas succumbs to unfettered sharing.

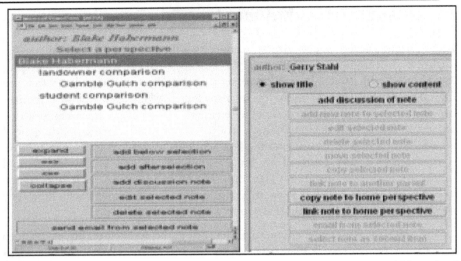

Figure 5. Two attempts to structure classroom practices. Left: in the middle school, students were only allowed to display their personal perspective or comparison perspective for groups to which they belonged. Right: in the graduate seminar, when students were not working in their personal perspective they were limited to adding simple discussion notes or copying information back into their personal perspective.

Conclusion

It has become a cliché that computer mediation has the potential to revolutionize communication just as the printing press did long ago. However, the real lesson in this analogy is that widespread literacy involved slow changes in skills and practices to take advantage of the technological affordances. Culture and technology co-evolved dramatically; the transition from orality to literacy involved a radical change in how the world thinks and works (Ong, 1998). Although social as well as technical changes can be propagated much faster now, it is still necessary to gradually evolve suitable mixes of practices and systems to support the move from predominantly individual, paper-based construction of knowledge to a new level of collaborative, Web-based cognition. This will involve the refinement of software support systems that are sophisticated, specialized and flexible, yet capable of becoming transparent in skilled practice. The design of such software will involve extended research into issues such as those raised in this paper.

Acknowledgments

The WebGuide research has been a collaboration of the author with Rogerio dePaula and other L^{3}D members, Ted Habermann and his group at NOAA, Dan Kowal and his middle school students, the participants in the WebGuide seminar, Thomas Herrmann and his students at Dortmund and the researchers in the ICS "Articulate Learners" project. The work reported here was supported in part by grants from NSF IRI-9711951, the McDonnell Foundation and NSF EAR-9870934.

References

Boland, R. J., & Tenkasi, R. V. (1995). Perspective making and perspective taking in communities of knowing. *Organization Science, 6*(4), 350-372.

Buckingham Shum, S., & Hammond, N. (1994). Argumentation-based design rationale: What use at what cost? *International Journal of Human-Computer Studies, 40*(4), 603-652.

dePaula, R. (1998). *Computer support for collaborative learning: Understanding practices and technology adoption.* Unpublished Masters Thesis, Telecommunications Department, University of Colorado, Boulder, CO.

Fischer, G., Nakakoji, K., Ostwald, J., Stahl, G., & Sumner, T. (1993). *Embedding computer-based critics in the contexts of design.* Paper presented at the Conference on Human Factors in Computing Systems (INTERChi '93), Amsterdam, Holland. Retrieved from http://www.cis.drexel.edu/faculty/gerry/publications/conferences/1990-1997/chi93/CHI93.html.

Halasz, F. G. (1988). Reflections on notecards: Seven issues for the next generation of hypermedia systems. *Communications of the ACM, 31*(7), 836-852.

Hewitt, J., Scardamalia, M., & Webb, J. (1998). *Situative design issues for interactive learning environments,* from http://csile.oise.on.ca/abstracts/situ_design

Koschmann, T., Ostwald, J., & Stahl, G. (1998). *Shouldn't we really be studying practice? [panel position paper].* Paper presented at the International Conference on the Learning Sciences (ICLS '98), Atlanta, GA. Retrieved from http://www.cis.drexel.edu/faculty/gerry/publications/conferences/1998/icls98/ICLS Workshop.html.

Ong, W. (1998). *Orality and literacy: The technologizing of the world.* New York, NY: Routledge.

Scardamalia, M., & Bereiter, C. (1991). Higher levels of agency in knowledge building: A challenge for the design of new knowledge media. *Journal of the Learning Sciences, 1,* 37-68.

Scardamalia, M., & Bereiter, C. (1996). Computer support for knowledge-building communities. In T. Koschmann (Ed.), *CSCL: Theory and practice of an emerging paradigm* (pp. 249-268). Hillsdale, NJ: Lawrence Erlbaum Associates.

Stahl, G. (1993). *Supporting situated interpretation.* Paper presented at the Annual Meeting of the Cognitive Science Society (CogSci '93), Boulder, CO. Retrieved from http://www.cis.drexel.edu/faculty/gerry/publications/conferences/1990-1997/cogsci93/CogSci.html.

Stahl, G., Sumner, T., & Owen, R. (1995). Share globally, adapt locally: Software to create and distribute student-centered curriculum. *Computers and Education. Special Issue on Education and the Internet, 24*(3), 237-246. Retrieved from http://www.cis.drexel.edu/faculty/gerry/publications/journals/c&e/.

Stahl, G. (1999). WebGuide: *Guiding collaborative learning on the web with perspectives.* Paper presented at the Annual Conference of the American Educational Research Association (AERA '99), Montreal, Canada. Retrieved from http://www.cis.drexel.edu/faculty/gerry/publications/conferences/1999/aera99/.

Stahl, G., & Herrmann, T. (1999). *Intertwining perspectives and negotiation.* Paper presented at the International Conference on Supporting Group Work (Group '99), Phoenix, AZ. Retrieved from http://www.cis.drexel.edu/faculty/gerry/publications/conferences/1999/group99/group99.pdf.

Stahl, G. (2000). Collaborative information environments to support knowledge construction by communities. *AI & Society, 14*, 1-27. Retrieved from http://www.cis.drexel.edu/faculty/gerry/publications/journals/ai&society/.

Vygotsky, L. (1930/1978). *Mind in society.* Cambridge, MA: Harvard University Press.

11. Intertwining Perspectives and Negotiation

Cooperative work typically involves both individual and group activities. Computer support for perspectives allows people to view and work in a central information repository within personal contexts. However, work in personal perspectives encourages divergent thinking. Negotiation in group perspectives is needed to converge on consensus, shared understanding and cooperation. Negotiation processes on their own can delay progress. By intertwining perspective and negotiation mechanisms, individual results can be systematically merged into a group product while work continues. Personal perspectives on shared information are thereby intertwined and merged into a shared group understanding. WebGuide is a prototype system that integrates perspective and negotiation mechanisms; its user interface has been mocked up in detail to work out the many issues involved. We have begun to use partial implementations of WebGuide to support cooperative intellectual work in small research groups.

Support for Individual and Group Perspectives

The World Wide Web (the Web) provides an obvious medium for cooperative work. However, it provides no support for the interplay of individual and group understanding that drives collaboration. First, we need ways to find and work with information that matches our needs, interests and capabilities. Then we need means for bringing our individual knowledge together to build a shared understanding and cooperative products.

In this paper, we explore the possibility of providing computer support for intertwining perspectives in cooperative work by means of an integrated system of perspective and negotiation mechanisms.

Our approach combines previous research we conducted individually on computer support for perspectives [23] and for negotiation [10, 11]. The term *perspective* means that a particular, restricted segment of an information repository is being considered, stored, categorized and annotated. Computer support for perspectives allows people in a group to interact with a shared, global information source; everyone views and maintains their own perspective on the information without interfering with content displayed in the perspectives of other group members. The problem is that perspectives of group members tend to diverge instead of converging as work proceeds.

Computer support for *negotiation* provides a solution to the divergence of ideas in different perspectives by allowing members of a group to communicate about what information to include as mutually acceptable. The problem with negotiation is that it delays work on information while potentially lengthy negotiations are underway. Here, perspectives provide a solution, allowing work to continue within personal perspectives while the contents of shared perspectives are being negotiated.

We believe that perspectives and negotiation are each important CSCW concepts in their own right, but that when combined they can offset each other's major weaknesses and provide powerful support for using shared information sources. We propose an approach to intertwining the mechanisms of perspectives and negotiation to help cooperative groups intertwine the personal perspectives of their members into an effective shared network of perspectives on task-relevant information. Our proposal is based on the normative standpoint that even in the case of distant and asynchronous cooperation people should have a chance to contribute to the convergence of their ideas.

The first section of this paper characterizes perspective and negotiation mechanisms that the authors developed independently in the past, followed by a section on related work to differentiate our approach from others. CSCW approaches often deal with the problem of joint editing of a shared document by several users and the subsequent merging of different versions. By contrast, in our approach many short segments (from selected and inherited individual perspectives) are dynamically extracted from a shared information source and intertwined to construct personal and team perspectives.

The paper's third section describes a student research project that helped us to define the requirements for computer support of this kind of cooperative work. This motivated the design of **WebGuide**, a prototype system that is then described in some detail. The paper concludes with current work – introducing our software into classrooms and small research groups for testing its use – and future work to evaluate its effectiveness.

Previous Work on Perspectives and Negotiation

This paper integrates two previously independent approaches: collaboration using perspectives and negotiation of shared information.

Perspectives

The most important characteristics of Stahl's [23] perspective mechanism are:

- Individual team members have access to what appears to be their own information source. This is called their *personal perspective*. It consists of items from a shared central information repository that are tagged as being visible within that particular perspective (or in any perspective inherited by that perspective).

- Team member A can integrate an item from B's perspective into her personal perspective by creating a *virtual copy* of the item. If B modifies the original item, then it changes in A's perspective as well. However, if A modifies the item, a new item is actually created for A, so that B's perspective is not changed. This arrangement generally makes sense because A wants to view (or inherit) B's item, even if it evolves. However, B should not be affected by the actions of someone who copied one of B's items.

- Alternatively, team member A can *physically copy* the contents of an item from B's perspective. In this case, the copies are not linked to each other in any way. Since A and B are viewing physically distinct items now, either can make changes without affecting the other's perspective.

- When A creates a virtual copy of an item from B's perspective, A can decide if she will also get virtual copies of items related to that one or if she will create her own sub-network for her copy of that item. Arbitrarily large sub-networks of information can be inherited with no overhead in time or memory using the virtual copy mechanism.

- Items of information can be created, edited or deleted by users within their own personal perspective without affecting the work of others.

- New perspectives can be created by users. Perspectives can inherit from existing perspectives. Thus, a team perspective can be created that includes virtual copies of all contents of the inherited perspectives of the team members. There is an inheritance tree of perspectives; descendants inherit the contents of their ancestor perspectives. Changes (additions, edits, deletions) in the ancestor are seen in descendent perspectives, but not vice versa. A hierarchy of team, sub-team and individual perspectives can be built to match the needs of a particular application.

This model of perspectives has the important advantage of letting team members copy the content of their team's perspective and other information sources without having to generate it from scratch. They can then experiment with this content on their own without worrying about affecting what others see. This is advantageous as long as one only wants to use someone else's information to develop one's own perspective. It has frequently been noted in computer science literature [5, 8] that different stakeholders engaged in the development and use of a system (e.g., designers, testers, marketing, management, end-users) always think about and judge issues from different perspectives and that these differences must be taken into account.

However, if one wants to influence the content of other team members' perspectives, then this approach is limited because one cannot change someone else's content directly. It is of course important for supporting cooperative work that the perspectives maintain at least a partial overlap of their contents in order to reach successful mutual understanding and coordination. The underlying subjective opinions must be intertwined to establish intersubjective understanding [9, 25].

Negotiation

The concept of computer-mediated negotiation addresses the problem of making changes to a system design or an information repository when the changes may conflict with the interests of others. Such a change must first be proposed by someone. The same software that is used to prepare and propose the change should also inform the people affected and help them to respond to the proposal. According to Herrmann [10], the following options for voting and discussion should be offered: Accept, reject or modify the proposal. Furthermore, the proposal can be accepted until revoked or the computer-supported negotiation process can be interrupted in order to discuss the matter face-to-face, through telephone inquiry or in other ways of more direct communication. Each of the above options can be accompanied by commenting on the choice.

This concept of negotiation was originally developed within the context of software design for situations in which two users of a computer system discuss whether a system feature should be implemented or not. The approach was intended to support "controllability" and "suitability for individualization" (cf. ISO 9234, Part 10) for groupware. Such negotiation can take place in multiple cycles of a proposer and a responder reacting to each other. Negotiation rules must be established to define how many negotiation cycles can take place, how much time is allowed to pass before a decision must be reached, what happens when a time limit is reached, etc. The goal of this negotiation mechanism is to get through routine cases of agreement, abstention or simple modifications of proposals as quickly as possible in order to determine efficiently which proposals require a more intensive communication process. This provides a common starting point from which cooperation can proceed.

A disadvantage of this negotiation mechanism is that it was designed for just two people. If applied to several participants, the time for arriving at a common starting point stretches out too much. The original negotiation concept assumed that a modified item would not be worked on further until the negotiation process was complete. This might make sense in the case of a change of software system functionality, but it seems unduly restrictive for modifications of information and analysis. By contrast, the approach of intertwining multiple perspectives into a common one has the advantage that participants can continue to work in their own perspective while awaiting the results of negotiations. This allows the negotiation mechanism to be extended from pairs of participants to small groups.

Related Work

This work builds on ideas from a variety of CSCW approaches.

Hypertext and Hypermedia.

Hypertext and hypermedia structures provide an important mechanism for supporting cooperative work with shared materials. To some extent, this is now provided by the Web itself, although many hypertext mechanisms have been explored that go beyond the Web's simple model [2]. The perspectives mechanism of Stahl [23] is a hypermedia implementation, based on a node and link structure; relationships among contents in different perspectives are defined by links. Internal manipulation of nodes and links allows multiple perspectives to share large information sources without unnecessary duplication. The use of "virtual copying" or "delta storage" is well known in system software [7], but was not previously used in CSCW hypermedia systems. We have chosen to implement our own hypermedia substrate – rather then use something like Lotus Notes – for reasons of granularity, control and speed.

Context Mechanisms

The importance of perspectives in cooperative work has been recognized at a theoretical level by Boland [5] and others, primarily based on the hermeneutic tradition in philosophy: Heidegger and Gadamer (see [23]). The application of virtual copying to perspectives on data was explored at Xerox PARC [4], but abandoned as too complicated for users at that time. A related mechanism of *transclusion* was proposed by Nelson [16] for hypertext. McCall applied a similar approach for organizing hypertext information by domain and version in Phidias [15]. Stahl [23] extended McCall's approach in Hermes, implementing a hypertext version of virtual copying in a productivity tool for professional design teams. He subsequently adapted this mechanism in CIE, a cooperative information environment for supporting peer group management of ISO 9000 documentation [22].

Computer Supported Collaborative Learning

A number of software systems have been developed to support collaboration of research teams in schools; CSCL [13] has become an important new research direction within CSCW. CSILE [19], for instance, is a threaded discussion system customized to scaffold classroom research. Systems like CoVis [17] and CaMILLE [21] also provide a shared workspace or notebook area for collecting research results. Rather than supporting negotiation through the system, they rely on face-to-face interactions to make choices about what materials get entered into the team repository. The prototypes of WebGuide are intended to demonstrate how current CSCL systems – which lack explicit representations of perspectives – can be enhanced.

Organizational Memories

By organizational memories we mean an approach to building a structured digital library of various forms of information that can be shared by community members through computer supported collaboration and communication mechanisms [1, 14]. Intertwined perspectives can help to structure an organizational memory. For instance, when a group of community members undertakes a new project they can create a new perspective on the memory and negotiate which items from existing perspectives should be included for use in the new project.

Collaborative Filtering

Collaborative filtering (e.g. GroupLens, [18]) is typical of approaches that try to automate the construction of perspectives. It displays available information in accordance with individual or team preferences. Statistical analyses are used to automatically determine which members of a group are interested in similar topics. Items of information that are of interest to one member are then sent to other group members with similar interests. Rather than relying entirely on automated mechanisms, WebGuide allows active selection or modification of information by users.

Conflict Management

The above approaches lack any computer supported negotiation mechanisms. Wulf [27] proposed the support of negotiation and developed it for conflict management in groupware. Wulf focuses on negotiation between two persons and he distinguishes various ways in which a groupware user can avoid or reduce the effects of another user's actions. However, we believe that it should always be possible for users to react to each other, at least by commenting. Ideally, these reactions back and forth should take place with support from the same system that presents the content under discussion.

Decision and Meeting Support

The clearest parallels to computer-supported negotiation are decision support and meeting support systems. In these systems, one can respond to proposals from others by extending them with one's own proposals or amendments. One can also annotate the proposals. In more elaborate systems, such as those derived from Argnoter [24], annotations can be classified as pro or con the argument. Several systems keep track of votes for or against a proposal [6]. Sen, et al. [20] describe an application of this for meeting scheduling. Our negotiation mechanism emphasizes the possibility of continuing the work on a perspective before the decision process is completed.

Due to space limitations, we cannot compare our work with approaches that are focused on synchronous collaboration and WYSIWIS problems or deal with merging and access mechanisms in the field of joint editing. As pointed out above, these approaches are related to another type of problem where the shared information is relatively limited and can be described by a small set of document versions.

The WebGuide Design

This section recounts the motivation and history of the design of our integration of perspective and negotiation CSCW mechanisms. It discusses a context in which future researchers are being taught how to engage in cooperative work and how to use computer technologies to support their work.

Supporting Cooperative Student Web Research

In summer 1997 we decided to apply our vision of intertwining perspectives and negotiation to a situation in middle school (6th grade, 12 year olds) classrooms we work with. The immediate presenting problem was that students could not keep track of Web site URLs they found during their Web research. The larger issue was how to support team projects. The more we discussed computer support for cooperative student Web research, the more complicated and detailed the issues became.

To facilitate our own collaboration we adopted two representations: (1) the design of a detailed user interface using HTML and (2) a formal model of the software procedures, data elements and context of use. You will see both representations below. The result of our collaboration is (1) an interface design for **WebGuide**, a Web-based prototype that integrates perspective and negotiation mechanisms to support collaborative learning and (2) a model of such a system in use. To make our design concrete, we focused on a project-based curriculum [3] on ancient civilizations of Latin America used at the school. The example of this student research project is well suited to illustrate the level of complexity that our approach can and must handle.

WebGuide was first conceived of as a glorified Web bookmark manager [12] and electronic notebook application [26], enhanced with perspective and negotiation mechanisms as described below. Students can conduct Web searches, collect, annotate, categorize and organize bookmarks for sites they like. They can summarize or excerpt the Web page contents (there is no need to copy the full contents because it is already available through the active bookmarks). Students are encouraged to use the facilities of **WebGuide** to make the results of their research more self-explanatory for themselves and their teammates by defining a hierarchy of headings or categories, arranging bookmarks under these and adding concise summaries of the content or importance of the bookmarked sites.

Figure 1. Part of Kay's personal perspective.

Figure 1 shows a view of a student's personal perspective in WebGuide. There are three topics visible in this view. Within each topic are short subheadings or comments, as well as Web bookmarks and search queries. At the bottom is access to search engines.

Varieties of Information

In compiling a list of requirements for WebGuide, we focused on how computer support can help structure the merging of individual results. Such support should begin early and continue throughout the research process. It should scaffold and facilitate the decision-making process so that students can learn how to build consensus. WebGuide combines displays of individual work with the emerging group view. Note that the topic on Aztec Religion in Figure 1 has been proposed by another student to be part of the team perspective. Kay has made a virtual copy of Que's topic so she can keep track of his work related to her topic. The third topic is an idea that Kay is preparing to work on herself. Within her electronic workspace she inherits information from other perspectives along with her own work.

Each student should be able to view the work of other team members as they work on it, not just when it is submitted to the team. Students should be able to adopt individual items from the work of other students into their own perspective, in order to start the collaboration and integration process. This can be done with the comparison perspective (see Figure 2). From early on, they should be able to make proposals for moving specific items from their personal perspective (or from the perspective of another) into the team perspective, which will eventually represent their team product, the integration of all their work.

The Web pages of a student's personal perspective should not only contain live link bookmarks and search queries, but also categories, comments, notes and summaries authored by the student. All these elements are representations of what we have abstractly called "items" of information. Comments can optionally be attached to any information item. Every item is tagged with the name of the person who created or last modified it. Items are also labeled with perspective information and time stamps.

The requirement that items of information can be copied, modified and rearranged presupposes that information can be collected and presented in small pieces. This is also necessary for negotiating which pieces should be accepted, modified or deleted.

In addition to bookmarks, the WebGuide page can contain Web search queries for finding current sites on a given topic. WebGuide is designed to help students learn to do Web research and the sharing of successful query formulations is important for that. WebGuide pages are structured by topic headings or categories for organizing the bookmarks and queries. These categories can initially be created without any bookmarks or queries as preparation for looking for relevant information, as Kay has done for the topics of Mexico City and Live Sacrifice (in Figure 1) that she intends to research. The categories are structured hierarchically to create a tree of information.

Because of the hierarchical nature of items, something that appears as a unit of information that can be proposed for negotiation may actually consist of many parts, some of which appear differently in different students' perspectives. The possibility of information items having a complex but hidden internal structure is required for the intertwining of perspectives and negotiation.

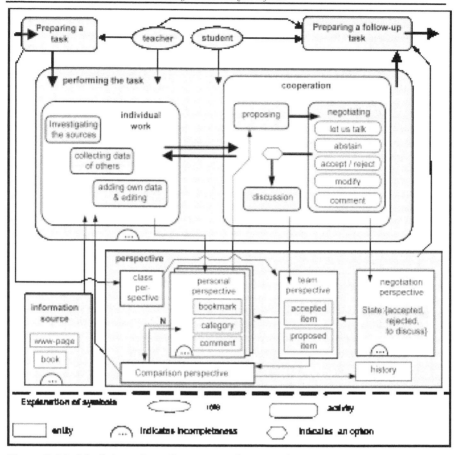

Figure 2. Model of the task performance and perspectives.

Types of Perspectives

WebGuide provides six types of perspectives to help students compile their individual and joint research (Figure 2 shows how they are related to each other and to the activities):

- The student's *personal perspective* is their private workspace. It inherits a view of everything in the team perspective. Thus, it displays the owner's own work within the context of items proposed or negotiated by the team and class – as modified by the student. Students can each modify (add, edit, delete, rearrange, link) their virtual copies of team items in their personal perspectives. They can also create completely new material there.

- The *team perspective* contains both items that have already been accepted by the team and items that are currently proposed for negotiation (like the Aztec religion topic in Figure 1). This perspective is pivotal. It includes accepted and proposed items. It gradually collects the products of the team efforts.

- The *class perspective* is created by the teacher to start each team off with some initial bookmarks and suggested topics. It typically presents a structure for classroom activities and provides the space used to instantiate the goal of collecting the products of cooperative intellectual work. It has the organizational function of structuring the team perspective.

- The *comparison perspective* combines all the personal perspectives of team members and the team perspective, so that anyone can compare all the work that is going on. It inherits from the personal, team and class perspectives. Students can go here to get ideas and copy items into their own personal perspective or propose items for the team perspective.

- The *negotiation perspective* contains all the information related to the current status of negotiation on the items proposed for the team perspective. It inherits proposed items from the team perspective. When they are approved or rejected at the end of negotiation, their status in the team perspective changes. It has the organizational function of making the process of negotiation more comprehensible.

- The *history perspective* is an archive of all information that has been entered in **WebGuide**. It is primarily for the teacher (or researchers), but can also be used by students to retrieve previous versions of items. It inherits from the comparison perspective, which contains information from all the other perspectives.

Of course, there is not really such a multiplicity of information in the central database. The perspectives mechanism merely displays the information differently in the different perspectival Web pages, in accordance with the relations of inheritance. Organizational information as well as content are represented in a consistent way by using the perspectives mechanism.

Practices and Perspectives

To design software for collaborative learning in schools means to design curriculum and classroom process as well. Computer support has to be matched with appropriate content on the Web and with a constructivist pedagogy [19]. The design of the WebGuide interface and the perspective and negotiation mechanisms is accompanied by the design of informative Web pages and of a use scenario.

Figure 2 shows a model of the process involving the teacher, the students and tasks using WebGuide. It shows the relation of individual to cooperative work and the mediating roles of the perspective and negotiation processes.

The model in Figure 2 represents the process flows. Students research using sources available to them: the Web, books, encyclopedia, CD-ROM, discussions or other sources. Students can review the contents of the class perspective, their team perspective and the personal perspectives of their teammates. All of these contents are collected in the comparison perspective, where they are labeled by their perspective of origin. Students extract from the research those items that are of interest to them. Then they organize and develop the data they have collected by categorizing, summarizing, labeling and annotating. The three stages of investigating, collecting and editing can be repeated as many times as necessary.

To support these steps of the work, WebGuide provides a menu of functionality for each information item. The following menu options are included: show/hide detail, Add a new item, Move this item, Edit this item's text, Delete item, Copy to my perspective, Propose to team and Negotiate this item.

The class project ends with each team producing an organized Web site about one of the civilizations. These Web sites can be used by members of the other teams to learn about the civilizations that they did not personally research. The sites can also provide a basis for additional class projects, like narrative reports and physical displays. Finally, this year's research products can be used to create next year's class perspective starting point, so new researchers can pick up where the previous generation left off – within a World Wide Web that will have evolved substantially in the meantime.

Negotiation Procedures

A student can make proposals for the team perspective from the Propose to team option within his or her personal perspective. This is how new items get introduced into the team perspective. A student can also propose an item from someone else's perspective by locating it in the comparison perspective. If she wishes to modify it, she can first copy it into her own perspective. If someone wishes to modify an item that is already in the team perspective, she must copy it into her own perspective, make the modifications there and then propose the modified item.

It should be possible when proposing – just as with copying – to treat a set of related items in one step. It is important to be able to treat a set of proposed changes together. For example, if a student deletes a bookmark at one spot in order to replace it with a better, richer bookmark elsewhere, then the deletion and the replacement should both be proposed and negotiated together. Of course, students should be discouraged from grouping too many items together.

When a student selects the Propose to team menu option for an item, a dialog box opens (see Figure 3). The student can decide whether the new proposal item should be combined with a previous or future proposal. The proposer also sees a list of all the other students who will be involved in the negotiation of the item. The determination of who should be involved is a matter for installation settings that define a local negotiation policy. These settings are system parameters of WebGuide, so they can be easily varied by teachers or research user communities.

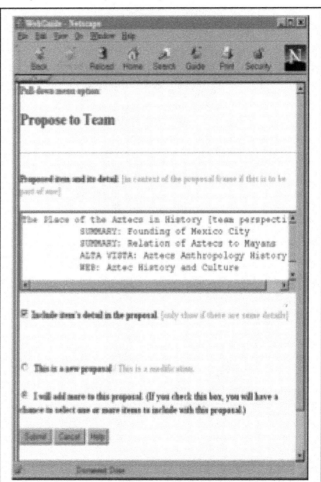

Figure 3. A dialog for proposing an item for negotiation.

For example, one might want to establish a rule that all new items must be negotiated by all team members – or alternatively that they do not require negotiation at all – while modified items require just those people to participate who either originally created the item or subsequently modified it. Another plausible rule would be to accept all annotations without negotiation.

As soon as an item is proposed, it appears in the negotiation perspective. Through perspective inheritance, it also appears in the team perspective and in the personal perspective of all team members, labeled as Proposed by name-of-proposer. A student can select the Negotiate this item menu option for the item to switch to the negotiation perspective for that item.

There are three windows (see Figure 4). The top window includes buttons corresponding to the negotiation options: Accept, Reject, Abstain and Let's talk. The second window displays the proposed item or items within the context they would have in the team perspective once accepted. The bottom window contains the results of negotiation decisions already made about the proposal and the commentary of team members concerning these decisions. No editing of the proposal is allowed in the negotiation or team perspective.

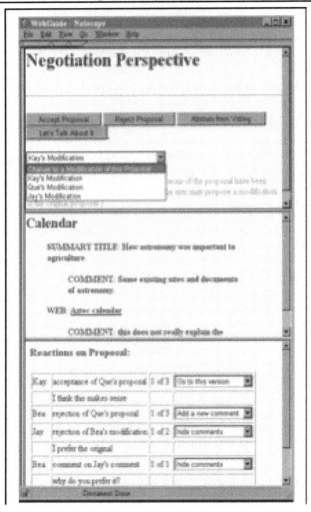

Figure 4. The Negotiation Perspective.

Several negotiation responses to the proposal are possible at this point. A negotiator can indicate that she abstains, that she does not care to participate in the negotiation. Alternatively, she could indicate with "Let's talk" that she would like to discuss the proposal face-to-face in the team. In the later case, the label on the proposed item changes to Proposed by name-of-proposer, Let's talk. In addition, an automatically maintained agenda of points for group discussion is extended to include this proposal.

Of course, the primary options are to Accept or Reject the proposal. It should be noted that a proposal can have been modified by other group members so that there may be several versions of the same proposal. If Accept is selected for one alternative, then all the others are assigned Reject and the negotiation is over for that student. If Reject is selected, then the next version of the proposal is displayed. When several versions are available, a student can either accept precisely one or reject them all.

After making a negotiation decision, a student should comment on the reasoning behind her response. All students who view the negotiation perspective after that can see her response with her comment. Although it may not be sensible in a negotiation situation involving several participants to allow cycles of responses to responses because the negotiation process would quickly become too confusing, WebGuide does allow students (and teachers) to comment on all actions, including comments on comments. This allows a simple kind of threaded discussion. Even after a student has completed her voting on a proposal she can comment on other people's choices or change her vote.

The procedure for amending a proposal is a bit involved. Once a student has rejected all the existing versions of a proposal, she can modify (see Figure 2) the proposal in her personal perspective and propose her amended version. This is how more than one version of a single proposal can become part of the negotiation perspective. Then the new version will be automatically integrated into the negotiation process of the original proposal. The label of the proposed item will be altered to read, Proposed by name-of-first-proposer amended by name-of-second-proposer. Students who have already voted will see this new label and can decide if they want to return to the negotiation perspective and reconsider their vote on this proposal. It might also make sense to have a more intrusive mechanism to alert people to newly proposed versions. The design decision to restrict modifications this way in the negotiation process results in a simplification of the process. To avoid confusion, it is only possible to edit the original proposal, not proposals that already have the label amended. While a proposal can be rejected by its original proposer when she prefers an alternative version, it cannot be recalled because that would create an asymmetry between the proposer and other participants.

The negotiation process for a proposal cannot exceed a time limit, determined by the negotiation policy parameters. At the end of the time period, the system determines whether the proposal or a modified version is accepted or rejected. Again, installation parameters determine what kind of majority is required: 2/3 of those voting, majority of those eligible, simple majority, etc. If the results are indecisive, the proposal will be labeled proposed for talk and added to the discussion agenda. Then students will have to get together in the classroom and decide what to do about the proposal. When matters are decided in group meetings, someone with a special password can enter changes directly in the team perspective, short-cutting the computer-supported negotiation process.

WebGuide in Practice

Cooperative Definition of Keywords for a Bibliographic Database

The concept of intertwining perspectives and negotiation is a general one which can be tailored to fit many cooperative work domains. For instance, we have experimented with the negotiation procedures described above in a system for use by academic researchers who share a collaborative on-line bibliography. This system was implemented and used in our research center at the University of Dortmund. The system is based on **WebGuide** mechanisms and functions.

We started with a literature database that was created in 1988 for our research group. It originally contained about 500 entries. The literary references were classified according to their content using a set of about 50 keywords. The database quickly grew to about 3,000 entries indexed by 200 keywords. The quality of the system deteriorated with this growth: it accumulated duplicate and outdated entries, many entries were inadequately indexed and the keywords became overlapping and outdated as well. A clear need for convergence could be empirically observed.

To address these problems, we created an experimental new system. Each member of the research group was given their own perspective on the database of entries and keywords; they are now responsible for maintaining the information they are interested in. Information they are interested in but do not want to maintain themselves they can access by virtual links to other perspectives. All literary references and keywords that one considers important for the team can be proposed for the team perspective and negotiated.

Consider the following use scenario: Andy browses the comparison perspective and finds an interesting keyword, K_1, from Barbara. He makes a virtual copy of it in his personal perspective. Andy can now use the keyword to retrieve all entries that are classified with it. However, before Andy can use K_1 himself to classify a new entry, he must make a physical copy of it ($K_1 K_2$). This will protect Barbara from being affected by Andy's classification activities. If Andy had continued to use a virtual copy of K_1 then he would retrieve not only his own but also Barbara's classifications of K_1 when he did a search for K_1. Andy can also introduce a new keyword, K_3 and propose it to his team if he thinks it is an important keyword. Even while his team is negotiating the acceptance of this keyword and can already begin to classify references using K_3. If and when K_3 is accepted by the team, all the references that had been classified with K₃ will be automatically proposed for acceptance in the team perspective for negotiation, one at a time.

This prototype system has been explored by a team of six researchers working cooperatively on various projects. Based on these trials, the following principles were proposed as preconditions for regular use of such a system:

- In order to reduce the complexity and the burden of excessive negotiation processes, negotiation should only take place when a new entry is proposed to the team, when the classification of an entry by a keyword is to be changed or when a keyword itself is being altered. All other changes should simply be accepted automatically without negotiation.

- There should be system functionality to notify team members when a new keyword is introduced (even in a personal perspectives), when someone creates a virtual link to a keyword and when someone makes a new proposal.

- Proposals make sense not only at the team perspective level; it is also useful for one team member to propose a new item to another team member.

- It should be possible to define sub-team perspectives to represent the interests of small research units and projects.

Negotiating Environmental Perspectives

We are now using an early implementation of WebGuide in a middle school classroom in Denver. (See Figure 5 for a screen image of this Java applet running on the Web). For the past five years, this class of students researched the environmental damage done to mountain streams by "acid mine drainage" from deserted gold mines in the Rocky Mountains above Denver. They actually solved the problem at the source of a stream coming into Boulder from the Gamble Gulch mine site. In 1998/99 they investigated the broader ramifications of their past successes, looking at the issue of acid mine drainage from various alternative perspectives. They interviewed adult mentors to get opinions from specific perspectives: environmental, governmental, mine owners, local residents, scientists, etc.

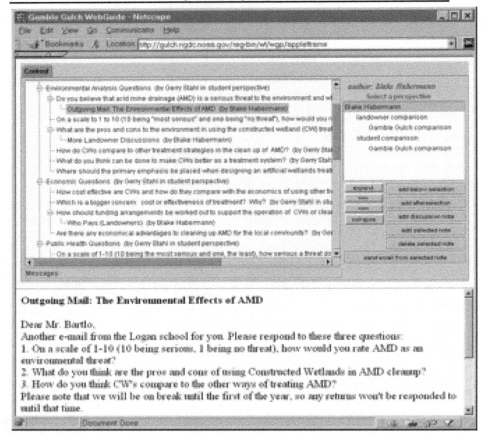

Figure 5. WebGuide for negotiating environmental perspectives.

WebGuide serves as the medium through which the students cooperatively research these issues with their mentors and with each other. Each student and mentor has their personal perspective and these perspectives inherit from the content-based perspectives (environmental protection, governmental regulation, etc.) depending upon which intellectual perspective they are working on constructing. Even email interactions happen through WebGuide and are retained as notes in its perspectives. The goal of the yearlong course is not only to negotiate within teams to construct the various positions, but also to negotiate among the positions to reach consensus or clarify differences.

As an initial field testing of the WebGuide system, this trial has resulted in valuable experience in the practicalities of deploying such a sophisticated program to young students over the Web. The students are enthusiastic users of the system and offer many ideas for improvements to the interface and the functionality. Consequently, WebGuide is benefiting from rapid cycles of participatory design. One main result is that the possibilities of achieving convergence of the contributions have to be improved. It proved to be a serious lack that this early version of WebGuide did not provide support for negotiation. The ideas of the students diverged within WebGuide and the teacher had to bring them together and build a consensus during face-to-face class discussions.

Constructing Perspectives on CSCL

An interdisciplinary graduate seminar on computer mediation of collaborative learning is also using WebGuide in several ways during 1999:

- As a communication medium for their internal cooperation.

- As an example CSCL system to analyze.

- As an electronic workspace for them to construct their individual and shared ideas.

This version of WebGuide stresses the use of perspectives for structuring collaborative efforts to construct shared knowledge.

Students in the class can form sub-groups either within or across their different disciplines. They develop ideas in their personal perspectives and then debate these ideas in the various comparison perspectives of their sub-groups. Here, it is an important result that the comparison perspectives are directly used to conduct a kind of pre-negotiation process. This helps to determine which notes are promoted to the class or team perspective.

A major hypothesis being explored by the course is that the use of a shared persistent information space can support more complex discussions than ephemeral face-to-face conversations.

Future Work

WebGuide is currently under intensive development and testing. Now that we have initial demos of our concept, we are engaging in participatory design with teachers, students and research groups to refine the approach. Initial evaluation of some of its concepts will be conducted in middle school, high school, college and graduate classrooms in Boulder, Colorado. We will investigate how different features are used in practice. For instance: Do students move fluidly and effectively among the different perspectives? To what extent do students group related proposals together? How much do students comment on their negotiation decisions or on those of others? Can students handle the process of modifying proposals? We will also explore different negotiation policy parameters: What happens to proposals that just one or two students slate for group discussion? What time limits, voting methods, negotiation participation rules are meaningful and effective?

In parallel with the testing of WebGuide in Colorado, the system will be used in courses at the University of Dortmund. In these courses, future teachers in various disciplines will be trained in the fundamentals of computer technology and its use in the classroom. These teachers-in-training will gain both theoretical knowledge and practical experience through their work with WebGuide.

The system for cooperative use of the bibliographic database described above will be developed further and used on a more regular basis. Thereby, we will explore whether the concepts there can also be applied to support organizational memories. As more of the WebGuide functionality is implemented and deployed in a variety of CSCW and CSCL applications, we will see how effective the intertwining of perspectives and negotiation can be.

Acknowledgements

The research reported here was begun during a six month visit by Herrmann to Boulder in 1997. It is being continued by Herrmann and his students at Dortmund, Stahl and his students, Ted Habermann and his group at NOAA, Dan Kowal and his middle school students and the researchers, teachers and students in the "Articulate Learners" project. The work reported here is supported in part by grants from NSF IRI-9711951, the McDonnell Foundation and NSF EAR-9870934.

References

Ackerman, M. S. (1994) Augmenting the organizational memory: A field study of Answer Garden. In: Proceedings of CSCW '94, ACM Press, 243-252.

Bieber, M., Vitali, F., Ashman, H., Balasubramanian, V., Oinas-Kukkonen, H. (1997) Fourth generation hypermedia: Some missing links for the World Wide Web. *International Journal of Human-Computer Studies*. Special issue on HCI & the Web.

Blumenfeld, P., Soloway, E., Marx, R., Krajcik, J., Guzdial, M., Palincsar, A. (1991) Motivating project-based learning: Sustaining the doing, supporting the learning. *Educational Psychologist*. 26, 369-398.

Bobrow, D. & Goldstein, I. (1980) *An experimental description-based programming environment: Four reports.* Technical Report CSL-81-3. Palo Alto, CA: Xerox Palo Alto Research Center.

Boland, R. J. & Tenkasi, R. V. (1995) Perspective making and perspective taking in communities of knowing. *Organization Science. 6*, 4, 350-372.

Ephrati, E., Zlotkin, G., Rosenschein, J. (1994) Meet your destiny: A non-manipulable meeting scheduler. In: *Proceedings of CSCW '94.* ACM Press. 359-371.

Fitzgerald F., Rashid R. (1986) The integration of virtual memory management and interprocess communication in accent. *ACM Transactions on Computer Systems, 4*, 2, 147-166.

Floyd, C. (1992) Software development and reality construction. In: Floyd, C., Züllinghoven, H., Budde, R., Keil-Slawik, R.. *Software Development and Reality Construction* Springer-Verlag. 86-100.

Habermas, J. (1981) Theorie des kommunikativen Handelns. Band 1. Handlungsrationalität und gesellschaftliche Rationalisierung. Suhrkamp Verlag.

Herrmann, T. (1995) Workflow management systems: Ensuring organizational flexibility by possibilities of adaptation and negotiation. In: *Proceedings of COOCS '95. Conference on Organizational Computing Systems.* ACM Press, 83 - 95.

Herrmann, Th., Wulf,V., Hartmann, A. (1996) Requirements for a Human-centered Design of Groupware; in: Shapiro, D.; Tauber, M.; Traunmüller, R. (eds):Design of Computer Supported Cooperative Work and Groupware Systems, Elsevier, Amsterdam, S. 77 – 100.

Keller, R., Wolfe, S., Chen, J., Rabinowitz, J., Mathe, N. (1997) A bookmarking service for organizing and sharing URLs. In: *Computer Networks and ISDN Systems. 29*, 1103-1114.

Koschmann, T. (ed.) (1996) *CSCL: Theory and Practice.* Lawrence Erlbaum Associates.

Lindstaedt, S., Schneider, K. (1997) Bridging the gap between face-to-face communication and long-term collaboration. In: *Proceedings of the International ACM SigGroup Conference on Supporting Group Work. The Integration Challenge.* ACM Press. 331-340.

McCall, R., Bennett, P., d'Oronzio, P., Ostwald, J., Shipman, F., Wallace, N. (1990) Phidias: Integrating CAD graphics into dynamic hypertext. In: *Proceedings of ECHT '90.* 152-165.

Nelson, T. H. (1981) *Literary Machines.* Mindful Press.

Pea, R. (1993) The collaborative visualization project. *Comm. ACM. 36*, 5, 60-63.

Resnick, P., Iacovou, N., Suchak, M., Bergstrom, P. (1996) GroupLens: An open architecture for collaborative filtering of netnews. In: *Proceedings of CSCW '94.* ACM Press. 175 -186.

Scardemalia, M. & Bereiter, C. (1991) Higher levels of agency for children in knowledge building: A challenge for the design of new knowledge media. *Journal of the Learning Sciences, 1*, 37-68.

Sen, S., Haynes, T., Arora, N. (1997) Satisfying user preferences while negotiating meetings. *Int. J. Human-Computer Studies.* 407-427.

Soloway, E., Guzdial, M., Hay, K. (1994) Learner-centered design: The next challenge for HCI. *ACM Interactions. 1*, 2, 36-48.

Stahl, G. (1996) Personalizing the Web. Available at http://www.cs.colorado.edu/~gerry/publications //techreports/www6/PAPER82.html.

Stahl, G. (1993) *Interpretation in Design: The Problem of Tacit and Explicit Understanding in Computer Support of Cooperative Design*, Chapter 9. Unpublished Ph.D. Dissertation. available at http://www.cs.colorado.edu/~gerry/publications/ dissertations/Ch09.html.

Stefik, M., Foster, D., Bobrow, D.G., Kahn, K., Lanning, S., Suchman, L. (1988) Beyond the chalkboard: Computer support for collaboration and problem solving in meetings. In: Greif, I. (Ed.) *Computer-Supported Cooperative Work.* 335-366.

Tomasello, M., Kruger, A.C., Ratner, H. (1993) Cultural learning. *Behavioral and Brain Sciences.* 495-552.

Torrance, M. (1995) Active notebook: A personal and group productivity tool for managing information. In: *Proc. AAAI Fall Symposium on Artificial Intelligence in Knowledge Navigation and Retrieval.* 131-135.

Wulf, V.(1995): Negotiability: A Metafunction to Handle Access to Data in Groupware; in: Behaviour & Information Technology, Vol. 14, No. 3,,S. 143 – 151.

Part IV: Applications to Health Care, Education and Publishing

12. Reflections on Supporting and Studying Collaborative Team Formation in Post-Cardiac Surgery Care: Lessons of CSCW for Collaborative Care Software Support

The fields of Computer-Supported Cooperative Work (CSCW) and Computer-Supported Collaborative Learning (CSCL) are multidisciplinary research fields that have studied the theory, design, implementation and adoption of software systems that support people in work and educational settings where people interact with each other strongly as part of their central activities. During the past decade, these fields have reached widespread conclusions that contrast dramatically with previous or naive assumptions and approaches. These conclusions have significant implications for any attempt to provide computer support for team approaches in hospital settings. In this section, a number of the main findings will be mentioned that seem particularly *a propos* based on our studies to date. In the following section, a proposal for software development will be sketched that is in accordance with these principles. Finally, a third section will propose the kind of study of the introduction of this system into practice that is indicated as needed by these findings.

Finding 1. Software support often fails

Despite the impressive progress of computerization throughout society, attempts to computerize have failed massively. So many large, custom system development efforts have failed in industry that it has been debated whether the overall corporate benefits have justified the actual expenses. The impressive successes in computer adoption are the result of the widespread use of a small number of fundamentally simple applications: word processing, databases, email, web browsing. These are basically simple applications oriented to individual users and broadly generic. They each started with simple functionality that was gradually expanded by large software developers like Microsoft in response to huge markets and with systematic user studies.

Attempts to develop software for group usage is far more complex than single user applications. CSCW and CSCL have repeatedly documented failures at various levels. Often, attempts at implementation discover that actual available technology is not up to the detailed requirements of appealing designs. Implemented software frequently meets widespread user indifference and even resistance to adoption. When group software is adopted, it can cause unforeseen catastrophic consequences due to the elimination of replaced tacit procedures. The CSCW literature is filled with cautionary tales even though people prefer to advertise successes.

Finding 2. Build one to throw away

The minimal conclusion is that designers should never expect their first implementation to be the final, successful system. The transformation of a "good idea" into usable software is in the best case a non-trivial exploration in which many unanticipated issues are uncovered. The software that results will need to be thrown out and rewritten from scratch based on what was discovered, probably multiple times. The recognition of this conclusion was itself a major shock for the engineering approach to software development. The traditional approach was a "waterfall model" of successive stages that were done sequentially with no thought to returning to a previous stage upstream: concept, design, implementation, testing, user studies, dissemination. The new approach requires cyclical revisions to the concept, design, technology, etc.

Finding 3. User-centered design

The whole field of human-computer interaction (HCI) was established in response to the failure of software development by engineers. HCI is based on a user-centered approach that does not rely on the instincts of engineers (or people with "a good idea") to come up with workable concepts and designs for software, but insists on involving users in the process from the start. The software concept itself should be based on empirical studies of how users work and what their needs are. The field of HCI has come up with a number of techniques for assessing user needs and integrating them into the software development cycle. Unfortunately, few of these techniques address the special and complex needs of software for groups.

Finding 4. It always takes longer, even assuming that

Because the process of transforming an enticing concept into usable software is a highly exploratory process; it is extraordinarily hard to predict the time, effort or cost involved. The more innovative the concept, the more unanticipated findings are likely. It is an underestimation to say that the process always takes longer than imagined, even if one takes into account this principle in estimating.

Finding 5. Study practices and artifact usage

The most important thing is to study carefully how the people you want to support really do their work. A technical trick or "good idea" will not get far. One slogan is "tradition and transcendence": provide software tools that do the same thing that traditional tools and procedures have been doing in the workplace and then consider how the computer support can gradually transcend the old ways. New systems must fit well into the established work-flow or they will not be used. People will need to understand the functionality, purpose and processes of the computerized work based on their largely tacit understanding of current practices. What artifacts and symbols are used now? How will they be taken up and/or replaced in the new system? How will people understand the features of the software as they do their work (not from a manual)? How will life be improved for the people who must actually do the new work?

Finding 6. Design for the socio-cultural context

The larger context must be taken carefully into account. For instance, in a hospital setting, what is the power hierarchy, what are the financial constraints, what are the institutional priorities? What about legal restrictions on sharing patient information? Can users be tracked in how they use the system and is that itself a violation of their privacy? Who has the legal right to see information on patients, on minors, on employees? What are the potential consequences for different people of their putting information, opinions or recommendations in written or electronic format? During many interviews at a hospital we studied, for instance, hospital staff and medical professionals uniformly said they did not use electronic communications to conduct their business because they did not want a persistent record of the kinds of information that they were willing to share face-to-face or on the telephone.

Finding 7. Iterative evolution instead of deductive waterfall

Virtually all system development in CSCL today is conducted as "design-based research." The software design process is tightly integrated with cycles of testing prototypes in realistic settings with groups of users. The idea is to start out with a very simple initial system that groups can readily use and that meets a felt need of theirs. As they use it, researchers study what problems arise and what needs are not met. A next prototype adds some simple functions in direct response to these findings. As cycles of design, implementation and trial take place, the developers gradually learn what works and how to integrate it into the use situation. The software design emerges from this exploratory, user-centered process rather than from some preconception. Of course, a vision of general priorities must guide the process as well – but this is a matter of *what* the software should support, not *how* that should be done.

Finding 8. Build on and extend current practices

Often, if the time for an innovation has really come, some "early adopters" will have already started to explore, however amateurishly, the new potential. The ideal is to work with them, providing missing technical expertise, but leveraging their tacit understanding of what is needed and what might work.

Proposal for Computer Support of Post-Cardiac Collaborative Care

This is a computer support proposal for a post-cardiac patient support system. The central idea is that the system should emerge from an initial combination of (a) a website with health care information for the life-long well-being of people who have had heart surgery along with (b) a peer support online community of former patients and their families, within a context of (c) certification and monitoring of information by trusted health care professionals.

This approach is based on the lessons of CSCW presented above. It also responds to a sense that a more ambitious attempt to design a knowledge management system that met the needs of hospital staff as well as patient families would suffer from at least the following problems:

- It would be a multi-million dollar undertaking requiring years of work

- It would have to be part of the hospital recordkeeping system, which has its own set of priorities and constraints

- It would be subject to unmanageable legal, financial and bureaucratic requirements as part of the hospital administration

- It would be subject to crippling restrictions from governmental privacy regulations and insurance considerations

- It would quickly lose sight of the patient and family needs and be overwhelmed by the complex needs of hospital staff, that are easier to define in terms of functional requirements engineering approaches

- Development of computerized patient records is no doubt being done anyway, although without a concern for usage by the patient and family, by consortia of hospitals

- Hospital staff will be reluctant to enter information into a public, persistent system as part of their role within the hospital

The proposed approach builds on major successes in the CSCW field and nascent developments that could be strongly supportive:

- Internet sites with generic health information are very popular. Many patients and families turn to these sites first to inform themselves about health issues. The overwhelming problem with such sites is that the information there has not necessarily been carefully vetted by a reliable source; it is impossible for the public to determine what is trustworthy online information.

- One of the most successful collaborative uses of the Internet is support groups. It is helpful to many people who have had major, life-changing illness to interact online with others who have had similar experiences.

- Mass General Hospital has developed a site (www.braintalk.org) with vetted information for a wide range of neurological problems, threaded discussion (currently 100,000 threads with 800,000 postings) and chat. There are 40,000 registered members and many more guests (with limited access).

- A small group of former cardiac patients at Concord have banned together to provide information and support for post-cardiac patients.

The proposal is to build an Internet portal site modeled on braintalk.org that would provide threaded discussion, chat and links to basic information relevant to post-cardiac patients and their families. Volunteers from the small group at Concord could initially seed and monitor the different parts of the portal, responding to visitors and collecting the most important questions into a summary page of "frequently asked questions" (FAQ). Medical school staff (e.g., interns supervised by professors) could compile and organize relevant medical information (Public Library of Science, Medical Dictionary & Thesaurus, PubMed, Drug Info, etc.) in a format understandable by the public. Cardiac unit staff could develop a description of the procedures used in pre-surgery, surgery and post-surgery, as well as recommendations for home care and life-long post-cardiac health.

This approach would get the project off to an important, concrete start, without running into the imposing obstacles presented by alternative approaches. Given the cooperation of the braintalk.org staff, some technical support from the Cincinnati Hospital computer staff, some volunteer time from former patients from Concord, some cyber-librarian research by medical interns and input from the cardiac team, this approach could get off the ground with minimal staffing. A part-time project manager to coordinate everything and a part-time web designer should be able to launch the portal in a half year.

A next step might be to support communication between the cardiac medical team and patients/families after discharge from the hospital. This could take the form of email, with some facility for posting interesting interchanges to the relevant threaded discussion forum or FAQ. Working this out would involve addressing some of the concerns of hospital staff, as well as starting to build out the software system in manageable stages.

Of course, part of the post-op procedure while the patient is still in the hospital would be to orient the patient and family to this online resource. This could start to affect the procedures within the hospital. For instance, verbal and written explanations of a patient's medicines could be combined with redundant information online. At some point, the portal could be further extended to provide a personalized view for a particular patient that would provide immediate access to drug and other information that is directly relevant to his or her case. As the personalized information became more extensive, provisions would have to be added to protect patient privacy. The system will gradually evolve to meet more needs and to overcome obstacles in small steps.

As people start to use the system it will become obvious how it could be extended and improved. The idea is to start very simply and to let the real needs emerge through use. By starting with the needs of the patient and family after the hospital stay, the focus of the project is tied to the life-long needs of the patient in a way that it will not be distorted by institutional, financial, legal and bureaucratic needs of the hospital system, that would otherwise impose an insurmountable inertia.

Proposal for Social Science Study of Post-Cardiac Collaborative Care

The need for social science study is two-fold:

1. In order to design software to facilitate an evolution from a traditional practice of medicine to a transcendent practice oriented to the life-long needs of the post-cardiac patient, the actual detailed practices of the

affected people (medical professionals, patients, patient families) must be understood both pre and post transformation.

2. In order to reproduce the change in practices in hospital units other than the ones being studied, it is important to have documentation and understanding of what was involved in the studied cases.

The practices that we want to study are those largely taken-for-granted ("tacit", unstated, non-verbalized) procedures and behaviors that make up the daily life and interactions of those people who interact in the post-cardiac unit. For instance, how do certain people, through their gestures, tone of voice, word selection, manner, etc. set the tone for how things will unfold – who will pose questions, make decisions, end interactions. These detailed interaction and communication practices function to construct the relationships between people and determine how things get done.

The clearest way to identify the nature of these generally unnoticed practices is often to contrast different versions of them in distinctive settings. For instance, we might be particularly concerned with how it is that a patient is given the opportunity to raise an issue that has been bothering him but that he has until this point not felt it was appropriate to raise. In a traditional hospital setting this might be done in one way, in a setting with family rounds in another, in a setting with collaborative teams yet another and in a setting with computer mediation still another way. We would want to study, document and contrast each of these ways.

Various theories of social practice propose different ways to study interactions and relationships (Engeström, 1987; Koschmann, Stahl, & Zemel, 2005; Shumar & Renninger, 2002; Stahl, 2006; Star & Ruhleder, 1996; Vygotsky, 1930/1978; Zemel, Shumar *et al.*, 2005; Zemel, Xhafa, & Stahl, 2005). The theory of mediated cognition recommends that one analyze how interactions are mediated by artifacts. Here, the term *artifact* is extended to include both symbols (like language) and tools (like paper forms and computer screens). A further development of this theory, cultural-historical activity theory, adds the subtle mediations of the socio-cultural context, specifically community relations, the division of labor and social rules. Ethnomethodology argues that *social order* is not some external force imposed on interpersonal interaction, but is actually constructed and reproduced through the ways in which people interact. For instance, the fact that a patient can only raise certain kinds of issues when talking to a surgeon is not some law of proper etiquette, but is a result of the details of how the patient and surgeon (and others) have interacted. It may never have been explicitly discussed by the participants, but a trained observer can discover through careful analysis of an adequate record of the relevant interactions how it was in fact established.

In order to transform the rules of interaction in the post-cardiac setting and in order to provide computer support for the transformed version of the interactions, we should try to understand how the rules are made under certain circumstances and how they might be made differently. That is the goal of this social science research. The exact behaviors or rules of interest cannot be determined in advance. They will emerge from our comparative study, as they began to in our preliminary investigations.

Medical practice stands at a crossroads today. The technical requirements of treating heart disease (at least patching up presenting problems) are basically solved. It is possible for almost all cardiac patients to survive surgery. The challenge now is to deal with the less well-defined problems of helping patients to re-define their post-surgery life with dignity and wholeness. This requires a reorganization of the resources of the medical team and an integration of the patient and his or her family support system into the team as active members with important roles to play. This, in turn, requires a transformation of the interpersonal, relational practices. This is a complex matter, exceeding the schematic views of social science theories. We must adapt and expand the theories and their associated methodologies.

Consider the schema of activity theory: the direct and abstract relation of a subject to an object is mediated first by artifacts and secondly by community, division of labor and social rules. In any given situation, there are likely to be tensions between these various mediating factors, producing problems and/or driving changes. In our study, the subject must be replaced by a team of people, some with medical training (surgeon, PA, social worker, pharmacist, physical therapist, nurse, etc.) and some without (patient, family members). The different team members have different expertise, assignments, interests – yet they need to work together, to make joint decisions, to share information, to work toward a common goal. The object is also complex: to guide the patient into a fulfilling life despite any changes due to the heart problems. This object changes over time, initially day-by-day.

The mediating factors are each manifold. The artifacts include language and medicines that are hard for a lay person to understand. They must be made intelligible if patients are to use them effectively to understand their changed circumstances, to communicate and to heal. The community is intricately structured: a hospital is a world of its own, with confusing hierarchies, subcultures, machinery, restricted spaces. The patient's support community may be extensive or dysfunctional in many possible ways. We may want to offer new community supports through former patients. The division of labor is necessarily well-defined in modern medicine, but it may need to become more flexible to involve patients or their relatives of varying levels of understanding or interest in taking more control of their medical destinies.

Based on our understanding of the core issues involved in transforming post-cardiac care and based on the results of our past year's exploratory studies, we propose a three year social science study. The study will track the changes that take place in specific local units of post-cardiac care at the Hospital of the University of Cincinnati and will document and compare the detailed social practices that take place within those units, primarily those interactions involving the patients and their family members. This study will define different models of teamwork as the units evolve and will document the different forms that specific interactional practices take in these different models. Particular concern will be placed on questions of how the units could take advantage of computer mediation

The explicit purpose of this study is to aid the transformation of the post-cardiac care process to be one that increasingly involves the patient and family in defining the patient's new life. To the extent possible, the project will follow the patient home to see how the patient interacts with the Internet portal proposed above. In this sense, the study is an instance of involved action research. The research team will exert its influence through periodic reports and meetings with Vice President Dr. Paul Uhlig.

References

Engeström, Y. (1987). Learning by expanding: An activity-theoretical approach to developmental research. Helsinki, Finland: Orienta-Kosultit Oy.

Koschmann, T., Stahl, G., & Zemel, A. (2005). The video analyst's manifesto (or the implications of Garfinkel's policies for the development of a program of video analytic research within the learning sciences). In R. Goldman, R. Pea, B. Barron & S. Derry (Eds.), Video research in the learning sciences. Retrieved from http://www.cis.drexel.edu/faculty/gerry/publications/journals/manifesto.pdf.

Shumar, W., & Renninger, K. A. (2002). Introduction: On conceptualizing community. In K. A. Renninger & W. Shumar (Eds.), Building virtual communities (pp. 1-19). Cambridge, UK: Cambridge University Press.

Stahl, G. (2006). Group cognition: Computer support for building collaborative knowledge. Cambridge, MA: MIT Press. Retrieved from http://www.cis.drexel.edu/faculty/gerry/mit/.

Star, S. L., & Ruhleder, K. (1996). Steps toward an ecology of infrastructure: Design and access for large information spaces. Information Systems Research, 7 (1).

Vygotsky, L. (1930/1978). Mind in society. Cambridge, MA: Harvard University Press.

Zemel, A., Shumar, W., Stahl, G., Dominguez, C., Brown, J., Zipperer, L., et al. (2005). Communications analysis of the concord collaborative care model. Paper presented at the Safety and Health Insurance (SAHI 2005), Saint Louis, Missouri.

Zemel, A., Xhafa, F., & Stahl, G. (2005). Analyzing the organization of collaborative math problem-solving in online chats using statistics and conversation analysis. Paper presented at the CRIWG International Workshop on Groupware, Racife, Brazil.

13.   Internet Repositories for Collaborative Learning: Supporting both Students and Teachers

Most efforts to create computer-supported collaborative learning environments have been focused on students. However, without providing appropriate integration of collaborative activities into curricula, these efforts will have little widespread impact on educational practices. To improve education through technology, learning environments for students must be integrated with curriculum development tools for teachers to create an integrated collaboration-oriented classroom. This paper describes how software tools for Internet repositories can aid fundamental collaboration activities— locating, using, adapting and sharing—at both the teacher level (with the Teacher's Curriculum Assistant) and the student level (with the Remote Exploratorium). It illustrates how tools for educators and tools for students can be orchestrated into integrated classroom support.

1. Collaborative Activities Require Support

The goal of encouraging groups of learners to engage collaboratively in problem-solving activities has much merit. Social interaction fosters deep learning in which students develop intellectual structures that allow them to create their own knowledge [27]. It promotes social skills that help people participate in the social construction of their shared reality [3]. It increases student engagement and brings out the relevance of learning [16]. It allows the educational process to be more student-centered, less disciplinary and more exciting [14, 15].

The use of technology to foster collaborative learning is often seen as a key to reforming science education—on the principle that the best way to learn science is to engage in the practice of science [10]. The practices of modern science involve the use of technologic tools for:

- observing and measuring interesting phenomena in the world,

- generating representations and visualizations of the data and

- creating simulations to understand observed processes and to test hypotheses.

Importantly, the practice of modern science is highly collaborative. Scientists work together to incrementally design experiments and simulations, to convergently develop hypotheses and theories and to test and evaluate their work [17, 22]. Many projects have successfully combined these elements to foster innovative forms of collaborative science education among students [8, 12, 24, 26].

However, research projects have often been unable to transfer their successful results to other sites or schools because they did not replicate the initial teacher learning that occurred implicitly in the teacher-researcher and teacher-teacher collaborations [21]. For educational change to succeed, teachers too must be supported in changing from an isolated teaching model to one of collaborative learning with other educators [4]. We believe that for collaborative learning to succeed in the classroom, collaborative learning activities for students must be integrated with collaborative curriculum development resources for teachers. To implement collaborative learning in the classroom, students can be offered activities that provide a focus for group exploration; teachers need curriculum to provide contexts for these activities. Student activities can, for instance, build upon simulations of scientific or mathematical phenomena. Classroom contexts for these activities can include background information, ideas of approaches for students to try, ways for teachers to provide guidance, complementary activities for other groups in the same classroom or for outside of class, supplementary readings, examples of what other groups produced through similar activities and possible variations to adapt the activities to specific local circumstances or to personal preferences.

Toward this end, we have developed two innovative software systems: one primarily for students and one primarily for teachers. They illustrate how tools for teachers and students can be orchestrated into integrated classroom support. The **Remote Exploratorium (RE)** [1] supports students and teachers in collaboratively using and developing interactive learning simulations of scientific phenomena. Our experience testing **RE** in schools is that efforts to use these simulations are largely futile without appropriate integration into curricula and without providing teacher support. The **Teacher's Curriculum Assistant (TCA)** [25] addresses this shortcoming by helping teachers and learners locate, use, adapt and share lesson plans that illustrate how systems such as **RE** or **KidSim** [23] can be used in classroom settings.

For innovative forms of collaborative education to achieve widespread use, dissemination mechanisms are required that make tools and materials available to parties other than those participating in particular research projects. We have chosen to use the Internet and the World Wide Web (www) as distribution mechanisms. However, our work and other experiences [9] have shown that simply making materials available is not sufficient to foster a collaboration medium where teachers and students share innovative ideas. Computer support for students and teachers should also assist with several activities associated with collaboration—especially locating, using, adapting and sharing.

Consider how the Internet functions now, as an unstructured repository of ideas for activities and for curriculum. People have posted their pet ideas on diverse Internet sites and in various formats. It is difficult for students or teachers to find sites that have offerings and to search through the offerings to retrieve those that are relevant. There is no support for adapting the activity ideas to actual classroom situations or for sharing experiences using these ideas with other students and teachers. In particular, the following activities are problematic:

- **Locating**. Students and teachers have no systematic guide to where to look on the Internet. They may hear of www locations from various sources and then surf around looking at individual offerings until they become lost or tired. Once repositories of ideas for activities are found, there is no uniform way to search through the offerings to find those that meet current needs. Some sites may provide primitive query mechanisms, but these vary from site to site.

- **Using**. Most Internet postings give only brief descriptions of ideas for activities. They do not provide the resources needed to carry out the activities, nor do they provide curriculum to create a productive context for the activities.

- **Adapting**. For learning to be effective, students must make the activities their own; they must be able to modify the activities and put their stamp on them. Teachers must also be able to adapt the activities and curriculum to the personal learning styles of the students and to the characteristics of the classroom and the priorities of the local school district. Simple postings do not facilitate this.

- **Sharing**. For the Internet repository to work as a collaborative medium, students and teachers who benefit from the repository must be encouraged to participate in its growth and evolution. They need tools that make it natural and easy to contribute their new versions of activities and curriculum and to annotate repository offerings they have used with their experiences. Students and teachers cannot post responses at most sites where items are found.

The remainder of this paper begins by presenting a use scenario that illustrates collaboration-oriented classroom support. Next, we present the two systems we have developed, RE and TCA. Finally, we discuss barriers we have encountered developing and using these systems. It is our hope that by identifying such barriers we can instigate further discussion and promote directions of change that will help make the Internet and the www more effective media for educational collaboration.

2. Collaboration-Oriented Classroom Support

The following diagram illustrates a scenario of classroom use of RE and TCA. The scenario shows how this software supports locating, using, adapting and sharing simulations and related curriculum. On the left and the right of the diagram are two classrooms (see Figure 1). They may be widely separated in time and space.

The teacher on the left has downloaded a TCA curriculum on ecology. This teacher has posed the question, "Why are ecosystems fragile?" The students have been told to find simulations of ecologies. They have turned to RE and located a simulation of a frog pond. After downloading it, they run it; populate it with frogs, flies and alligators; and observe what happens. Then they use it, varying the parameters that describe the quantities and behaviors of the creatures. If they are advanced users, they create their own new creatures with interesting behaviors and study the consequences of their introduction. Finally they upload their new simulation for others to use. The teacher extends the ecology curriculum to include activities targeted at introducing new species into existing ecosystems and observing population dynamics.

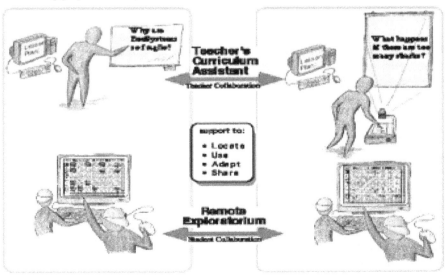

Figure 1. TCA and RE support collaboration of teachers and of students to develop repositories of simulations and of associated curriculum.

The teacher on the right uses TCA to search for curriculum on ecology and locates the version that the first teacher modified. Students in this classroom select a simulation of sharks in the ocean from RE. Their teacher adapts the curriculum to the new simulation and poses the question added as a result of the first class' work, "What happens if too many of one species are added to an ecosystem?"

3. Remote Exploratorium: Tools for Students

We have developed a design environment called Agentsheets [20] that can be used to create construction kits, simulation environments, visual programming languages and games. Design environments are tools that allow groups of learners to construct artifacts meaningful to them. The process of designing serves as a vehicle to create opportunities for learning [2] and the use and modification of simulations of scientific phenomena forms a basis for collaborative activities in the classroom [12]. Many of the existing Agentsheets titles allow groups of students to set up, run and modify simulations of scientific and mathematical phenomena [19].

Recently, we have combined the Agentsheets design environment with the Mosaic networking medium to create the Agentsheets Remote Exploratorium [1], providing learners access to interactive exhibits (Figure 2). Students can actively interact with exhibits including Electric World (an exhibit to experiment with electricity) and Waves (an exhibit to experience the Doppler effect and supersonic booms). The easy inclusion of additional information, such as instructions, learning motivation and even related references for further exploration, is supported through the use of Mosaic and creates an interactive exhibit which contextualizes educational use. RE supports fundamental collaboration activities by allowing students to progress through several layers of usage:

3.1. Locating: Navigating through the Exploratorium

Exhibits are linked to other sources of related information located on the www. The learner makes use only of the Mosaic part of the virtual exploratorium to find interesting related information consisting of text, pictures and videos. The Exploratorium   may   be   visited   on   www   at   URL: http://www.cs.colorado.edu/~l3d/remote-exploratorium/AgentsheetsRemoteExp.html.   Classrooms   must   have   the Agentsheets player to run simulations.

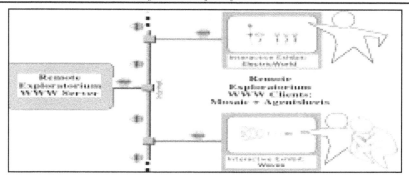

Figure 2. Remote Exploratorium: Servers and Clients

3.2. Using: Downloading and Running Exhibits

If learners are interested in a deeper understanding of an exhibit, they can download it and run it. For instance, the Electric World exhibit is about electricity. In the Electric World Mosaic page (Figure 3, left), the learner can click the download option to access the interactive exhibit. In response, Mosaic sends a compound document to **Agentsheets**. The **Agentsheets** design environment loads sounds, installs agent depictions, compiles agent programs and stores agent documentation. The learner sees two new windows on the screen: a worksheet in which the simulation takes place (Figure 3, right top) and a gallery of agents (Figure 3, right bottom) containing electrical components. Simple documentation describing the behavior of agents and means to interact with agents can be accessed through Macintosh Balloon Help. The balloons, like the code, depiction and sound of agents have been transferred from the RE server via the Mosaic www client to the **Agentsheets** design environment. In the Electric World learners can operate switches and observe reactions. For instance, operating the left most switch in the lower row of switches will put the circuit into a feedback mode in which an electric coil and the electromagnetic switch located left of the coil will interact with each other.

3.3. Adapting: Constructing New Simulations and Extending Behavior of Exhibits

Exhibits are not static artifacts to be observed. Learners have all the components to create new simulations or to change existing ones. In Figure 4 (left side), the learner has added a column of switches. By doing this, learners can directly and tangibly apply knowledge gained from the exhibit.

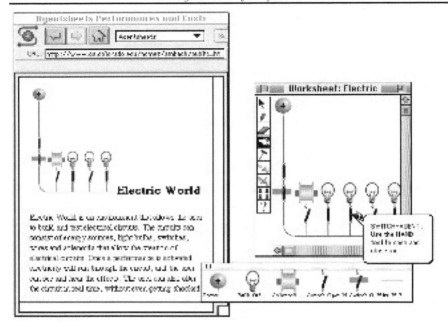

Figure 3. The Electric World Exhibit

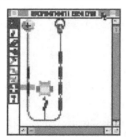 

Figure 4. The changed Electric World is shown on the left. Adding a buzzer to the circuit is shown on the right.

Students can also change their role from end-users to designers by using **Agentsheets** functionality to modify the behavior of an exhibit. For example, learners can add their own agents to exhibits. In the Electric World a learner introduces a buzzer by first defining its depiction, 🔲 , using the **Agentsheets** depiction editor and then defines the behavior of the buzzer either using a textual programming language called **AgenTalk** or using graphical rewrite rules. The new buzzer agent is ready to be used in the Electric World (Figure 4, right side). It serves as a replacement for the bulb. When the buzzer receives current, it plays a sound. This extensibility allows an exhibit to be customized to support what is most relevant to the learner and to reflect shifts and changes in the learner's acquired knowledge.

3.4. Sharing: Adding New Exhibits

Efforts are underway to extend RE to support participants in posting changes to existing exhibits and even adding entirely new exhibits. Currently, contributors must contact the Exploratorium curator via email.

4. Teacher's Curriculum Assistant: Tools for Teachers

The Teacher's Curriculum Assistant [25] is a design environment to support the curriculum development needs of classroom teachers. It accesses a special TCA curriculum repository on the Internet that points to educational resources such as RE and other learning resources available over the Internet. The design of TCA supports fundamental collaboration activities in the following ways:

4.1. Locating: Searching for Distributed Curriculum Sources

The first problem with using the Internet as a source of curriculum ideas is the distributed nature of the Internet. Resources may be located at thousands of sites around the world and there is no central listing of all these locations. TCA addresses this problem by requiring all postings to adopt a standard form of indexing and to register their indexes at a central site for TCA users. Thus, when someone wants to offer a new Agentsheets simulation, they fill out a form specifying what grades, subjects, etc. the title is appropriate for. An index record is created for the title, including this information and the location of the title on the Internet. Periodically, teachers using TCA update the database on their computers with new index records. All curriculum structure as well as indexes for the multimedia resources are kept on the teacher's desktop computer; only the resources themselves (text, pictures, video clips, spreadsheet templates, HyperCard stacks, software applications) need to be downloaded.

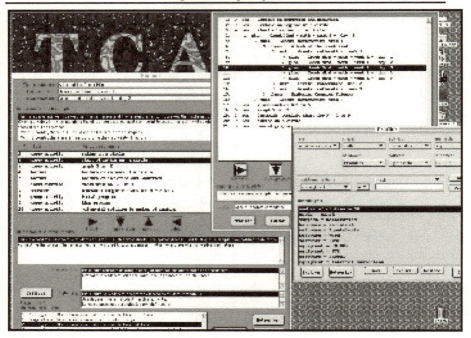

Figure 5. The TCA Profiler, Explorer and Planner windows.

TCA provides a combination of query and browsing tools for searching the indexes in its database. This combination is designed to respond to problems in information retrieval in unobtrusive ways. Queries are notoriously difficult to formulate and brittle to execute. People cannot generally articulate specifications for the information they want. They need to see what is available and then gradually focus in on a set of interesting results [18]. Simply browsing through large information spaces, however, has its own pitfalls. People become distracted and lost; they lack an overview and focus [7].

TCA provides a classroom Profiler (Figure 5, far right blue window) for teachers to specify the characteristics of their classrooms. The Profiler gathers information for queries by collecting facts about a teacher's classroom. For instance, what is the grade level and subject; what hardware and software are available; what pedagogical approaches are preferred? Then, when a teacher decides to explore curriculum on the Internet, TCA automatically generates a query for just those curricular resources.

Once teachers have located a promising set of curriculum using the Profiler, the Explorer (Figure 5, middle red window) can be used to browse through this smaller, more manageable amount of information. The Explorer lets a teacher traverse through four levels of curriculum: semester themes, weekly units, daily lesson plans and individual resources. In Figure 5, for example, a teacher displayed a number of resources for ninth grade mathematics in the Explorer window. She then expanded the third resource to find a lesson plan built around this resource by pressing the up arrow. Continuing, she found a weekly unit that included five coordinated lesson plans. In this way, the teacher found sample curriculum to use with the selected resources and to adapt for a week of activities that would promote her pedagogical goals.

4.2. Using: Downloading Educational Resources

Teachers can efficiently perform searches on their own computers to find which of all the curricular resources on the Internet are most suited to their needs. Only when it comes time to actually use the resources do they need to download the ones they want. TCA downloads them automatically using the location information in the indexes.

4.3. Adapting: Tailoring Educational Resources and Curriculum to Local Needs

TCA provides several support mechanisms to help a teacher adapt curriculum and resources to actual classroom needs:

- Computational critics (rule-based mechanisms for evaluating designs [6]) in the TCA system compare the user's profile with the indexes for a given curricular item and suggest changes to eliminate incompatibilities

- The TCA system uses case-based reasoning adaptation rules [11] to make changes automatically, based on incompatibilities between the profile and indexes; the teacher can accept or reject these changes.

- A teacher can use commercial applications from within TCA (word processors, spreadsheets, Agentsheets) to modify resources created in those applications.

The lesson Planner in TCA can be used to modify curriculum themes, units and plans, while the Editor window can be used to change the indexing of resources.

The lesson Planner (Figure 5, left green window) allows teachers to build lesson plans by adding and rearranging resources, such as textual readings, group activities, collaborative research topics and class presentations. Teacher preparation instructions and materials requirements from all the resources in the lesson plan are displayed together to help the teacher get ready for a class.

4.4. Sharing: Posting New Curriculum to the TCA Server

The networker component of TCA allows teachers to download and post to Internet sites and thereby to share in the collaborative process of curriculum development. It lets teachers download any indexes that have been posted since they last updated. It also lets them upload their contributions, for instance to post modified versions of curriculum or new resources. This component is used to set up details for Internet usage, such as phone numbers and sites for maintaining TCA indexes.

5. Discussion

We encountered several issues while creating RE and TCA that we believe to be barriers to the use of Internet and www technology as collaboration media:

Reliability: Imagine if a student were using a textbook and that textbook periodically disappeared without warning. This situation, although an Internet reality, is unacceptable in widespread educational use of distributed educational resources such as RE.

Efficiency: Exhibits in RE require not one, but several files containing various types of information (e.g., sound, pictures, code). Participants have a low tolerance for files that require many minutes to be downloaded successfully, however file compression and aggregation is not supported within the network media. To address this problem in TCA, the information teachers need for planning is maintained on their computer. Options are provided which allow teachers to schedule the downloading of large educational resources overnight or in other less critical times.

The Sharing Bottleneck: Barriers to true two-way collaboration over the Internet and www fall into two categories: technical and institutional. On the technical side, only very limited mechanisms for feedback are currently supported within www client software. For the most part, interaction is limited to selecting from provided options or entering small amounts of text into forms. On the institutional side, there are many policy decisions to be made and processes to be worked out concerning verification and authentication of posted materials. For instance, who should verify (if anyone) that posted exhibits actually compile and run? On a more ominous note, what policies and mechanisms are required to ensure that simulation agents with malicious behaviors, such as deleting or scrambling data, are detected before widespread dissemination occurs? Many institutional issues are also raised by the attempt to establish a curriculum repository. Sanctioning and endorsements of TCA require policy decisions. For instance, should posted curriculum be reviewed against some criteria concerning suitability for the claimed audience or other educational content concerns? Who will make these decisions and what are the criteria? One solution is to have several curriculum servers, some mediated by providers of curriculum, others open.

Standards are Required: We have tried to design computer support tools to help students and teachers take advantage of the Internet as a repository of activities and curriculum. In doing this, we have found that the repository itself must take on structure. The Internet imposes little structure; that is why the world's largest library is the messiest that has ever existed [13]. The www imposes useful structure with its hypertext mark-up language (html) and newer alternatives like Hyper-G are imposing more structure to permit higher functionality [5]. RE introduces a file type for transmitting Agentsheets titles. TCA defines indexing formats for curriculum. The construction of our tools for students and teachers takes advantage of these structures. In suggesting structures, we have tried to balance the needs of standardization with the goals of open-ended collaboration.

Institutional Collaboration is Required: Before a system such as TCA can achieve widespread use, the indexing scheme it proposes must be accepted as a standard by providers of curriculum and educational resources. Institutions such as federally funded curriculum development efforts, textbook publishers and software developers must collaborate to seed TCA with a critical mass of information and a community of teachers must begin to use it.

6. Summary

We started with Agentsheets, an environment for creating simulations that can be used for collaborative activities of students. This needed to be supplemented with a means for distributing new titles and allowing students to find titles that met their needs. RE was designed to use the www as a medium for students and educators to share simulations and other interactive learning environments. Classroom experience with Agentsheets showed the need for providing curriculum contexts for the simulations. TCA is an attempt to establish a medium for teachers to collaborate around a growing body of curriculum. This effort in turn points out the need for institutional collaboration to form a community of users that accepts the standards proposed by TCA. In conclusion, we have found that classroom support requires support for teachers as well as for students. Such support should cover the activities of locating, using, adapting and sharing. Only when these activities are supported, can networking media be transformed into collaboration media.

Acknowledgements

The Teacher's Curriculum Assistant is under development at Owen Research, Inc. with support from DOE grant DE-FG03-93ER81588, NSF grant III-9360544 and NASA grant NAS9-18921. The Remote Exploratorium is under development at the Center for LifeLong Learning and Design, University of Colorado at Boulder, with support from Apple Computer, Inc., NSF under grant RED 925-3425 and ARPA under CDA-940860. We wish to acknowledge the encouragement and feedback from administrators and teachers of the Boulder Valley Public Schools, especially Len Scrogan, Scott Dixon, David Clark and Stevan Kalmon.

References

1. Ambach, J., C. Perrone and A. Repenning, "Remote Exploratoriums: Combining Networking Media and Design Environments to Support Engaged Learning," *To appear in: Computers in Education (Special Issue on the Internet in Education)*, August, 1995.

2. Balestrie, D., S. C. Ehrmann and D. L. Ferguson, *"Learning to Design, Designing to Learn: Using Technology to Transform the Curriculum,"* Taylor and Francis, New York, 1992.

3. Berger, P. L. and T. Luckmann, *The Social Construction of Reality: A Treatise in the Sociology of Knowledge*, Doubleday, New York, 1989.

4. Ellis, J. D., "Teacher Development in Advanced Educational Technology," *Journal of Science and Technology*, Vol. 1, pp. 49-65, 1992.

5. Fenn, B. and H. Maurer, "Harmony on the Expanding Net," *Interactions*, Vol. 1, pp. 26-38, 1994.

6. Fischer, G., K. Nakakoji, J. Ostwald, G. Stahl and T. Sumner, "Embedding Computer-Based Critics in the Contexts of Design," *Conference on Human Factors in Computing (Interact '93 and CHI '93)*, Amsterdam (24-29 April), 1993, pp. 157-164.

7. Halasz, F., "Reflections on Notecards: Seven Issues for the Next Generation of Hypermedia Systems," *Communications of the ACM*, Vol. 31, pp. 836-852, 1988.

8. Harel, I. and S. Papert, "Software Design as a Learning Environment," *Interactive Learning Environments*, Vol. 1, pp. 1-32, 1990.

9. Kay, A. C., "Computers, Networks and Education," *Scientific American*, (Special Issue: The Computer in the 21st Century), pp. 148-155, 1995.

10. Kearsley, G., B. Hunter and M. Furlong, "Scientists at Work," in *We Teach with Technology: New Visions for Education*, Ed., Beedle & Assoc., Wilsonville, OR, 1951, pp. 63-78.

11. Kolodner, J., *Case-Based Reasoning*, Morgan Kayfmann, San Mateo, CA, 1993.
12. Linn, M. C., "The Computer as Learning Partner: Can Computer Tools Teach Science?," in *Technology for Teaching and Learning*, K. Sheingold, L. Roberts and S. Malcom, Ed., 1991, pp. 31-69.
13. Marchionini, G. and H. Maurer, "The Roles of Digital Libraries in Teaching and Learning," *Communications of the ACM*, Vol. 38, pp. 67-75, 1995.
14. Papert, S., *Mindstorms*, Basic Books, New York, 1980.
15. Papert, S., *The Children's Machine*, Basic Books, New York 1993.
16. Penner, L. A., G. M. Batsche, H. M. Knoff and D. L. Nelson, *The Challenge in Mathematics and Science Education: Psychology's Response*, APA, Washington, D.C., 1993.
17. Popper, K. R., *Conjectures and Refutations*, Harper & Row, New York, 1965.
18. Rao, R., J. O. Hearst, J. D. Mackinlay, S. K. Card, L. Masinter, P. K. Halvorsen and G. G. Robertson, "Rich Interaction in the Digital Library," *Communications of the ACM*, Vol. 38, pp. 29-39, 1995.
19. Repenning, A., "Programming Substrates to Create Interactive Learning Environments," *Journal of Interactive Learning Environments (Special Issue on End-User Environments)*, Vol. 4, pp. 45-74, 1994.
20. Repenning, A. and T. Sumner, "**Agentsheets**: A Medium for Creating Domain-Oriented Visual Languages," *IEEE Computer (Special Issue on Visual Programming)*, Vol. 28, pp. 17-25, 1995.
21. Riel, M., "A Functional Analysis of Educational Telecomputing: A Case Study of Learning Circles," *Interactive Learning Environments*, Vol. 2, pp. 15-29, 1992.
22. Roschelle, J., "Learning by Collaborating: Convergent Conceptual Change," *The Journal of Learning Sciences*, Vol. 2, pp. 235-276, 1992.
23. Smith, D. C., A. Cypher and J. Spohrer, "KidSim: Programming Agents without a Programming Language," *Communications of the ACM*, Vol. 37, pp. 54-67, 1994.
24. Songer, N. B., "Learning Science with a Child-Focused Resource: A Case Study of Kids as Global Scientists," *Technical Report,*, School of Education, University of Colorado at Boulder, 1993.
25. Stahl, G., T. Sumner and R. Owen, "Share Globally, Adapt Locally: Software Assistance to Locate and Tailor Curriculum Posted to the Internet," *To appear in: Computers in Education (Special Issue on the Internet in Education)*, August, 1995.
26. Tinker, R. F., "Educational Networking: Meeting Educators' Needs," *INET '93*, 1993.
27. Vygotsky, L., *Thought and Language*, MIT Press, Cambridge, 1989.

14. Evaluating Affordance Short-circuits by Reviewers and Authors Participating in On-line Journal Reviews

Elizabeth A. Lenell and Gerry Stahl

This paper presents the results of a "by-hand" analysis of the on-line interactions that occurred during seven peer reviews of articles submitted to JiME (Journal of Interactive Media in Education), an academic e-journal. JiME has been specifically designed to promote open, on-line dialogue between article reviewers and authors as part of the article review process. When articles are published, edited versions of the review comments are included with the articles. The purpose of this study was to examine pre-publication interactions between reviewers and authors as they debated over article submissions, with an eye to how affordances of the JiME review medium were utilized. The goal was to determine whether those affordances contributed to what was seen as a computer-supported collaborative effort, or whether commentators somehow circumvented the affordances. Based on the findings, a set of design and editorial interventions are recommended.

For about three semesters, we have been engaged in a series of seminars on CSCL. In 1999, we reviewed theories of mediation and experimented with several CSCL media. Currently we are looking at the role that artifacts more generally play in cognition and collaboration. This paper reports on a study of a specific designed medium to support the review and publication of scholarly articles: JiME (the Journal of Interactive Media in Education, available at http://www-jime.open.ac.uk).

Although promising, it is clear that there are many challenges and practical barriers to the use of computer technology in collaborative learning (Stahl, 1999). This paper attempts to characterize some specific issues that arise in the JiME medium. We focus on the initial review process in which a small group of reviewers and the author engage in a critical dialogue. JiME is not strictly a learning environment, but does encourage social interaction via computer-based affordances. The users of those affordances are the multidisciplinary reviewers and authors of articles submitted to JiME. The goal of JiME is to support a limited community (later broadened during open review and eventual publication) to engage in knowledge building. The desired product is a scholarly publication that incorporates the author's ideas in a way that is compatible with the reviewers' critical reception. Starting with a draft expression of the author's ideas, the knowledge-building process subjects that draft to the multiple interdisciplinary perspectives of the reviewers. This leads to a dialogue in which questions are posed and issues raised. The author responds and in some cases enters into more prolonged discussions with the reviewers. In the end of closed review, the editor makes recommendations that typically summarize the knowledge-building process and delineate a view of the collaboratively constructed ideal article.

One of the unique and central concepts behind the design of JiME (Sumner, et al., 2000) is its artifact-centered structure. The idea here is that the knowledge-building activities of the review process are grounded in the artifact of the author's text. Each section of the text is automatically linked to comments on that section. Furthermore, the JiME interface displays the section of text and its associated discussion side-by-side. A usual outcome of the review is that some of the review discussion is kept linked to the text when the article is revised and published.

New users such as the volunteer reviewers must gradually learn how to use a medium like JiME. In some cases, they discover or are instructed in the intended usage patterns and they come to master these; in others, they adapt or appropriate the technology as best they can to their personal preferences and constraints. Thus, the JiME communication medium with its specific affordances can be conceptualized as a cognitive artifact that can be either "mastered" or "appropriated" (Wertsch, 1998) by its users. If the JiME affordances are mastered, then article reviewers and authors will use them in ways similar to those intended by the designers. If the affordances are appropriated, they will be modified to suit the users' purposes. Those purposes may not necessarily meet the intention of the artifact designers. While artifacts come with physical (or virtual) affordances, the uses of the artifact are not always obvious to the users, particularly with computer-based media which are inherently complex to use and which come with many associated technical problems (e.g., monitor resolution). The degree to which users learn to take advantage of JIME's affordances can seriously affect the progress of the knowledge-building process as envisioned by the JiME designers.

In this paper, we look in some detail at the usage patterns in a series of JiME reviews. From this analysis, we draw some conclusions about how well reviewers master the affordances of the JiME medium as a collaboration artifact, in particular, how well they take advantage of the intended links between the text artifact and the review discussion.

Data source

The Journal of Interactive Media in Education is an electronic publication that was designed as a "document-centered discourse" environment (see esp. Sumner, Shum, Wright, Bonnardel & Chevalier, 2000). The journal is designed to link the discourse between peer reviewers and authors directly to the content of the reviewed article itself. Of particular interest for the study reported here is the fact that the discourse interface itself is designed to encourage interaction between the multidisciplinary reviewers and authors through use of a pre-assigned hierarchy within which reviewers and authors can enter comments about article sections or abstract areas. The standardized discussion hierarchy features five General (abstract) review categories:

- Originality and Importance of Ideas

- Clarity of Goals

- Appropriateness of Methods

- Clarity and Credibility of Results

- Quality of Writing

Additionally, each article is assigned Specific categories that correspond to particular sections of each article. These categories are unique to each article and assigned by the article editor.

At the beginning of the JiME review process, for a period of about one month (the "Closed" review period), the invited reviewers and the article authors "debate" the merits of the articles. This debate consists of the reviewers entering comments under whatever headings/categories they choose. Authors and other reviewers see the comments after they are posted and can respond by posting comments at the same level (Level 1 if entered at the same hierarchical level as the original comment), or at a subordinate level (e.g., Level 2 would appear indented and below the comment being responded to, etc.).

In addition to entering and responding within the General hierarchy itself, comments may be linked directly to the Specific article sections. The idea behind this design was that the debate entries thus constitute a kind of footnoting to the original text.

Editors can and do modify both the linked and original comments when the articles are published in JiME. Because of this, for this project, only pre-print archives are used for analysis. These pre-print versions of the review debates have not been altered by editors and so represent the original way reviewer and author interactions occurred. Also, while it is an important knowledge-building and collaborative affordance of JiME, aspects of the linked text are ignored for this project due to space and time limitations. Finally, there are occasions when an editor directs reviewers or authors. These directives are not studied here, although there will be a brief commentary regarding this in the concluding section.

Between 1996 and 1999 there were twenty-two articles submitted and archived in JiME. These were made available to the investigator by JiME editors as part of coursework at the University of Colorado, Boulder. Of these 22 articles, seven were chosen to be examined based on the fact that each had one or more Level 3 comments in their debate hierarchies—this collection of seven articles constituted the entire body of articles with more than 2 levels of interaction. That is, at least one instance of the following type of interaction was present in some aspect of the debate hierarchy of the seven examined reviews:

- Reviewer makes an initial comment (Level 1)

- Author or another reviewer responds or enters a comment corresponding to the initial entry (Level 2)

- A third comment or response is entered (Level 3)

The decision to choose articles based on depth of debate was made because a primary interest of this project is to understand how JiME affordances for collaborative exchange were used (or not used). Level 3 interactions were rare among the 22 archived articles and it was hoped that the seven with Level 3 interactions would provide points of insight that could not be seen in articles with less depth of interaction.

Research questions and analysis

If the primary affordance for collaboration is presumed to be the debate hierarchy, then the first question to be addressed is: "Do contributors follow the hierarchical format?". A simple qualitative examination of all categories in every article was conducted to answer this question, with notes made about how reviewers and authors use the predetermined categories.

The second major question to be addressed regarded how reviewers and authors interact. In order to answer this question, a descriptive statistical analysis is performed to reveal the degree of interaction by Level of commentary. Supplementing this is a qualitative analysis of the timeliness by which debate comments are entered relative to each other—an analysis that answers the question of "when" reviewers and authors respond to each other. This last provides clues as to the limits of the collaborative interactions that are reported in the results.

Analysis

Do contributors follow the hierarchical format?

Reviewers and authors do not strictly follow the pre-determined hierarchy established before the review debates begin. For instance, reviewers do not tend to make entries in every possible category. This is not surprising, since even in traditional reviews it is unlikely that a reviewer would comment on every possible section of an article. However, JiME affords collaborative exchange in two categories for all articles. A General comment section is designed for comments regarding abstract consideration of articles (Quality of Writing, Clarity of Goals, etc.). The Specific category allows for exchanges on specific subsections of each article. For illustrations of the JiME hierarchy, see Appendix A.

The primary pattern that emerges from examination of the seven articles studied in this project is that it is common for individual reviewers to make comments in either the General or the Specific categories, but in not both. Of the 25 reviewers, more than half (14) made comments predominantly in one kind of category— either General or Specific. Table 1 provides an example.

Table 1. Example of how reviewers and authors tend to choose either General categories or article-Specific categories for their comments.

Article 1 Author/Reviewer	Date entered	Time entered	Category		Level
			General	Article Specific	
Reviewer 1	22-Oct	7:38 gmt	Orig. & Imp. of Ideas		1
		7:44	Approp. of Meth		1
		7:47		1. Bkgrnd	1
		7:48		1.1 The Course	1
		7:50		2. Res. Questions	1
		7:51		2.1 Res. Ques/Pop Topics	1
		7:53		3. General results	1
		20:29	Re:Orig. & Imp. of Ideas		
	Nov. 2	GMT			3
Reviewer 2	Oct. 23	17:57	Orig.& Imp. of Ideas		1
		18:05	Clarity		1
		18:16	App of Meth		2
		18:30	Cred of results		1
		18:20	Qual of Writing		1

	Date	Time	General	Specific	
				References	2
Reviewer 3	26-Oct	2:27	Approp of Meth		1
Reviewer 4	Nov. 1	19:27		1. Background	2
		20:07		2. Research Questions	2
		21:07		3. General results	2
		2:02		4. Conclusions and results	1
Author	1-Nov	19:52	Orig &Imp. of Ideas		2
		20:34	Approp of Meth		2
		23:41		1.1 The Course	2
		23:55		2.1 Res. Quest/ Pop Topics	2
	Nov. 2	3:18		1. Background (A)	3
		4:14		1. Background (B)	2

As exemplified in Table 1, although reviewers may make entries in both General and Specific categories, there tends to be a preference for one type or the other. In the case of Reviewer 3, for example, only one comment is made. In this case, the reviewer made a substantial single entry that covered several facets of the article.

The most serious implication of this "single-category" pattern is that the JiME affordance for an individual to consider an article from two perspectives is short-circuited. The two types of category should allow review comments to be input at two different levels: an abstract level exemplified by the General categories and a more detailed level at the Specific level. But by segregating their comments to one or the other category, Reviewers in particular create a limiting factor in their interaction with other reviewers and the author.

For example, if a reviewer enters a majority of his or her comments in the General categories, then obviously this reviewer is not contributing debate comments in the Specific categories. The reviewer entering only General comments may be missed or ignored by those who are concentrating their comments on Specific categories. In this way, there is a kind of double barrier to interaction between reviewers: the reviewer may be self-limiting, plus other reviewers (also self-limiting) may miss interaction because they are not paying attention to the comments in categories they are not considering. This is suggested by Article 2, represented in Table 2.

Table 2. Example of category-specific responses. Reviewers tend not to respond across their category preferences.

Article 2 Auth./Reviewer	Date of Entry	Time of Entry	General	Article Specific	Level	
Reviewer 1	21-Jan	15:05	Orig/Imp of Ideas		1	A
		15:14	Clarity of Goals		1	a
		15:17	Approp of Meth		1	A
		15:19	Cred of results		1	A
		15:20	Qual of Writing		1	A
		16:12		1.1 What do pub do	1	
		16:28		1.2 How textbook op work	1	
		16:48		1.3 Exp w/multimedia adopt.	1	
		17:07		2. Causes of reluctance	1	
	22-Jan	14:39		3.1 What can author do: interface and support (A)	1	
		15:07		3.1 What can author do:interface and support (B)	1	
		15:08		3.2 What can pub do: workshop & class support	1	
		15:11		3.3 What can commun do: peer and user groups	1	
	3-Feb	17:11	Approp of Meth		3	
Reviewer 2	3-Feb-98	2:19	Orig & Imp of ideas		2	B
		2:26		3.1 What can author do	2	
Reviewer 3	3/5/1998	14:53	Orig/Imp of ideas		3	C
		16:45	Clarity of Goals		2	b
		16:58	Cred of results		2	B
		16:48	Qual of Writing		2	B
		14:43		2. Causes of reluctance	2	
Reviewer 4	2/22/1998	2:37	Orig/Imp of ideas		1	
		2:49	Approp of Meth		4	
Author	3-Feb	16:23	Approp of Meth		2	B
		15:41		3.1 What can the author do	2	

In this table, comments by Reviewers 2-4 and the Author are relatively restricted to the General comments entered by Reviewer 1. For instance, Reviewer 1 entered a comment on the Originality and Importance of Ideas on January 21 (indicated by *A*); Reviewer 2 responded to this on February 3 (*B*); finally, Reviewer 3 enters the last response for this category (*C*). The case is similar for the other General categories, where A indicates the first comment entered and B indicates the response.

The primary point of this table is that even though Reviewer 1 entered several comments in Specific categories, the other Reviewers chose to respond only to the General categories. For whatever reason, they did not further elaborate on the Specific categories and JiME has no current affordance to encourage more complete involvement by Reviewers across categories.

How do reviewers and authors interact?

Figure 1 shows the descriptive breakdown of comments based on the hierarchy level in which they occur.

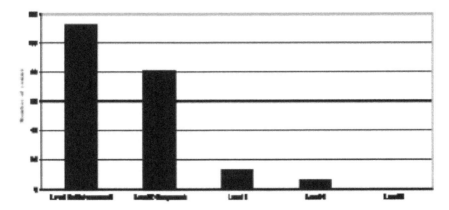

Figure 1.

Of the 112 entry-level comments examined in this study, 55% (62) have only one response and these responses tend to come exclusively from the article Authors. Only 12% (13) of the entry-level comments have two responses and about 5% (6) have three responses. The overwhelming pattern of interaction is that a Reviewer will make an entry-level comment, an author will respond and there will be no further responses. This pattern allows rejection of the hypothesis that there is a high level of interaction among JiME Reviewers and Authors.

One question that is raised by this pattern, however, is what kind of topics prompt Authors to respond to initial comments and is there reason to believe the answers have an inhibitory influence on other Reviewers. Although a more in-depth study of this is warranted, a superficial survey of the articles shows the following issues tend to elicit Author responses:

- Requests for more info

- Direct questions regarding methods

- Direct questions regarding concepts

- Terminology debates

- Conceptual debates (i.e., reviewer challenges conceptual definition)

- Claim debates (e.g., reviewer argues against a claim made by author)

- Debates about external issues ("The problem . . .. is that people are insufficiently critical.")

- Comments about "external" issues (such as relationships to experiences, books cited, etc.)

- Presentational issues ("[have] text popped up over the node . . . so as not to divert your attention")

- "Simple" agreements ("Good point!") (rare)

- Compliments (rare)

Given that an Author responds particularly to criticisms of the claims he or she has made, as well as conceptual and terminological issues, it would be reasonable to speculate that further commentary or questioning by other Reviewers might be unnecessary. This presumes, however, that Author responses are made in a timely manner relative to the initial entries—that is, that such criticisms are immediately countered by Authors and thus need no further questioning by other Reviewers. As will be shown in the next section, however, this is frequently not the case.

Time-related issues

In-depth exchanges (comments at Level 3 and beyond) are not common in JiME review debates. This could be interpreted as a simple matter of pragmatics. The closed debate period in which the invited reviewers have available for considering the articles is typically only one month long (with a different time period for other readers during the "open" review period). But even given this narrow time span, it is reasonable to ask what contributes to the lack of deeper interactions among reviewers and authors.

A closer examination of time issues across the seven articles studied in this project shows that Reviewers tended not to utilize more than one day for entering review comments. This pattern of entering comments on a single day is common across all the article debates reviewed in this study. Of 25 Reviewers in the articles studied here, only 32% (8) made entries on more than one day. It is possible that this indicates that the Reviewers wrote their observations elsewhere (in word processing applications, for instance) and copied them into the JiME hierarchical structure. This would amount to producing a traditional-style review, which essentially by-passes some of the affordances of the JiME hierarchy for collaborative work. There is some evidence to substantiate this idea of transference of a traditional review.

The time at which a commentary is input into the debate hierarchy is recorded by the JiME software. The record of input for all Authors and Reviewers provides further evidence that Reviewers may be producing their reviews external to the hierarchy and then transferring it into the debate structure. This pattern is apparent particularly in Table 1, where Reviewer 1 has made seven entries in about 15 minutes. Although these entries cannot be shown here due to confidentiality issues, the entries are large enough that it is unlikely they were composed and entered in JiME at the rate of one every two minutes.

If Reviewers do write their reviews in a traditional, non-interactive manner and then transfer their comments into the debate structure, then this may be contributing to restricted dialogue between both Reviewers and Authors. It seems logical that there is a disincentive for Reviewers to go back into a debate looking for comments to respond to after they have made such entries.

On the other hand, consider the article represented in Table 3. This article, which is atypical in that almost all contributors made entries on more than one day, there is no interaction between Reviewers at all. Rather, Reviewers have merely added comments under various sections and at Level 1. They are not interacting with previously entered comments, but simply adding their observations to the relevant categories. Even under the title "5. Whose Value", where there appears to be a Level 2 response by Reviewer 3 to Reviewer 2, there is only a confirmation of what was said with additional comments added. Only the Author responds to the comments in this section, with a short clarification of a point made particularly by Reviewer 3.

Otherwise, responses to Reviewer comments in this paper are exclusively from the Author. The JiME affordance for collaboration in this case is reduced to an affordance for collection of sectioned review comments. The Reviewers are not considering each other's views or points, or at least they are not responding to them more than superficially.

Table 3. Representation of an article in which Reviewers enter comments at Level 1, suggesting non-interaction with other commentators (Reviewers or Author).

The pattern of lack of Reviewer to Reviewer interaction is in evidence to some degree across all articles in this study. Consider Table 4, for example.

Table 4. Incidence of comments by Reviewers and Authors(A) by hierarchical level.

Table 4 shows that most debate entries by Reviewers are at Level 1. With rare exception, Level 1 entries are non-responsive to either Reviewers or Authors. While the reason for this is unclear, it points to the need for a remediation via either the JiME medium or from an editor if more collaboration is desired. This will be addressed in a later section of the paper.

What is also apparent from Table 4 is that Authors make the most responses. This is probably not surprising, since Reviewers direct their comments to the content of articles. What is important for this paper is that if a medium like JiME is to support more collaboration or interaction between debate commentators—be they Reviewer or Author—a way must be found to remedy the lopsidedness of responses. If a medium like JiME were to be used for collaborative knowledge building, a serious redesign of affordances and editor mediation would be needed.

Discussion

There is a distinct trend for Reviewers to engage in the review debate from either the General perspective or the article Specific perspective. There is also a tendency for Reviewers to enter comments over a narrow time period. It has been argued here that both contribute to a subversion of the JiME affordance for collaboration and interaction among Reviewers and Authors.

One way to counter this would be to change the affordance of the hierarchical structure in such a way that Specific categories were presented to Reviewers and Authors at a time before the General categories were accessible. This could be accomplished in several ways, but simply removing the five General categories from the debate hierarchy at the beginning of the debate period might suffice. After a time period for review of Specific categories had passed, the editor could then open the debate to the more abstract General discussion—perhaps restricting access to the Specific categories at that time.

In this way, individuals could be encouraged to view the article from two perspectives. Depending on how the interface was changed, there might also be a second opportunity for Reviewers and Authors to read and respond more deeply to comments.

It is also possible that the editors themselves might mediate the debates in a more calculated way. Rather than just organizing the debate hierarchy into article-

Specific categories and directing actions to be taken by Authors, a new role might be undertaken—that of facilitating discussion of particular points within the debates. For instance, asking questions about whether or not consensus had been reached on terminological or conceptual issues might further deepen discussions. This, however, is not necessarily the goal for a journal like JiME, but might be more appropriate for a medium or context more directly concerned with knowledge building.

On the other hand, asking Reviewers to pick or summarize the most important commentaries would be another way editorial mediation could enhance a medium such as JiME. This could potentially also be incorporated into the JiME debate structure and be implemented as a final stage of the review process.

To return to a point brought up in the Introduction of this paper, we can see that both Reviewers and Authors contributing to the JiME reviews have generally appropriated the affordances of the system, but they have not mastered them. Both design and editorial remediation, as suggested above, may help.

Acknowledgements

The study reported on here is part of a larger project called the JIME Discourse Analysis Project, initiated as a joint project of students in courses offered by Tammy Sumner and Gerry Stahl at the University of Colorado, Boulder. Although the above collaborators have all had input into the JIME Discourse Analysis Project, the data representation, analyses and findings reported here, are solely those of the authors.

References

Koschman, T. (1996). CSCL: Theory and practice of an emerging paradigm. Mahwah, NJ: LEA.

Koschman, T. (1999). Toward a dialogic theory of learning: Bakhtin's contribution to learning in settings of collaboration. In: Proceedings of Computer Supported Collaborative Learning (CSCL '99), Palo Alto, CA, ppl 308-313.

Stahl, G. (2001). WebGuide: Guiding collaborative learning on the Web with Perspectives. JiME. Available at: http://www-jime.open.ac.uk/00/stahl.

Sumner, T., Shum, S.B., Wright, M., Bonnardel, N., & Chevalier, A. (2000). Redesigning the Peer Review Process: A developmental theory-in-action. Proc. Coop' 2000: Fourth International Conference on the Design of

Cooperative Systems. http://kmi.open.ac.uk/techreports/papers/kmi-tr-96.pdf.

Wertsch, J. (1998). Mind as action. New York: Oxford University Press.

15. Developing Summarization Skills through the Use of LSA-Based Feedback

Eileen Kintsch, Dave Steinhart, Gerry Stahl, Cindy Matthews, Ronald Lamb and the LSA Research Group**

Interactive Learning Environments. (2000) Vol. 8, No. 2, pp. 87-109.

This paper describes a series of classroom trials during which we developed *Summary Street*, an educational software system that uses Latent Semantic Analysis to support writing and revision activities. *Summary Street* provides various kinds of feedback, primarily about whether a student summary adequately covers important source content and fulfills other requirements, such as length. The feedback allows students to engage in extensive, independent practice in writing and revising without placing excessive demands on teachers for feedback. We first discuss the underlying educational rationale, then present some results of the trials conducted with the system. We describe the collaborative process among researchers and teachers which enabled the development of a viable and supportive educational tool and its integration into classroom instruction.

Summary Street is an educational software system that uses Latent Semantic Analysis (LSA) to support the reading and writing activities by which students develop and expand their knowledge in new topic areas. *Summary Street* determines the degree to which a student summary covers important source content and conforms to requirements, such as length. It tells the student what information in the source is missing, provides comments on redundancy, extraneous content and certain aspects of mechanics. Its current operation is described in more detail later. First, however, we discuss the underlying educational rationale and review the course of its research and development.

Text-based activities are indisputably a major vehicle for acquiring basic content knowledge in most school settings, across a range of pedagogical models, from those that emphasize traditionally structured classrooms to those in which students direct their own paths of inquiry. One form of computer support for comprehension and learning that our team has developed uses LSA to provide students with immediate feedback on how well their summaries of informative, expository texts cover the topic they are working on. We intend for this tool to be used by students independently, though still within a classroom setting, so that they can assess their own initial attempts to compose and revise their summaries. We hope thereby to provide students with more experience in extended writing and revising, while leaving teachers more time for other kinds of educational activities, such as coaching and modeling writing and summarization techniques, providing individual help, planning and delivering instruction, evaluating final versions of students' writing and other projects. Thus, in no sense is the tool intended to replace the teachers' role, for it is they who must teach the skills and, at least in our implementation, evaluate the final products of students' writing. Even though students are able to use the summarization tool on their own, we want to emphasize that it is a system that seeks to complement classroom instruction, rather than existing as a stand-alone system. Its purpose is to reinforce what is being taught rather than just provide an adjunct learning activity. Thus, in designing our first prototype, called *State the Essence*, we began with the premise that this would take place in collaboration with teachers who were the intended users. The summarization tool in its many transformations and its integration into the instructional curriculum represents a collaborative effort of researchers and teachers.

The current system evaluates only the completeness of the content, for the most part, leaving other important aspects of writing, such as sentence structure, organization and style, for traditional instructional methods. Nonetheless, we believe that in addition to improving their writing skill, students will benefit metacognitively from working independently, guided by the immediate feedback they receive. With frequent practice in assessing and revising the content of their summaries, we believe that students will also become more attuned to their own thinking and writing processes; they will be more likely to realize what they do and do not understand and better able to express what they mean in writing.

Importance of Summarization as a Learning Skill

Our initial discussions quickly converged on summarization as the kind of learning activity that LSA technology could effectively support and that conformed well with the teachers' instructional goals. The sixth-grade classrooms in which the tool is being tested employs a problem-based learning approach for instructing the district mandated curriculum. Learning how to summarize text is emphasized throughout the school year as a crucial study skill that helps students acquire a basic understanding of difficult and novel subject matter which they can then apply to solving problems or developing a project. Summarizing is more constrained than an open-ended writing task, with which young students often flounder, and it has a number of advantages over simply reading text and answering "comprehension questions", including the following:

- Summarizing not only provides practice in extended expository writing, it also teaches important study skills, such as identifying important content and separating main ideas from details. The fact that students at this age tend to highlight everything in a text – creating a "sea of yellow" – is symptomatic of their inability to do this. This happens especially when students are dealing with content that is completely new to them.

- Summarizing for a given purpose (e.g., to write a report on Mayan religious beliefs) requires even deeper thinking and analysis to select the relevant information.

- Summarizing is a way to develop solid understanding of complex material and also to articulate one's understanding so that it can be shared with others. The teachers with whom we work have noted clear differences in depth of understanding of topics that students have summarized as opposed to those they have only read about. Students appear to retain appreciably more information over longer periods of time if they have summarized it, and in classroom discussion they display an ownership of those topics, which shows up in their ability to contribute detailed and well reasoned ideas.

- Having to express content adequately yet concisely makes students aware of the need to learn summarization strategies that go beyond just adding and deleting single words, phrases or sentences. This awareness becomes a starting point for introducing students to higher-level strategies, such as how to reformulate text content by combining several ideas in a single sentence and generalizing across details.

- Summarizing requires active meaning construction to a much greater degree than choosing a response on a multiple-choice recognition test, or even than writing short answers to isolated questions. Thus, not only is summary writing an effective means to construct and integrate new knowledge, it is also a more authentic method for assessing what students do and do not understand than traditional comprehension tests.

The Use of LSA to Provide Writers with Content Feedback

As the rationale as well as technical details about LSA can be found in various other publications, we will not review them here (please see Landauer & Dumais

(1997), Landauer (1998), Landauer, Foltz & Laham (1998), as well as the introductory article by Landauer & Psotka in this volume). Essentially, LSA is an automatic statistical method for representing the meaning of words and text passages based on the analysis of a large amount of textual input. A semantic space is generated in which words, sentences, and whole texts can be represented as vectors. How closely related these vectors are to each other is measured by the cosine between them. We use this cosine measure to calculate what feedback to provide writers.

The most general LSA space available today is based on an input of about 11M words from carefully selected texts that form a representative sample of what a single student finishing high school might have read during his or her school years. This space is sufficient for our analysis, except for technical topics. Thus, for students writing on the functioning of the pulmonary and cardiac systems, or students writing on Meso-American civilizations, the general space does not have enough information to make the fine distinctions required. It has some basic information about the Inca and Maya cultures, for instance, but not enough to tell apart details of their religion or agricultural practices. Therefore, a specialized space must be constructed in order to use LSA. For instance, the Heart space discussed below was constructed from an input of 830 documents comprising about 17,688 words describing the function of the heart. The Meso-American space was based on 530 documents, comprising 46,951 words dealing with this topic. At the moment we do not yet have a good understanding when specialized spaces are required and when the general space suffices. Thus, ad hoc decisions must be made based on the performance of the system.

Because misspelled words are not considered words by LSA, we first have to correct spelling. For this purpose, all misspelled words (or rather, all strings LSA does not recognize) are flagged with asterisks, and the student is asked to make sure that they are spelled correctly. In principle, although this is not done in the present system, a standard spell checker can provide the student with alternatives, and LSA can select the most promising alternative(s) by looking at the cosine between each alternative identified by the spell checker and the immediate neighborhood of the word. Most likely, words with a higher cosine to the context are the right choice.

Content feedback is provided in the following manner. Suppose students are asked to summarize a text T containing the sections $\{T1, T2, \ldots, Tk\}$. The teacher requires that each of these sections be covered in the student's summary. What we do is to compute the cosine, Ci, between the summary a student wrote and each of the sections Ti. If $Ci \leq ti$, where t is an empirically determined threshold value, the student is told that section Ti is not adequately covered in the summary. The student then has the option to look at the appropriate section of the text on the computer screen and add some material about this section to the summary. If

$C_i \geq t$ for all sections, the student is told that he or she has now covered all parts of the text.

Since the teachers require summaries to be of a given word length to avoid extensive copying (about one quarter of the source text), students are told how many words they have written so far and whether this is within the allowed limits. If the text is too long, the student is given two kinds of feedback to help shorten it. One the one hand, irrelevant sentences in the summary are identified. The cosine is computed between each sentence in the summary and the text as a whole. If it is below some lower threshold, the sentence is identified as (possibly) irrelevant. This relevancy check tends to pick up sentences that are truly irrelevant (such as "I hope you like the summary I wrote") or sentences that refer to obscure details in the text that are not appropriate for a summary. On the other hand, redundant sentences are identified by computing the cosines among all sentences in the summary. If a cosine is greater than some upper limit, the two sentences are highlighted in the text and the student is told to inspect them for the purpose of combining them or deleting one. Sixth-grade students tend to repeat themselves, so this is a very useful check. Note, however, that both the relevance and the redundancy check occasionally pick up false positive: sentences, for example, with several overlapping words, but distinct meanings. This has the positive result that students must critically evaluate the computer's advice and decide whether they agree with it or not. Upper and lower limits for the relevance and redundancy checks are, once again, set empirically. For example, sentences with a cosine to the text that are below .30 might be termed irrelevant, and sentences with a cosine greater than .80 between themselves might be termed redundant.

The system itself is thus quite simple. However, what was not simple was to determine the best ways to provide this kind of feedback to students and the optimal sequencing of this feedback, as described below.

History of Trials Using State the Essence: Fall 1997 – Fall 1998 Instruction

Two team-taught classes participated in trials using an early version of the summarization tool called *State the Essence* during the 1997-1998 school year, and a subsequent trial took place in the fall of the next academic year. The system was designed to support students' summary writing in three curricular units, each lasting about three-to-four weeks: Energy Sources (September, 1997 and September, 1998), Ancient Civilizations of the Western Hemisphere (January, 1997) and The Human Circulatory System (April, 1998). Students first composed their summaries using a word processor or pen and paper in advance. They then pasted or typed them into *State the Essence* in order to receive feedback on how to revise them. For the trial on the circulatory system, we collected summaries that students wrote using traditional means as well as those written with *State the Essence*, which allowed us to make within-subject comparisons. However, our main goal during this initial period was to test the system rather than to collect learning and performance data.

1. <u>Sources of Energy</u>. In addition to teaching students about the new content, during the first unit the teachers' instruction introduced students to the concept of summarization and the appropriate strategies. The teachers' instruction included directly explaining the strategies and their purpose, together with modeling the strategies and class discussion of good and poor examples of summary writing.

Students read 10 brief texts (two to two-and-a half pages) about different sources of energy (nonrenewable: coal, natural gas, nuclear, petroleum, propane; and renewable: biomass, geothermal, hydropower, solar, wind) and wrote one summary (75 - 200 words) of each energy type. Students used this task as the starting point for their projects, which involved becoming an expert in one energy source, organizing a science station and teaching the subject to other students in small groups.

2. <u>Ancient Civilizations</u>. For this unit students were required to summarize three texts (each about two-and-one-half to three pages) about the Maya, Aztec and Inca civilizations, again to develop basic knowledge about the cultures. The summaries were to be between 200 to 300 words long. Each class then divided into three groups, each focusing on one of the cultures, and each member of a group researched one particular aspect of the culture (e.g., history, religion, artistic or scientific contributions, social structure). Finally, each group made a joint presentation with visual props to the class as a whole, each member filling in a piece of the topic in jigsaw fashion. The summarization instruction this time focused on higher-level strategies, such as sentence combining and constructing generalizations to achieve conciseness. Students prepared two of their summaries in the traditional manner, using a word processor or pen and paper, and revised a third summary guided by feedback from the summarization software.

3. <u>Circulatory System</u>. Unlike the preceding units, the instructional focus here was primarily on developing a deep understanding of the content - a challenging topic with a great deal of unfamiliar technical vocabulary and difficult concepts. Summarization of two texts about the lungs and the heart was used to help students integrate this information and to assess their conceptual understanding of the dual-loop circulatory system. The summaries were to be 150-250 words in length, and students used *State the Essence* to work on one of these summaries. They wrote the other summary using traditional means.

Evolution of State the Essence

Initial trials with *State the Essence* were beset by technical problems from overloading the system with too many simultaneous submissions. However, these problems were overcome in our later trials. In general, the school trials with the summarization software were a success in terms of student enthusiasm and teacher satisfaction, at least to some degree: the system worked well, was relatively easy to learn, and using *State the Essence* did not interfere with students' learning of the content (there was no significant difference between summarizing conditions in scores received on a short-answer test on the unit of study). However, as mentioned, the purpose of these school trials was not a formal evaluation of the system but rather to further develop and refine it.

There are three classes of changes that we explored:

1. How the student's writing is to be evaluated by LSA: There are several options here; for example, a given essay can be matched against a set of pre-graded essays, or against an expert summary prepared by the teacher or expert writer. In the end we adopted a more practical method that would only require a teacher to submit the text to be summarized, subdivided into topic sections, a method that has been incorporated into the later versions of the system.
2. What feedback to give the student, and in what order: It is easy to overwhelm users and confuse them with the rich feedback the system is able to provide. Over the course of the year we experimented with several different feedback formats before arriving at a system that is somewhat constrained yet still flexible to use. "Less is more" was our take-home message - less feedback and more support.
3. How to embed our system into classroom instruction: Use of the summarization tool as a stand-alone system is rather inefficient for middle-school students. Most students at this level need explicit instruction on how to summarize, and how to revise. Furthermore, available technology has made it difficult to use the system in a classroom without taking too much time away from other instructional activities. Our trials therefore took place over one or two sessions with the entire class – a practical necessity, though not an optimal way to learn revision skills.

Evaluating the summaries

Our initial problem in delivering feedback to the students was to decide what text to use as a basis for comparison. Several different approaches to evaluating college students' essays are described in Landauer, Foltz, and Laham (1998), some of which we also applied to evaluating the students' summaries. One approach is to compare a summary to a corpus of previously graded summaries. The summary which is the closest match in terms of the LSA cosine becomes the basis for assigning a grade of A, B, or C, and so on. Since we had not yet accumulated a set of graded summaries to draw on, this option was not open to us. Hence, we first tried matching the sixth-graders' summaries against a set of four or five summaries written by expert writers (teachers and researchers). Given that even expert writers do not completely agree on what content to include or exclude, the student's overall score was based on the best fit (i.e., the highest LSA cosine) to one of the expert texts. Section scores were based on a comparison of the summary to each section of a "golden" summary that incorporated the main content in all the expert summaries. Although this method worked quite well, putting together a set of expert summaries for each novel text proved too cumbersome in the long run.

An alternative basis of comparison is to use the source text itself. A holistic score can be obtained from the cosine between the student's summary and the original source text. In addition, section scores may be derived by dividing the text into distinct topic sections, approximately equal in length, and comparing the entire summary to each of these sections. As described earlier in this paper, a set of empirically determined thresholds is used as the basis for the feedback given to the student on how adequately each section was covered. The summary "passes" when all sections have met the criterion for each section within the given length constraints. This method underlies all the versions of the summarizing software described here.

Presenting the Feedback

LSA-based feedback goes far beyond other forms of automatic feedback, such as spelling and grammar checks, by evaluating the semantic content of a piece of writing. For essays and summaries, it can tell the writer whether or not all the important subtopics have been covered and what kind of information is missing; it can point out sentences that appear to have too much overlap in content with each other or with the original text; and it can suggest sentences that seem to have little relevance to the topic of the text.

In addition to this content information, in our initial trial on Energy Sources we provided students with feedback on the length of their summaries. Length constraints across all three trials varied between 100 to 300 words for texts that ranged from about 800 to 1450 words. Students received an overall score weighted to reflect appropriateness of length, the adequacy of section coverage and overall content coverage. In addition, they could request checks for (a) redundancy, (b) relevance (both based on a comparison of sentences in the summary with those in the original text), and (c) repetition (based on a comparison of all sentence pairs in the summary). Our sixth-grade students, although appreciative and highly motivated, seemed confused and floundered in their attempts to revise their summaries. In addition to solving various technical problems, it was clear that we needed to provide better editing tools, a clearer presentation, and more support for summarizing and revising both within the system and through classroom instruction. We especially needed to present the feedback in a way that was easier to understand than the set of numerical scores that were initially presented simultaneously.

In our second trial on Ancient Civilizations the feedback was given in three stages, accessed by the user's request first for general feedback, then successively more. The general feedback included length (*too long, too short*), an overall score, and adequate/inadequate section coverage, as before. Requests for more feedback first displayed irrelevant and relevant sentences (the latter were praised); then, at an advanced level, feedback was provided on redundant sentences (summary sentences with too much overlapping content). In addition, we added an overview of summarization strategies to the Introduction to *State the Essence* and hyperlinks to further hints and examples. Links were also provided to the Maya, Aztec, and Inca source texts and to additional background information.

The results of this classroom trial were both encouraging and revealing of significant weaknesses in the system. Again, the overall point score was a great motivator: students were challenged to try to improve their scores and remained focused on the task. However, the scores were not always reliable, tending to be inflated and too sensitive to small local variations. Sentence level feedback was especially problematic, with too many inappropriate flags (both good and bad), and difficult to use because problematic sentences were presented in a list, out of context and on a separate screen from the writer's textbox. Presenting misspelled words as a list posed similar difficulties for making corrections. Even though presented in stages, or at different levels, students were still overwhelmed by the amount of feedback they received and often dismayed at the multiplicity of problems to deal with. Further, many students needed extensive and quite explicit guidance on how to make meaningful changes in revising their summaries; in particular, they needed to be shown how to generalize across sentences or how to combine ideas from several places into a single sentence in the context of their own work. This need clearly goes beyond what LSA-based feedback provides, but highlights an area where the teacher's classroom intervention can be helpful.

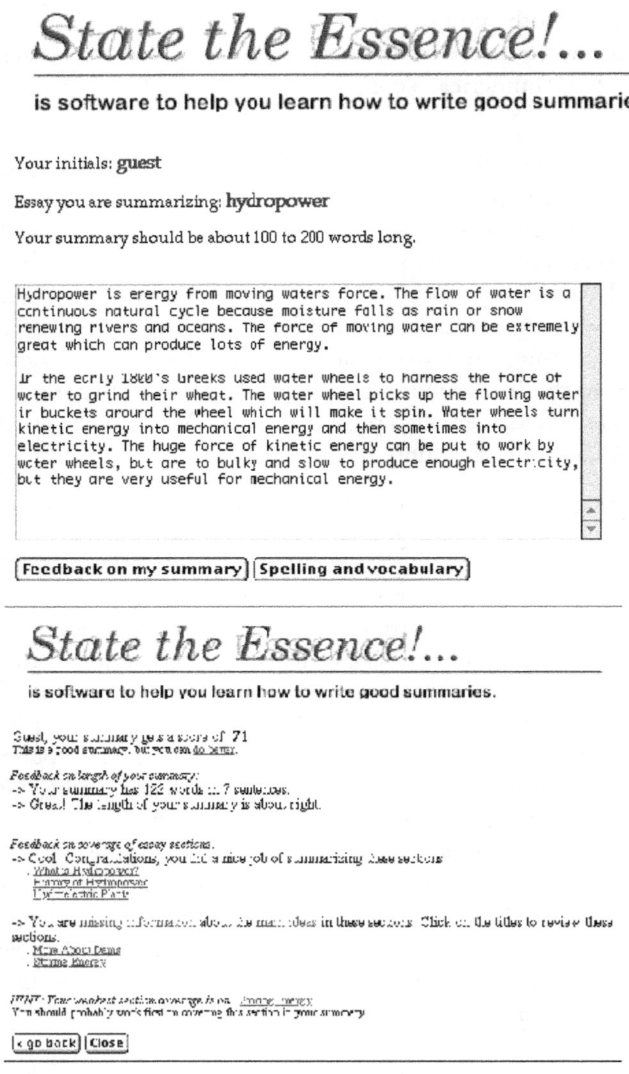

State the Essence!...

is software to help you learn how to write good summaries.

Your initials: **guest**

Essay you are summarizing: **hydropower**

Your summary should be about 100 to 200 words long.

> Hydropower is energy from moving waters force. The flow of water is a continuous natural cycle because moisture falls as rain or snow renewing rivers and oceans. The force of moving water can be extremely great which can produce lots of energy.
>
> In the early 1800's Greeks used water wheels to harness the force of water to grind their wheat. The water wheel picks up the flowing water in buckets around the wheel which will make it spin. Water wheels turn kinetic energy into mechanical energy and then sometimes into electricity. The huge force of kinetic energy can be put to work by water wheels, but are to bulky and slow to produce enough electricity, but they are very useful for mechanical energy.

[**Feedback on my summary**] [**Spelling and vocabulary**]

State the Essence!...

is software to help you learn how to write good summaries.

Guest, your summary gets a score of **71**
This is a good summary, but you can do better.

Feedback on length of your summary:
-> Your summary has 122 words in 7 sentences.
-> Great! The length of your summary is about right.

Feedback on coverage of essay sections.
-> Cool! Congratulations, you did a nice job of summarizing these sections
   . What is Hydropower?
   . History of Hydropower
   . Hydroelectric Plants

-> You are missing information about the main ideas in these sections. Click on the titles to revise these sections.
   . More About Dams
   . Storing Energy

HINT: Your weakest section coverage is on . Storing Energy.
You should probably work first on covering this section in your summary.

[< go back] [Close]

<u>Figure 1</u>. Screen shots showing a student summary and first-level feedback from *State the Essence*: overall score, word length, sections with adequate content coverage, and sections with missing information.

16. Designing Collaborative Learning Environments using Digital Games

César A. Collazos, Luis A. Guerrero,José A. Pino,Sergio F. Ochoa,Gerry Stahl

Abstract: Collaborative learning environments require carefully crafted designs –both technical and social. This paper presents a model describing how to design socio-technical environments that will promote collaboration in group activities. A game was developed based on this model. This tool was used to conduct experiments for studying the collaborative learning process. Testing with this system revealed some strengths and weaknesses, which are being addressed in the on-going research.

Introduction

Quantitative research in CSCL is hard to conduct because quantitative measures of collaborative interactions tend to lose the collaborative context [Stahl, 02]. There are many causes for the difficulty of measuring the collaboration processes [Collazos, 07]. However, advantages of collaborative learning are clear and they are well documented [Johnson, 86, Slavin, 88]. The design and measurement of collaborative activities continue playing a key role on both: (a) the learning results that can be obtained and (b) the improvement capability of such activity. Currently there are several proposals to design or measure collaborative processes in learning environments; however, there are just few ones able to integrate these two key elements. Unfortunately, these integrated proposals are complex to apply; therefore, it is not clear they can be used by most teachers and instructors.

This paper presents a model to guide the design of socio-technical environments to promote collaboration in group activities in order to deal with these challenges. A collaborative learning environment was designed using the model, and it was applied in a real scenario. The model allowed us to determine the interactions among subjects, the initial conditions and the design of the shared workspace structure.

The proposal also includes a set of indicators that have shown to be useful to measure collaboration in learning environments [Collazos, 03a]. These indicators complement the design model, allowing teachers and instructors to measure and analyze the students' performance. Thus, it is possible to design effective collaborative learning environments (CLE).

Next section presents some related work. Section 3 describes the model for designing environments that promote collaboration. Section 4 introduces the collaborative indicators to be used to measure and analyze collaborative learning activities. Section 5 presents the CLE which was designed using the model. Section 6 shows and explains the experimental results obtained using this CLE. Finally, Section 7 presents the conclusions and further work.

Related Work

There is no doubt collaborative games could be useful for learning. The most important issue is to investigate the requirements that game-based learning should satisfy to get the best results. Thus, Di Blas et al. report an experience in which educational, relational, and organizational settings are at least as much important as technology for the success or failure of a collaborative learning case [Di Blas, 05]. They also found the teacher's participation and motivation was crucial. Focusing on the cognitive capabilities and needs of the learner has produced several innovative computer-mediated micro-worlds aimed at helping students learn a specific domain [Anderson, 93]. Activity Theory (AT) [Wertsch, 79] can also be a source of inspiration for designing collaborative learning environments [Gifford, 99]: AT claims that internal activities emerge out of practical external activity and thus the unit of analysis must include the person and the culturally defined environment.

Instead of designing systems that compensate for meta-cognitive deficiencies by becoming increasingly directive, we should develop systems supporting the learner's meta-cognitive activities (or even better, that develop their meta-cognitive skills) [Dillenbourg, 92]. Furthermore, particular forms of interactions are needed to trigger the desired learning mechanisms in collaborative learning environments [Dillenbourg, 99]. There is, however, no guarantee that those interactions occur. Hence, the idea is to develop mechanisms for increasing the probability that they will happen. One of these ways is by designing well-specified collaborative scenarios [Santoro, 05]. Thus, we need to design the learning task and the learning environment. The design of the learning task needs to draw on the best we know about how people learn, on knowledge of academic subject matter and/or vocational competencies, and on knowledge of the learners. A task needs to be sufficiently well-specified that the chances of a learner engaging in unproductive activity are kept within tolerable limits. The learning environment is the physical environment or physical settings within which learners work.

The Proposed Model

The proposed model involves three interrelated activities. Each of them provides feedback that allow designers to establish the best design of the collaborative learning environment (Figure 1). The model attempts to assist collaboration in two ways: establishing the situation in which the collaboration takes place (set up initial conditions), and structuring the collaboration itself through coaching or self regulation (maintaining the collaboration).

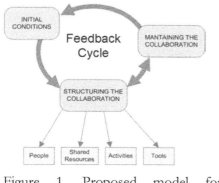

Figure 1. Proposed model for supporting collaboration

The cycle starts with the definition of the initial set of conditions that probably will be present during the collaboration process. Such a definition influences the elements that will be used in the process and the role of each one of them. These two elements establish restrictions on the strategies that can be used for maintaining the collaboration among the participants. The strategies to maintain the collaboration will make a difference between a successful or unsuccessful activity.

As a result of applying this model it is expected the collaborative activity carried out on the learning environment promotes collaboration among group members. Next section describes these three key elements.

Establishing Initial Conditions

A first way to increase the probability that some types of interactions occur is to carefully design the situation where the collaboration will take place. Numerous independent variables have been studied in order to determine the conditions under which collaborative learning is efficient and effective. Based on Bannon's work [Bannon, 89], the proposed model defines a set of elements to consider for specifying the initial characteristics of the groups. Next, these elements are briefly explained.

Type of activity. Specify the type of activity that will be performed by the members of the group in order to solve a problematic situation. It could, e.g., include tasks such as: puzzle solving, editing a newspaper or writing a letter.

Nature of collaborators. Specify the types of interaction that occur. It could include three types of interactions: peer-to-peer interaction, teacher-student interaction, and student-computer interaction.

Group heterogeneity. This covers several independent variables such as: size of the group, gender and differences within the group. Typically, the smaller the group, the more each member talks and the less chance there is someone will be left out. Also, smaller groups require less group management skills and they can usually decide faster [Kagan, 92]. Gender specifies the male/female group composition.

Positive interdependencies. This is one of the key elements in successful groups. Based on many studies, psychologists working in education identified positive interdependence as a feature of good learning groups [Slavin, 90]. Collazos et al. have developed various ways of structuring positive interdependencies in software tools based on the interface design to ensure students think "we" instead of "me" [Collazos, 03b].

Setting of collaboration. It corresponds to the place where the collaborative activity will be held. It could be the classroom, workplace, home or a virtual space.

Conditions of collaboration. These conditions specify the kind of mediation. It could be physically co-present or computer-mediated.

Period of collaboration. This specifies the time interval in which the collaborative activity will occur. It could be specified in minutes, hours, days, weeks, or months.

These elements are instantiated, as it is shown in Table 1, and then they are considered during the collaboration structuring process. Section 4 shows how to instantiate and use these elements to make design decisions.

Structuring Collaboration

The teacher/instructor cannot simply ask students to start the projects and encourage peers to learn together, but s/he should specify a collaboration process. Such process could include several activities. At each activity, the team has to produce something as a result, and team members have some role to play. The elements we propose to use to design the collaboration process are the following ones:

Activities. This element represents the tasks that must be performed by the group members during the collaboration process. This includes the workflow of (individual and collaborative) activities that make up the process. It also includes the goals and rules of each task. There are activities performed by the group associated to the main goal, and other activities done by every member of the group related to the partial goals. On the other hand, the rules of the group activity should be specified. These rules mediate the subject-community relationship, and refer to the explicit and implicit regulations, norms and conventions that constrain actions and interactions within the activity system [Engestrom, 87]. These rules permit reviewing boundaries and guidelines for the activity. The activities included in the collaboration process must be designed so that every member of the group has a similar work load [Kagan, 94].

People. This element determines the roles that should be present in the collaboration process. Each group member has a role to play in each activity. The role assigns responsibilities and grants to the users. For example, a student can play the role of reader in a pair reading exercise. This role will be played for a while, and then it is assigned to the other student of the pair [Johnson, 98].

Tools. This component represents the tools used by people to perform the collaborative activities. These tools must allow collaborators to communicate, coordinate and participate in the process. Members of the group must communicate and coordinate among themselves in order to accomplish tasks that are independent, that are not completely described or that require negotiation [Fussell, 98]. Regarding participation, the idea is to define scenarios where members of the group have the same chances of participation to solve the situation.

Shared Resources. These resources represent the knowledge that is shared by the group members during an activity. This knowledge can include digital objects, a portion of the user interface, coordination strategies, decisions, goals and awareness mechanisms. For example, the discussion of the strategies to solve a problem helps group members to construct a shared view (shared resource) of their goals and tasks required to be executed [Fussell, 98]. This shared view can improve the coordination during an activity, because each learner knows how his/her task matches the global team goals.

These four elements can be used to structure the collaboration process, by considering the constraints imposed by the initial conditions. The goal of this design should be maximizing the knowledge acquired about a subject (learning goal) or the ability of the student to assimilate and reproduce a certain skill (transversal goal), such as negotiation capability or leadership.

Maintaining the Collaboration

The last aspect to consider is related to the strategy that can be used to maintain the collaboration among members of the group. Such strategy could be coordinated by a cognitive mediator or by the team members themselves.

There is no guarantee interactions among team members actually occur. Hence, some external regulation is needed to promote the occurrence of those interactions. One way to provide that kind of regulation is through the cognitive mediator. The role of mediator will not be to intervene at the task level, but to guarantee all the group members participate, and to frequently ask questions such as: What happened? What does it mean? The role of the cognitive mediator is to maintain the focus of the discussion, guiding students through the knowledge construction process. As the collaboration goes on, the state of interaction is evaluated [Pinheiro, 03]. Remedial actions may be proposed to reduce discrepancies between these states. Indicators that have shown to be useful to measure and analyze the collaboration process in learning environments are presented below.

The Indicators

Collazos et al. [Collazos, 03a] have defined five Indicators of Collaboration (IC) that allow measuring and analyzing an activity carried out in a collaborative learning environment. These indicators are the following ones:

Applying strategies (IC1). This indicator tries to capture the ability of the group members to generate, communicate and consistently apply a strategy to jointly solve the problem.

Intra-group cooperation (IC2). This indicator refers to the use of collaborative strategies previously defined during the work.

Success criteria review (IC3). This indicator measures the degree of involvement of the group members in reviewing boundaries, guidelines and roles during the group activity. It may include summarizing the outcome of the last task, assigning action items to group members, and noting times for expected completion of assignments.

Monitoring (IC4). This indicator is understood as a regulatory activity. The objective of the indicator is to oversee if the group maintains the chosen strategies to solve the problem, keeping focused on the goals and the success criteria.

Performance (IC5). This indicator refers to the quality of the proposed solution to the problematic situation. The evaluation of collaborative work takes into account three aspects: Quality (how good is the result of collaborative work), Time (total elapsed time while working) and Work (total amount of work done).

The Collaborative Learning Environment

As explained above, a Collaborative Learning Environment (CLE) involves, at least, four elements: people, activities, tools and shared resources. For developing our environment we use a game-based learning approach.

The tool used in our learning environment is a game —called *Chase the Cheese*—, which is played by four persons, each one using a single computer. The computers are physically distant. Thus, the players need to use a computer-mediated-communication tool. All activities made by participants are recorded for later analysis and players are made aware of that. Players are given very few details about the game. The main game rules and obstacles must be discovered by participants while playing. They have to develop joint strategies to succeed.

The game window has four quadrants. The goal of the game is to move a mouse figure (in quadrant 1) to the cheese (quadrant 4). Each quadrant has a coordinator –one of the players– permitted to move the mouse with arrows; the other persons can only help the coordinator sending messages which are seen at the right-hand side of the screen. In this way, each player has two predefined roles: coordinator (only one per quadrant and randomly assigned) and collaborator. In fact, there are four partial goals –one per quadrant- that must be achieved in order to obtain the main goal. The game challenges the coordinator of the quadrant in which the mouse is located because there are obstacles that impede the mouse movements. Most obstacles are invisible to the quadrant coordinator, but visible to one of the other players. This feature of the game must be discovered by the players in order to achieve the goal. The players must then develop a shared strategy to communicate the obstacle locations to the coordinator. Each participant has a partial view of the labyrinth and s/he must interact with her/his peers to solve the problem. Each player (and quadrant) has a colour associated. When starting the movement of the mouse, the coordinator has an individual score of 100 points. Whenever the mouse hits an obstacle, the score is decreased 10 points. The coordinator has to lead the mouse to the cheese (in the case of the last quadrant) or to a bridge between quadrants. When the mouse passes to another quadrant the coordinator role is switched, and the previous score is added to the total score of the group. If any individual score reaches a value below or equal to 0, the group loses the game. The goal of the game is to move the mouse to the cheese and to do it with a total score as high as possible.

Let us see how we design the CLE according to the model proposed in the previous section. Table 1 presents the initial conditions in our game software tool. Table 2 presents the way we structured the collaboration among members of the group in our tool.

Elements	Description
Type of activity	Solve a labyrinth
Nature of Collaborators	Peer to peer interaction
Group heterogeneity	The game is played by four people, randomly selected.

Positive Interdependence	Goal interdependence, because, there is a common goal, in that case, lead the mouse to its cheese.
	Role interdependence: There are two predefined roles, coordinator and collaborators.
	Resource interdependence: Every member of the group has information that the other ones need. They have a partial view of the labyrinth, because they have information about their own colourful obstacles.
	Reward interdependence: Group members not only must lead the mouse to its cheese but arrive with the highest score.
Setting of Collabor.	Classroom
Conditions of Collabor.	Computer-mediated
Period of Collaboration	45 minutes

Table 1. Initial conditions for the software tool

Elements	Description
Activities	Global: Lead the mouse to its cheese.
	Partial: Pass through every traffic light icon.
	Rules: The coordinator is the only person able to move the mouse. When the score gets to 0, the game is over.
People (roles)	Coordinator: one per quadrant.
	Collaborators: the three remaining persons.
Shared Resources (Communication)	The system provides some dialogue boxes, where every participant can send messages to a member or the group. Also, there is a message reception mailbox.
Shared Resources (Participation)	In order to guarantee equal participation of all members of the group, the labyrinth was designed with a similar complexity in every quadrant. The number of obstacles and their distribution was similar in all the quadrants.

Table 2. Structuring the collaboration

The third part of the model (i.e., maintaining the collaboration), includes participation of a cognitive mediator. Our first experiments using this CLE did not include it in an explicit way. We only presented the information at the end of the activity. However, we re-built the collaboration processes through semantic analysis of the messages, and so, we determined the degree of collaboration measured by some IC. The cognitive mediator and/or participants could interpret the results and decide what actions (if any) to take, in order to improve the collaboration [Collazos, 03c]. It could be possible that students, who view and analyze the IC values [Collazos, 03a] may learn to understand and improve their own interaction.

Experiments

The designed CLE was used in an experiment involving 11 groups of four students, whom carry out the collaboration process. The groups that participated in the initial experiment were the following ones:

Group 0: A group of graduate students from the "Collaborative Systems" course at the University of Chile, with some experience in collaborative work techniques.

Group 1-4: Four groups of high school students. They were about 15 years old. Two of the groups were randomly chosen (Gr.1 and Gr.2) and the remaining ones included friends (Gr. 3 and Gr. 4).

Group 5: A randomly selected group, i.e., people that have never worked together.

Group 6: Friends who have worked as a group many times before this experiment and that have a good personal relationship.

Groups 7-10: Four groups of graduate students, from the University of Cauca, Colombia (Gr. 7, Gr. 8, Gr. 9, Gr. 10).

Table 3 presents the obtained results. Every IC is computed with a 0-1 range, where 1 means the highest score. Although some groups got a good score in some indicators, we can see that almost all groups were ineffective collaborative groups because they were weak in collaborative attitudes (IC3). The rest of the indicators are acceptable, since most of them are over 0.5.

Students have two responsibilities in cooperative learning situations: (a) learn the assigned material, and (b) ensure that all members of the group learn the assigned material [Johnson, 78]. The second aspect is something that never occurred during the collaborative learning processes of our groups. Of course, nobody told the group members they should have a collaborative attitude. Many hypothesis can be developed to explain why these attitudes did not appear spontaneously: perhaps the students initially thought the game was very easy, or maybe they felt pressured to play instead of stopping to carefully think what to do, etc.

Table 3: Experimental Results

By means of educational games, learners should be able to apply factual

	IC1	IC2	IC3	IC4	IC5
Gr. 0	0.69	0.69	0.2	0.75	0.65
Gr. 1	0.31	0.71	0.2	0.80	0.57
Gr. 2	0.71	0.74	0.8	0.78	0.66
Gr. 3	0.75	0.84	1	0.86	0.61
Gr. 4	0.68	0.62	0.2	0.80	0.69
Gr. 5	0.48	0.61	0.5	0.74	0.63
Gr. 6	0.71	0.72	1	0.85	0.52
Gr. 7	0.47	0.80	0.2	0.80	0.53
Gr. 8	0.27	0.75	0.2	0.82	0.54
Gr. 9	0.28	0.75	0.2	0.81	0.54
Gr. 10	0.48	0.80	0.2	0.83	0.53

knowledge, learn on demand, gain experiences in the virtual world that can later shape their behavioral patterns and directly influence their reflection. Learners are encouraged to combine knowledge from different areas to choose a solution or to make a decision at a certain point, learners can test how the outcome of the game changes based on their decisions and actions. Despite the fact our learning environment includes many of the elements proposed in our model the results obtained were not the best. What matters is not just the design of the environment, nor even the design of a single task or curricular unit. Rather, the cultivation of minds, which itself requires engagement in a social process of meaning appropriation, requires the whole environment, not just the computer program, be designed as a well orchestrated whole. This includes key elements, such as curriculum, teacher's behavior, collaborative tasks, mode of collaboration and interaction, tasks and learning goals.

Conclusions and Future Work

The design of well-specified environments could induce collaborative learning activities within a group. Thus, it is important to carefully define every activity that is part of the process in order to promote collaboration. This paper presented a model to design CLE and a set of indicators to measure the collaboration process in such environments. The design model is easy to apply; therefore almost any teacher/instructor could use it. This model attempts to support collaboration in CLEs through two ways: structuring the situation in which the collaboration takes place (set up initial conditions and structuring the collaboration), and structuring the collaboration itself through coaching or self regulation (maintaining the collaboration).

Based on the obtained results, we believe it is not only important to design the tool supporting the collaboration process, but also to consider other aspects such as teacher's participation and learning goals, in order to have an effective CLE. The use of the proposed indicators allows us to identify strengths and weaknesses of the CLE we designed. It means the indicators are useful to evaluate this kind of learning environments. In addition, the indicators fit with the proposed model, allowing teachers/instructors adjust the CLE based on the feedback given by these metrics. In future versions, we will build tools that allow on-line monitoring the state of the participants' interaction, modelling the state of the interaction, and providing collaborators with visualizations to self-diagnose the collaboration.

Acknowledgements

This work was partially funded by Spanish Ministry of Science and Tech., CICYT Project ADACO (TIN 2004-08000-C03-03), Colciencias (Colombia) Proj. N° 4128-14-18008 & 030-2005, and Fondecyt (Chile) grant N° 1040952 and 11060467.

References

[Anderson, 93] Anderson, J. Rules of the mind. Mahwah, N.J.: Lauwrence Erlbaum, 1993.
[Bannon, 89] Bannon, L. Issues in computer-supported collaborative learning, NATO Advanced workshop on computer-supported collaborative learning, Italy, Sept. 1989.

[Collazos, 03a] Collazos, C, Guerrero, L.A., Pino, JA.., Ochoa, S. Evaluating collaborative learning processes. Lecture Notes in Computer Science 2440, 2003, 203-221.

[Collazos, 03b] Collazos, C, Guerrero, L.A., Pino, J.A., Ochoa, S. Collaborative Scenarios to promote positive interdependence among group members. LNCS 2806, 2003, 356-370.

[Collazos, 03c] Collazos, C., Guerrero, L.A., Pino, J.A, Ochoa, S. Improving the use of strategies in Computer-Supported Collaborative Processes. Lectura Notes in Computer Science 2806, 2003, 247-260.

[Collazos, 07] Collazos, C., Guerrero, L., Pino, J.A., Stahl, G., Ochoa, S. A Model and a Game for Investigating and Designing Collaborative Learning Environments, SIIE 2006, León, Spain, 2006.

[Di Blas, 05] Di Blas, N., Paolini, P., Poggi, C. 3D Worlds for Edutainment: Educational, Relational and Organizational Principles. Proc. 3rd. Int. Conference on Pervasive Computing and Communications Workshops, 2005.

[Dillenbourg, 92] Dillenbourg, P. The computer as a constructorium: Tools for observing one's own learning. Elsom-Cook & Moyse (Eds.), Know. Negotiation, London: Acad. Press, 1992.

[Dillenbourg, 99] Dillenbourg, P. What do you mean by collaborative learning? In Dillenbourg (Ed.) Collaborative-Learning: Cognitive & Computational Approaches. Oxford: Elsevier, 1999, 1-19.

[Engestrom, 87] Engestrom, Y. Learning by expanding: an activity-theoretical approach to development research. Orienta-Konsultit Oy, Helsinki, 1987.

[Fussell, 98] Fussell, S. Coordination, overload and team performance: effects of team communication strategies. CSCW'98, Chapel Hill NC, 1998, 275-284.

[Gifford, 99] Gifford, B., Enyedy, N. Activity centered design: Towards a theoretical framework for CSCL. Proc. 1999 Conf. on Computer Support for Collaborative Learning, Palo Alto, CA, 1999.

[Johnson, 78] Johnson, D., Johnson, R. Cooperative, competitive, and individualistic learning. Journal of Research and Development in Education 12, 8-15, 1978.

[Johnson, 86] Johnson, D.W. Stanne, M. A comparison of computer-assisted cooperative, competitive, and individualistic learning. Am. Educational Res. J. 23, 1986, 382-392.

[Johnson, 98] Johnson D., Johnson R, Holubec, E. Cooperation in the classroom. Interaction Book Company, Edina, MN, 1998.

[Kagan, 92] Kagan, S. Cooperative learning. San Juan Capistrano, CA: Kagan Coop. Learning, 1992.

[Kagan, 94] Kagan, S., Kagan, M. The structural approach: six keys to cooperative learning. In S. Sharon (Ed.), Handbook of cooperative learning methods, Westport, CT: Greenwood Press, 1994, 115-133.

[Pinheiro, 03] Pinheiro, M. K., Lima, J. V., Borges, M. R. S. A framework for awareness support in groupware systems, Computers in Industry, 52(1), 47-57, 2003.

[Santoro, 05] Santoro, F.M., Borges, M. R. S., Santos, N. Learning to Plan the Collaborative Design Process, Lecture Notes in Computer Science 3168, 33-44, 2005.

[Slavin, 88] Slavin, R. Cooperative learning and student achievement. In R.E. Slavin (Ed), School and classroom organization. Hillsdale, NJ: Erlbaum, 1988.

[Slavin, 90] Slavin, R. Cooperative learning: Theory, research and practice. Englewood Cliffs, NJ: Prentice-Hall, 1990.

[Stahl, 02] Stahl, G. Rediscovering CSCL. In Koschman, T., Hall, R., & Miyake, N., (Eds.), CSCL2: Carrying forward the conversation, Lawrence Erlbaum Associates, Hillsdale, NJ., 169-181, 2002.

[Wertsch, 79] Wertsch, J. The concept of Activity in Soviet Psychology: An Introduction. In J. Wertsch (ed.): The concept of Activity in Soviet Psychology. Armonk, N.Y.; M.E. Sharpe, Inc., 1979.

17. Introduction: Computer Support for Learning Communities

GERRY STAHL, MARKUS ROHDE, VOLKER WOLF

This special issue emerged from two workshops on community-based learning: one at the Sixth International Conference on the Learning Sciences (ICLS 2004), held in Santa Monica, CA, and the other at the International Conference on Computer-Supported Collaborative Learning (CSCL 2005), held in Taipei, Taiwan. A call for papers was issued as a follow-up to these stimulating workshops; 16 papers were submitted, of which six were accepted following a rigorous double loop peer reviewing process. This special issue is part of a wider discourse on learning communities, specifically the conferences series on Communities and Technologies and related publications (Huysman *et al.* 2003; Ackerman *et al.* 2003; Huysman and Wulf 2004; Klamma *et al.* 2004; Stahl 2006).

Within the perspective of the history of computers, interest in computer support for communities represents a logical progression. In the mid-twentieth century, computers were viewed as self-contained machines; designer's concerns stressed internal efficiency in terms of logical operations and memory allocation. It took visionaries like Bush (1945) and Engelbart (1962) to conceptualize computers as extenders of human intellect. Then designers had to consider human-computer interaction, how individuals actually used computer tools. Although the visionaries provided glimpses of inter-personal implications, most software development focused on tools for individual users and at best took into account human psychology.

More recently, the fields of Computer Supported Cooperative Work (CSCW), Computer Supported Collaborative Learning (CSCL) and Communities and Technologies (C&T) have begun to think about how small groups and communities-of-practice relate to computational infrastructures. Consideration of small groups brought in anthropologists and communication analysts. As we now expand to consider computer support for communities, social theorists and business management specialists also become involved in the multidisciplinary effort. Consideration of the community already includes the ultimate expansion to thinking about computers and the world. Groupware bleeds unnoticed into global applications: The burgeoning variety of Internet-based communication media—

IM, email, wiki, blog—bring the world together into a maze of community. At this point, computer artifacts become pervasive infrastructure and social practices of usage, far outstripping the plans of technology designers.

Modern communities are learning communities in the sense that they evolve through the collective building of knowledge and the shifting participation of their members (Lave and Wenger 1991). Conversely, learning can be viewed in terms of a member's increasingly skilled participation in knowledge-based communities. The interplay of community members and the development of their participations are increasingly mediated by computers, networks, software, databases, websites, digital media, etc. The theme of computer support for learning communities is a timely and significant one.

The papers collected here not only recognize the irresistible potential of computer support for learning communities, but at the same time they delve into the ubiquitous barriers and social contradictions involved. They recognize that the design of community-based learning is not simply a matter of technological engineering, but integrally involves intransigent social issues. Existing community structures and educational institutions evolved to meet the needs of a bygone era; adapting them to a high-tech knowledge society confronts conflicts that would not even occur to armchair designers. To uncover and explore these realities of developing learning communities, each paper in this special issue (a) investigates a concrete real-world case and (b) subjects data from that case to scientific analysis. The results may not always be encouraging, but they are thought-provoking and important.

Learning about computing in the community. The first paper takes us out into the community, to a geographically-based nonprofit community organization. It asks how one can foster the kind of practical, technical learning within such an organization that it needs to achieve its goals today. The staffing of a nonprofit is not structured to support learning of its own participants, although its mission in the case study example depends upon educating the local population about ecological issues. In order to accomplish this mission, the organization must learn how to develop and maintain an effective Web site despite severe limitations on technical skills and financial resources. Issues of community computing under these conditions highlight a number of general problems and suggest some innovative responses for diversifying participation, managing organizational knowledge and enhancing social capital. The paper shows how carefully structuring technical training as participatory design can help the organization to learn in a sustainable way.

Re-engineering a learning community at school. Another study by the same group takes what they learned about the nonprofit Web site experience back into the public school. Just as the technical support experts learned from the community volunteers in a way that engaged and empowered the people in the organization, so the teachers in the school learned from their students in an interaction that benefited everyone. Students are often more technically facile than their teachers, so why not, argues this paper, let the students teach the teachers about technical matters. The experience results in authentic learning for the students and ties their learning to tangible practical ends that motivate engagement.

Implementing collaborative inquiry despite school. The kind of learning that builds inquiry skills is severely constrained by the social structure of conventional schooling, even in countries like Finland with successful, progressive education systems. The physical space and time of the school separates students and isolates teachers. It compartmentalizes learning into bite-size servings of unrelated disciplines. It divides lessons from testing—contradicting the formative role of assessment and focusing activity around a tyranny of grading. While this case study transformed some of those conditions, it still found that concerns about grading formed a major barrier to collaborative inquiry. Another, related problem was continued student orientation toward completing assigned work tasks, rather than pursuing progressive inquiry defined as the continuing improvement of knowledge objects (questions, ideas, explanations) within the learning community. Computer support can only facilitate knowledge building if the social relations and the epistemic orientation of teachers and students are already focused on pursuing collaborative inquiry.

Influences of student, group and task characteristics. A traditional mode of analysis within educational research is the statistical analysis of quantified independent variables upon dependent ones, such as exam scores and other operational indicators of learning outcomes. This paper illustrates a multilevel analysis that can distinguish effects of individual differences from effects of participation in small groups. Here, the "learning community" is a freshman college course of 230 students divided randomly into groups of 10. The "computer support" is a generic threaded discussion tool for each small group to communicate about assigned themes. Each student is required to post at least 2 messages to each theme within a 3 week period. A sophisticated statistical analysis is unable to find significant effects of this exercise on the learning within the small groups, despite all the literature that the authors cite on the benefits of CSCL. Perhaps the point is that it takes more than a vanilla communication medium and a minimal imposed interaction task among randomly collected students to constitute effective computer support or a consequential learning community.

Moderation strategies for learning communities. This study explores some techniques for building a more effective learning community through carefully designed computer support and skillful pedagogical facilitation. First, the small group of 12 college students was given an intensive two-month collaborative learning assignment. Second, they were given a sophisticated computer-based environment in which to work. While this software was also a threaded discussion system, it included extensive functionality to support and scaffold collaborative knowledge building, including tools for the students or for a moderator to link, highlight, annotate, manipulate and structure posted notes. The reported experiment is a unique attempt to investigate the applicability of small-group facilitation techniques to computer-supported threaded discussion. Interestingly, the designed functionality for moderation can be used by the students themselves as well as by an outside moderator.

Issues in building social capital in learning communities. The final paper takes the classroom back out into the community, into the reality outside of school walls. It tries to build an apprenticeship learning community consisting of future and current entrepreneurs. By building working relationships between a student community and an entrepreneurial community, it strives to increase trust and thereby build social capital as well as understanding. Although the students are university computer scientists, the computer support only plays a mundane role in the community building. The paper nicely details both the theory and detailed practicalities of trying to match two very culturally different communities, and evaluates the limited success. Perhaps this points to the moral of the special issue as a whole: that the complexities of the social issues dwarf the technical support issues, which however, still need to be respected.

In these six diverse papers we see a range of approaches to computer support for learning communities. Their contrasting experimental approaches and incompatible analytic methodologies illustrate major directions within this multidisciplinary field. The pros and cons of these alternatives are highlighted by the juxtaposition of the papers. Each paper presents its theoretical foundations and its scientific methodology, illustrating these with a concrete application. Despite sophistication of theory, complexity of method and extent of research effort, each study falls short of achieving desired learning and community outcomes. The papers not only present important findings; they also illustrate in their various shortcomings the abiding limitations of our current knowledge of this important question: how to provide adequate socio-technical support so that learning communities can achieve their manifest potential.

We would like to thank the following reviewers for their engagement in reviewing and selecting the papers of this special issue: Amy Bruckmann (Georgia Tech, USA), Hans Brüggelmann (Universität Siegen, Germany), Jörg Haake (Fernuniversität Hagen, Germany), Thomas Herrmann (Ruhr-Universität Bochum, Germany), Chris Hoadley (Penn State University, USA), Marleen Huysman (Vrije Universiteit Amsterdam, The Netherlands), Yasmin Kafai

(University of California at Los Angeles, USA), Markus Klann (Fraunhofer FIT, Sankt Augustin, Germany), Michael Koch (Technische Universität München, Germany), Thérèse Laferrière (Université Laval, Canada), Heinz Mandl (Universität München, Germany), Bernhard Nett (Fraunhofer FIT and International Institute for Socio-Informatics, Bonn, Germany), Volkmar Pipek (Universität Siegen and International Institute for Socio-Informatics, Bonn, Germany), Johann W. Sarmiento (Drexel University, USA), David W. Shaffer (University of Wisconsin, USA), Marcus Specht (Open University, Heerlen, The Netherlands), Gunnar Stevens (Universität Siegen, Germany). Thanks also to David Tietjen (College of Information Science, Drexel University, USA) for language editing.

References

ACKERMAN, M.; PIPEK, V.; WULF, V. (eds), 2003, Sharing Expertise: Beyond Knowledge Management, Cambridge: MIT-Press.

BUSH, V., 1945. As we may think. *Atlantic Monthly, 176* (1), 101-108.

ENGELBART, D., 1962, *Augmenting human intellect: A conceptual framework* (Vol. Summary Report 3578). Menlo Park, CA: Stanford Research Institute.

HUYSMAN, M., WENGER, E. and WULF, V. (Eds.)., 2003, Communities and technologies: Proceedings of the first international conference on communities and technologies (C&T 2003). Dordrecht, Netherlands: Kluwer.

HUYSMAN, M. and WULF, V. (Eds.)., 2004, Social Capital and Information Technology. Cambridge, MIT-Press.

KLAMMA, R., ROHDE, M. and STAHL, G., 2004, Special issue on: Community-based learning: Explorations into theoretical groundings, empirical findings and computer support. *SigGroup Bulletin, 24* (4), 1-100. Retrieved from http://www.cis.drexel.edu/faculty/gerry/publications/journals/cbl.pdf.

LAVE, J. and WENGER, E., 1991, Situated learning: Legitimate peripheral participation. Cambridge, UK: Cambridge University Press.

STAHL, G., 2006, Group Cognition: Computer Support for Building Collaborative Knowledge. Cambridge, MA: MIT Press.

Table of Contents

Special Issue on "Computer Support for Learning Communities"

Edited by Markus Rohde, Volker Wulf & Gerry Stahl

Introduction: Computer support for learning communities

Gerry Stahl, Markus Rohde & Volker Wulf

Supporting community-based learning: Case study of a geographical community organization designing its website

Umer Farooq, Craig H. Ganoe, Lu Xioa, Cecelia B. Merkel, Mary Beth Rosson & John M. Carroll

Fostering an informal learning community of computer technologies at school

Lu Xioa & John M. Carroll

Implementing virtual collaborative inquiry practices in a middle school context

Minna Lakkala, Iisa Ilomäki & Ture Palonen

Learning in asynchronous discussion groups: A multilevel approach to study the influence of student, group and task characteristics

Tammy Schellens, Hilda van Keer, Martin Valcke & Bram de Wever

Facilitating asynchronous discussions in learning communities: The impact of moderation strategies

Andrea Kienle & Carsten Ritterskamp

Reality is our lab: Communities of practice in applied computer science

Markus Rohde, Ralf Klamma, Matthias Jarke & Volker Wulf

18. Book review of Professional Development for Cooperative Learning: Issues and Approaches

Edited by C. M. Brody and N. Davidson, 1998, Albany, New York: State University of New York Press.

This book is about training K-12 teachers to adopt a cooperative learning paradigm in their classrooms. It provides a collection of solicited essays aimed at instructing future trainers of public school teachers in America. The book consists of 15 chapters by leaders in the field. In addition there is an introduction and an afterward by the editors. The contributions summarize the principles of major efforts in teacher professional development over the past decades. In addition to distinguishing among the various approaches within the rather incestuous family of practitioners represented, the book relates lessons from the frontlines and addresses the issue of systemic change.

Here is a selection of advice offered the reader (emphasis added): "Teachers need support to *continue* evolving their conceptions of cooperative learning" (p. 45). "Simply providing information and [in-service workshops] result in only a small minority of teachers actually *implementing* the ideas" (p. 60). "Teachers must *'live'* cooperative groupwork in formal training programs" (p. 69). "When teachers learn how to use a variety of cooperative learning structures they are empowered to reach various educational objectives" (p. 105). "The Child Development Project's model of cooperative learning builds on . . . teaching prosocial *values* and building a *caring* schoolwide and classroom community" (p. 148). Socially-Conscious Cooperative Learning "teaches about cooperation as an *idea and value* and links cooperative learning in the classroom to the broader goal of building a more *cooperative and just* society" (p. 203). "What happens *between and after* training sessions is more important than what happens during training sessions [and] teachers' behavior is largely determined by the organizational structure of the *school*" (p. 232).

As these excerpts suggest, the lesson learned in struggling to train teachers in non-traditional teaching methods is self-reflexive: the training must itself be non-traditional training. The old in-service presentations must be replaced with processes that involve the participants in cooperative learning activities, transformative practices, and values formation. This raises the question – ignored by the editors and the contributors – whether brief, didactic essays summarizing principles do not suffer the same limitations as instructionist teaching and in-service lectures. One has the nagging sense that this book ignores the very insights that it documents.

It is a sign of how fast the times are changing that just as people start to address the widespread dissemination of cooperative learning approaches, the once *avant garde* spirit of these reforms seems already archaic. What was leading edge in the 80's or even early 90's is not only now universally accepted in the research community, but feels like a relic of the 50's, when some of this research began. Unfortunately, the reality in most classrooms, textbooks, and even educational websites is pre-constructivist and non-cooperative. Since one cannot walk before one learns how to crawl, we will have to master the lessons of professional development for cooperative learning if we want to have any hope of transforming classrooms even further. And it *does* seem necessary these days to go qualitatively beyond the view of education espoused in this book.

To someone excited by the promise of *collaborative* (*sic*, not "cooperative") learning, this book is as old-fashioned and dull as it is still necessary. The pedagogy of collaborative learning, by contrast, is an active and still controversial field, presenting a strong challenge to traditional education, oriented as it was toward the individual student. In particular, computer and Internet technologies have been inspiring new approaches to supporting collaborative learning during the past decade (Crook, 1994; Koschmann, 1996; O'Malley, 1995). The field is now reaching the point where prototypes are establishing the viability of innovative ideas and the time has come for widespread dissemination. That is, we need to know how to conduct professional development of teachers for collaborative learning.

But the book under review fails to address the distinctive needs of collaborative approaches. In their introduction, the editors pay lip service to collaborative learning and say they "made a conscious decision to use the term 'cooperative learning' as the generic concept" (p. 9). In so doing they reduce collaborative learning to just a set of approaches within their concept. Given that every author has a somewhat different approach, collaboration loses its distinctiveness. However, there is in fact a coherent tradition of collaborative learning that goes beyond cooperative learning in its critique of the tradition. And this admittedly subtle distinction is missed by the editors.

Both cooperative and collaborative learning theories oppose the view that knowledge consists of facts told by teachers for students to repeat back. They may advocate a student-centered, constructivist approach in which students construct their own meaning using the ways in which they personally learn best. Social aspects of learning are considered theoretically important and the use of small group processes is emphasized in practice.

The difference may be defined in terms of the "unit of analysis." Cooperative learning still privileges the teacher as the orchestrator of the educational process and still looks to the assessment of individual student knowledge as the sign of learning. Collaborative learning – for instance in versions like Lave and Wenger (Lave & Wenger, 1991) – analyzes things at the level of the community. Here, the teacher is just another participant within the changing roles of the community, and learning consists of evolution of the group and the abilities of its members to participate within it. The classroom may be re-conceptualized as a knowledge-building community (Scardamalia & Bereiter, 1996) or a learning organization (Brown & Duguid, 1991), where the essential outcomes are measured at the group level not the individual. Thus, collaborative learning constitutes a distinct educational paradigm with a very different approach to defining and assessing learning. Whereas cooperative learning is still measured by post-test evaluations of individual student learning based on teacher-defined goals, collaborative learning is concerned with evidence of social cognition (Crook, 1994, pp. 132f; Koschmann, 1996, p. 15). Social cognition may involve the creation of new socially-shared meanings, the increasingly skilled enactment of social practices by students, or the evolution of the learning community as such.

Given this distinction, one can see cooperative learning as a halfway stage to collaborative learning in the sense that the dissemination of the former provides an important basis for the implementation of the latter. Collaborative learning – whether supported by computer technology or not – must adopt many of the classroom practices of cooperative learning, such as its refined use of small group processes. While it is disappointing that this new book that claims to encompass both cooperative and collaborative learning never mentions any of the seminal references in this review, the topic of the book is important for advocates of both flavors of educational reform. It might have been even more useful and less redundant if it included discussions of teacher training and educational reform within both paradigms. This would have been much harder, for successes in broadly disseminating collaborative learning are rarer and far less well known.

References

Brown, J. S., & Duguid, P. (1991). Organizational learning and communities-of-practice: Toward a unified view of working, learning, and innovation. *Organization Science, 2*(1), 40-57.

Crook, C. (1994). *Computers and the collaborative experience of learning.* London, UK: Routledge.

Koschmann, T. (Ed.). (1996). *CSCL: Theory and practice of an emerging paradigm.* Hillsdale, NJ: Lawrence Erlbaum Associates.

Lave, J., & Wenger, E. (1991). *Situated learning: Legitimate peripheral participation.* Cambridge, UK: Cambridge University Press.

O'Malley, C. (1995). *Computer supported collaborative learning.* Berlin, Germany: Springer Verlag.

Scardamalia, M., & Bereiter, C. (1996). Computer support for knowledge-building communities. In T. Koschmann (Ed.), *CSCL: Theory and practice of an emerging paradigm* (pp. 249-268). Hillsdale, NJ: Lawrence Erlbaum Associates.